THE STAKES OF POWER
1845 – 1877

THE STAKES
OF POWER
1845–1877

By

ROY F. NICHOLS

The Making of America
GENERAL EDITOR DAVID DONALD

American Century Series
HILL AND WANG · NEW YORK
A division of Farrar, Straus and Giroux

To the memory of two uncles,
Sayres Ogden Nichols and Joseph Bloomfield Osborne,
veterans of the conflict.

FIRST EDITION FEBRUARY 1961
THIRD PRINTING (FIRST AMERICAN CENTURY SERIES EDITION)
JANUARY 1964

20 21 22 23

Manufactured in the United States of America

Foreword

UNDETERRED BY THE mountainous literature on the Civil War era, which ranges from minute monographs to massive multivolume works, Dean Roy F. Nichols has set himself, in *The Stakes of Power,* the heroic task of integrating the political, social, economic, intellectual, diplomatic, and military history of the years between 1845 and 1877.

Few scholars could approach this ambitious undertaking with the experience and equipment of Mr. Nichols. As Dean of the Graduate School at the University of Pennsylvania, he has taught courses in this field for many years. In such previous books as *The Democratic Machine, Franklin Pierce: Young Hickory of the Granite Hills,* and *The Disruption of American Democracy,* he has exhibited his mastery of the sources of the period and his ability to analyze its complex problems. Through his numerous provocative articles and challenging book reviews, he has demonstrated his familiarity with the entire sweep of Civil War literature.

As a result, *The Stakes of Power* is a brilliant synthesis of the best modern scholarship on the years between 1845 and 1877. In his carefully developed early chapters Mr. Nichols shows how the Civil War was caused by "a highly complex mélange" of "pride, politics, patience, prudence, pique, petulance, and plotting." His conspicuously impartial account of the actual years of conflict is distinguished by his integration of military and political

v

history and by his understanding that Abraham Lincoln and Jefferson Davis as presidents faced essentially similar problems. On the Reconstruction period Mr. Nichols is a moderate revisionist, pointing out that, despite undeniable excesses and extravagances, the Radical governments in the South were not without positive accomplishments.

But *The Stakes of Power* is something more than just a summary of contemporary scholarship; it is also a fresh and provocative interpretation of the whole Civil War era. Mr. Nichols sees the central theme of the period in the contest for the control of the political and economic power of the Federal government. Convincingly, he argues that the struggles of the tragic 1850's centered about the efforts of the frustrated Northerners to break the "almost complete" dominance which the Southerners exercised over national offices and policies. Once the two sections were separated by war, each faced a new struggle for the control of power, and Mr. Nichols shows how Lincoln's superior genius was a powerful factor in the evolution of a new structure of power, both military and political, in the North. Instead of viewing the postwar years in simple moralistic terms, he maintains that they witnessed a contest over "a new politics emerging from a redistribution of power which was being directed not so much by the incidents of Southern Reconstruction as by more complex changes in the life of the nation."

Dean Nichols' absorbing study precisely fulfills the objectives of The Making of America series, a six-volume series designed to make the best of historical scholarship available to the general reader who is not a specialist in American history. Falling chronologically between Charles M. Wiltse's *The New Nation* and Robert Wiebe's history of the Populist and Progressive periods, *The Stakes of Power* is at once a broad-ranging account of the most crucial period in American history and a vigorous new interpretation of that era.

DAVID DONALD

Contents

Acknowledgments

THE AID AVAILABLE to anyone writing a book is varied and not always received from persons. I owe much to the power of the Great West, where I was privileged to write much of this book on the shores of Coulter Bay under the shadow of the Grand Tetons, in Sun Valley, and high up in Estes Park. Amidst such surroundings it is possible to learn as nowhere else of the enduring strength and grandeur of the nation. It is likewise a pleasure to make acknowledgments to David Donald, editor of this series, to Arthur Wang, its publisher, to Barbara Rex, discerning critic, and to Ruth E. Hamilton who made my scribbling legible.

Acknowledgment is also made for permission to reproduce the maps in this volume: pp. 7, 111: from *The Republic of the United States: A History* by Jeannette P. Nichols and Roy F. Nichols. Copyright, 1942, Roy F. Nichols and Jeannette P. Nichols. By permission of Appleton-Century-Crofts, Inc.; p. 86: from *The Civil War and Reconstruction* by James G. Randall, reprinted by permission of D. C. Heath and Company; p. 159: from *Empire for Liberty: The Genesis and Growth of the United States of America* by Dumas Malone and Basil Rauch. Copyright © 1960. Appleton-Century-Crofts, Inc.

Introduction

MANKIND IS CONFUSED by conflicting emotions impelling both to peace and war. Among the emotions are a love of ease and an itch to fight. The energy sources within the human organism seem to encourage indiscriminate loving and hating, affectionate interchange and the urge to hurt and kill. What is common among individuals can be duplicated in mass behavior. What is required by any who wish to comprehend the history of sectional conflict is an understanding of the will to fight.

When the masses of mankind left war-torn Europe for America, they came quite frequently to seek peace and happiness and a surcease from strife. In the years preceding the eighteen forties the American will to peace with foreign powers had only broken down once. Here the motive in broad terms had been to resent insult and to complete independence. These ends were achieved and, secure behind the great rampart of the Atlantic, the young nation had lustily proceeded to enjoy the fruits of liberty.

But it was not for long—the urge to fight welled up, and these descendants of men who had fled from war again reached for the sword. There is probably no simple answer to the question why. But a retelling of the story may suggest the compelling reasons Basically we are called upon to review the implications of the fact that it was an age of romanticism, of brittle and tingling emotion. It was not an age of calm and orderly development but of jangling nerves, poor health, uneasy conscience, and a wildly and widely ranging imagination. It was an age of liberty, of self-government. It was an age of tremendous enterprise, stimulated by a Midas dream of inexhaustible wealth and unlimited reward for ingenuity. It was an age of mystical dedication to the realization of a manifest destiny. It was an age marked by a subtle conflict over definition, an increasing schizophrenia that sprang from a division of social personality.

Most significantly it was an age of such uncertain definition of power that there was bound to be contest for it. For the desire to exercise the power of government shapes human behavior in many ways. It arouses among men the deepest of emotions and stirs them often to great exertion. These emotions and drives are no less strong when this power is the power of self-government in a variegated society than when the power is despotic and concentrated in the hands of a dictator or an elite. Power is desired to satisfy ambition, to give assurance of status, to afford material gain, to insure protection. Many will strive to secure it but an even more intense striving may be stimulated by fear of losing it. In democratic societies power and rights are inextricably entangled because there cannot be rights without power to secure and protect them, hence power can often be sought in the name of the cause of liberty. The loss of power, likewise, can be conceived of as synonymous with the loss of liberty. Power, therefore, can invite conflict to secure it; but it must also be recognized that it can cause conflict to prevent its loss. Indeed, a most significant conclusion can be drawn, namely, that the fear of losing power may be a stronger influence to conflict than the desire to obtain power. Such appears to have been the case in the history of the United States at mid-nineteenth century. From 1845 to 1861 tension grew, and then came the spilling of blood.

1

E Pluribus Duo

THE AMERICAN PEOPLE entered the 1840's in a frolicsome mood. Rollicking ditties, log cabins, and hard cider stimulated the romping voters in 1840 to sweep "Tippecanoe [Harrison] and Tyler, too" into the White House literally on wings of song soaring through clouds of alcohol-perfumed exhalations. Little did these carefree citizens dream that they were on the eve of two wars.

Such naïve unawareness was due to a general lack of interest in the significance of political power. Americans thought of the process of government as a sort of game, called politics, which it was not often necessary to take too seriously. But a change in this attitude was impending, little though they realized it. This change was drawing the United States nearer and nearer to the brink of disaster and, after a brief rehearsal, was to plunge the Republic into the fiery pit of civil war.

Nature had set the stage for this tragedy when it decreed that the American people should be divided. Life in the more northerly temperate zone had to be different from that in the semi-tropics; and differences in ways of living unfortunately had bred conflicting ideas and impulses. The presence of millions of Negro slaves, concentrated in the southern half of the new Republic, accentuated difference and eventually stirred controversy. This division made it inevitable that each section would create a brand

of politics designed to serve what it believed to be its best interests.
Such diversity had not appeared to be particularly dangerous in
the early days of the Republic. As the founding fathers from the
various states labored in Philadelphia, New York, and Washington to fight the Revolution and to create and perfect the Federal
Republic, they were held in step by a great sense of common
danger and of mission: to proclaim liberty in a world of monarchies. This taught them the art of compromising in the interests of
the great objective. Thus guided they had constructed an intricate
system of checks and balances and a nice division of power designed to keep any section or interest from obtaining a dominant
position in the government. They likewise had the wisdom to
realize that this new society would not be static. So they recognized the necessity for arranging for the political needs of an expanding and mobile population, and designed the Northwest
Ordinance to provide that new units of self-government, that is,
new states, be received into the Federal system on equal terms
with the original thirteen.

The system developed with reasonable smoothness even when
restlessness, imagination, and ambition for greater strength caused
American interests to seek territory beyond the original bounds of
the Republic. Even when the Louisiana Purchase caused certain
Eastern spokesmen to protest that it would destroy the balance
created in 1789, and to resist the admission of new states from the
area, the matter was settled by compromise. The new territory
was divided so that the number of free and slave states should
remain equal. This division was achieved when in 1820 a geographical line, 36° 30', had been projected westward into the Mis-
sissippi-Missouri Valley as an extension of the Mason-Dixon line
and the Ohio River, north of which relatively few slaves were
ever to be held.

Sectionalism in the early decades had in fact entered but little
into national elections. Men with wide horizons, truly dedicated
to the promotion of the nation's strength, enlightenment, and
power, had occupied the White House; if a majority of them

seemed to come from Virginia, their residence appeared not to color their policies too brightly. Washington, Jefferson, Madison, Monroe, and the two Adamses, all of them from the older regions, were succeeded in due time by Jackson from the new West. But these were all men of national outlook and of statesmanlike deportment. Though sectional issues were not unknown, the nation was the major concern of most with political interests. Yet it was true that the White House was generally occupied by a Southerner, one of the Virginia dynasty, and the prevailing leadership in Congress was Southern.

In the late thirties a change had come over the nature of American politics. The control of government began to have a new significance. In the first decades of the national government, the definition of its function had been rather narrow. Hamilton's ambitious plans for making it a source of subsidy to business had been fought by those of Jefferson's laissez-faire persuasion and eventually curtailed. But the new bursts of energy that were characteristic of the expanding society after its release from preoccupation with Europe during the war period, 1792-1815, meant that the enterprising imaginations of the Americans would turn to government as a source of aid to business promoters and their projects.

There were demands for the creation of a new government bank, for a protective tariff to foster the infant industries stimulated by the invention of machinery and threatened by England's competition, for Federal appropriations to build roads and canals, and to make harbors safe for commerce and obstructed streams navigable, and for a generous policy of cheap or even free distribution of the great areas of unused land owned by the nation. It was argued that with laws and appropriations of this character, not only would the nation develop more quickly and mobilize its wealth more speedily, but many communities and individuals, new corporations and promoters, would be enriched. Communities, groups, and individuals became rivals for these subsidies, and their success or failure, involving financial gain or loss, meant that the pressures upon public functionaries and lawmakers, even upon judges, would be great. Defeat might mean ruin, success a bonanza. The stakes of power became ever greater. Therefore, the lust for power was encouraged. Election contests, which were commonly merely sport, sometimes became struggles of desperation with no holds barred.

This political strife was kindled not only by the growing demands for aid, but by a less personal, a more general force. The nation was generating an unprecedented quantity of human energy because of the great increase of population, both from natural causes and from immigration. Had this new surge of humanity distributed itself evenly over the country, and had the tide of westward migration projected slave and free labor communities equally into the western part of the Mississippi Valley, there would have been a minimum of political reaction. The society east of the great river would have been projected west of it in parallel ranges, and the political balance between North and South, achieved earlier along the seaboard, would not have been disturbed. But geographical conditions changed at about the 95th meridian, and beyond that point slavery was not thought to be profitable. In this western region therefore, settlers seemed likely to establish free labor communities. This meant that the population base of the slave or Southern bloc in the Federal government would continue to shrink.

As certain Southern leaders looked ahead they saw their generally dominant position threatened. To them there appeared two disquieting possibilities. One was a loss of power and status; the other was disaster. Once their veto power was gone, they feared that the abolition of slavery would follow. This would be both an economic loss and a social catastrophe. In certain of the states in the Lower South, the whites would then be in the minority and theoretically at the mercy of their former slaves. To Southerners, with these thoughts coloring their emotions, the continued exercise of power was essential to the safety of their communities.

This intensity of apprehension and the consequent fanatical belief in the necessity of possessing power were to step up the tempo of politics of the 1840's. Election contests were to become charged with passion. Both Democrats and Whigs began to generate emotional overcharges. The former had come into power in 1829 largely as the personal following of Andrew Jackson, "Old Hickory," the Hero of New Orleans. As an Indian fighter and conqueror of the British he represented American love of two-fisted, rifle-firing fighting, and many grew hoarse shouting for him.

His actions appeared downright, hard-hitting, and often arbitrary. He would brook no opposition, and he breathed fire and brimstone on some bankers and secessionists. The Whig opposition called him a tyrant. For a while he was all-powerful, but then came the time to choose his successor. This precipitated a quarrel among the heirs. Jackson passed his mantle to his chosen successor, Martin Van Buren. This New York Democrat was one of the most crafty organizers in the Democratic party. His guile and his sandy hair earned for him the title "The Fox." When Jackson made him his choice he snuffed out the immediate chances of his first Vice-President, John C. Calhoun of South Carolina. He had disregarded the seniority of the most prominent leader of the South and had broken the succession of statesman Presidents, mostly Southern. Neither the tall, somewhat austere and humorless Southern statesman, nor his Southern colleagues, would forget this ruthless act. Calhoun, a public man who seemed all brain and logic, could not bring himself to learn the arts of the politician; perhaps he was incapable of acquiring them. Therefore, he was forced to bide his time while Van Buren, despite his political skill, was overwhelmed by misfortune originating largely in the financial panic of 1837, and was at length driven from office by the Whigs in 1840.

As the campaign of 1844 approached, the Whigs demonstrated their complete failure in office, and Calhoun and his backers thought they saw their chance. But they chose to promote his fortunes on an issue, the security of the South, which boded ill for the unity of the nation. A small inner group of supporters worked

hard in 1842-43. They raised money and undertook a press campaign, directing editorial policy in old newspapers and seeking
to set up new organs. They were adopting a line which they believed would rally the South solidly behind Calhoun. As one of
them described it: "The combinations in Christendom against the
slave holding interest, the course of English diplomacy abroad, the
state of Northern feeling at home and the present necessity for
maintaining the balance of power between the free and slaveholding states constitute a crisis which gives an importance to this question [Southern security] and also to the election of a Southern
president which I think our papers and speakers might turn to
good account. Yet it is not to be denied but that this question
will do much to divide parties sectionally . . . our papers ought
to take the initiative on this question and begin at once to develop
cautiously." What they meant was the South must keep control
of the Republic, or their way of life would be in danger. This
attitude had been a long time maturing and even in 1843 it was
not too generally held, but it was indicative of a belief which was
to spread and to provide a leading element in an ultimate conflict.
It could spell disaster.

This effort to nominate Calhoun as the Democratic candidate
for the Presidency did not catch on. Van Buren's organization had
complete control of the party machinery, and his third nomination appeared sure. The Calhoun forces then joined a number of
younger men from all parts of the nation who were organizing a
stop-Van Buren move. They sought to capitalize on the enthusiasm for the annexation of Texas which was welling up as part of
the demand for the fulfillment of the nation's manifest destiny.
Van Buren, fearing trouble with Mexico and the antislavery people, played into his opponents' hands by opposing the acquisition.
Enthusiasm for Texas proved to have a greater appeal than the
logic of Calhoun's demand for Southern security, as a symbol
around which to rally a united South.

That section was facing what seemed to many to be unpleasant
facts. Slavery was believed to have reached its limit of expansion

TRAILS BEYOND THE MISSISSIPPI

within the existing boundaries of the United States. The South seemed doomed to shrink in proportion to the rest of the nation unless more tropical territory to the South were acquired. Furthermore, Northern Democrats seemed willing to vote to destroy safeguards, like the "gag" rule, erected in Congress against abolitionist propaganda. There were rumors that Great Britain was working with Texas to bribe her to abolish slavery in return for loans. A great free society might be in the making in Mexico, next door to the Southern states, which would become a place of refuge for escaping slaves and a harbor for abolitionist propaganda. Also, British interests might gain a dangerous foothold there. In self-protection certain Southern leaders were thinking of Texas as a must, and they hoped that the traditional hatred of Great Britain and tear of her advance would persuade enough in the North to support the annexation.

A group of younger Senators and Congressmen, typical of whom was Robert J. Walker, speculative Senator from Mississippi, were ready, in effect, to demand that Van Buren support annexation or forfeit the nomination. However, Van Buren and the leading Whig candidate, Clay, were in agreement that the annexation of Texas probably meant war with Mexico, and this they opposed. They went so far as to issue statements to that effect on the eve of the conventions in 1844. The sentiment which this action aroused lost Van Buren enough of his Southern delegates to make it necessary to find a compromise candidate who could secure the support of the Jackson-Van Buren managers and the Southern annexationists. A compromise was reached whereby the acquisition of both Texas and Oregon, slave and free, was demanded in the party platform, and a Tennessee protégé of Jackson, James Knox Polk, was nominated. The Van Burenites took some comfort from the demand for all of Oregon and accepted Polk—but they would not forget.

The Whigs, on their part, nominated Henry Clay, Kentucky slaveholder, an aging but jaunty political veteran who was returning to the limelight. He had been on the political stage for many years, always seeking to organize a successful opposition to the Jacksonians. His chief talent was a capacity to save situations by promoting ingenious compromises. Magnetic, sporty, eloquent, he had made many friends but his many enemies had created a widespread distrust of him. Now he awakened that distrust again by his vacillation on Texas.

In the South fiery orators demanded Texas so vehemently, threatening a Southern convention, nullification and even secession, that Clay altered his position and announced himself in favor of annexation, if it could be achieved without war and by common consent. This shift contributed heavily to his defeat. A small group of antislavery enthusiasts had started a Liberty party in 1840 which in 1844 was campaigning a second time demanding that no more slave territory be acquired or slave states admitted. Clay's change on Texas caused enough of his Northern Whig supporters to vote for the Liberty party candidate, James G. Birney. Their defection cost him the election.

Polk, the first dark-horse presidential candidate, was chosen. He was an unimpressive, serious-minded Tennessee politician who was to prove a surprise. He had been prominent in Congress during Jackson's day and had been an able legislative adjutant of Old Hickory. Since then he had served a term as Governor of Tennessee. He had a genius for hard work and a complete innocence of humor. His determination was to prove phenomenal, and his will generally unshakable. Many were to underrate him to their sorrow. His election spurred Congress to annex Texas before he was inaugurated, and when he entered the White House he found Texas on the way into the Union and the Mexican government vowing vengeance. He was not very long in office before trouble came. Mexico refused to pay the claims of the United States confirmed by treaty but demanded that her northern neighbor keep away from the Rio Grande River. Polk on his part tried to be patient. He hoped to persuade that republic to accept the facts of life, and sent a minister to make the vain attempt. He likewise took the precaution to station General Zachary Taylor and a small army in Texas. Polk soon learned that in sending a minister he had only his trouble for his pains. Mexico refused to receive him and very insultingly ordered the United States away from southern Texas. At this point Polk commanded a military advance.

In January 1846 he ordered General Taylor to march to the Rio Grande. Taylor could not get off until March and it was toward the middle of that month that he approached the river and came within sight of Mexican patrols. For about a month Taylor, on the north bank with 2,700 men, faced the 6,000 to 8,000 Mexicans across the river. Inevitably, hostilities commenced and, on April 25, a Mexican detachment, deployed north of the river, attacked and captured an American patrol, killing eleven officers and men. Polk and his Cabinet were at this time debating the desirability of asking Congress to declare the existence of a state of war. Before they had come to a firm decision, Taylor's dispatch reporting the fighting arrived at the War Department on Saturday evening, May 9. Polk worked busily that Sunday and his message, sent to Congress on Monday, brought instant action.

Meanwhile Taylor remained on the banks of the Rio Grande, greatly outnumbered. He had established two posts, one at the mouth, at Point Isabel, and the other at Fort Texas, up the river opposite the Mexican town of Matamoros. As he was marching men up from the coast to strengthen Fort Texas he discovered, May 8, that a Mexican army was in battle array between him and the post. Despite the fact that he was greatly outnumbered he attacked them near some ponds at Palo Alto. The American artillery destroyed Mexican cavalry charges and set the prairie grass on fire. By sunset the Mexicans had had enough and retreated. The Americans had lost some fifty-five, and the Mexicans 500.

Taylor next day set out again but, within three miles of Fort Texas, found the Mexican army entrenched at a spot where it would be difficult to use his artillery. "Old Rough and Ready," sitting calmly on the back of knock-kneed Old Whitey, directed a more difficult battle which ended in a more smashing victory. The Mexican army was turned into a fleeing mob, abandoning arms, ammunition, flags, and baggage and losing 1,500 men or one-quarter of its strength. The Americans lost 110 at this battle of Resaca de la Palma. On May 18 the Americans entered Matamoros and chased the Mexicans sixty miles farther into the interior.

While these victories were being won, the President and Congress had gone into immediate action. The President's message was received Monday noon, May 11, and by Wednesday Polk had signed an act authorizing the recruiting of 50,000 volunteers and appropriating $10,000,000. He issued a proclamation recognizing the existence of war and called in General Winfield Scott to assume command of the military operations.

The President likewise resorted to diplomacy. While war clouds had been gathering over Texas there had been those who were demanding that Britain surrender all claim to Oregon and that joint occupation be ended. "Fifty-four forty or fight" was a bellicose slogan. However, even the somewhat ruthless Polk could not contemplate two wars at once, so in June he asked the advice of the Senate about accepting Britain's offer to split the region at 49°. The Senate advised and consented on June 12.

While the volunteers were flocking to the flag, predominantly from the South and West, Polk was summoning what he thought was another resource. Even before war broke out he had been asked to help a former President of Mexico, living in exile, to return to his native land. It was believed that if the one-legged General Santa Anna could get back home with American aid, he would help make a speedy peace. In the course of the mobilization, Polk arranged to permit the former President to return through a blockading fleet which the Navy Department had stationed off Vera Cruz. In the meantime General Taylor's army on the Rio Grande was building up in preparation for a campaign in northern Mexico.

Rather unexpectedly, while these military preparations were in process, Polk found himself confronted by "domestic" warfare. The pot of politics boiled over, particularly in the Democratic party. The initial session of Polk's first Congress, 1845-1846, had proved fiery. The Democrats, true to the tenets of the party, had lowered the protective tariff, thus arousing the hostility of the manufacturing interests. They had killed any hope of a third national bank by setting up an "independent" treasury which upset a good many financiers. Polk also was preparing to veto a Rivers and Harbors appropriations bill desired by many Northern communities. Finally, the President, after having acquired all of slave Texas, had accepted the compromise of only half of free Oregon. Both Texas and Florida had been admitted as slave states, while only one free state, Iowa, had been added. The pro-slavery interests now had a majority in the Senate. No wonder that, as the Northern Democrats sat together in their boarding houses, or met each other in the Capitol, they had grievances to share.

Revolt was simmering that hot August when Polk lit the spark. His hope had been that Santa Anna would regain the Presidency and make peace, and, at the same time, sell the California part of northern Mexico to the United States. If this was to be accomplished, Polk would need millions to hand over to Santa Anna at the signing of the peace treaty. So in August, as Congress was on the eve of adjournment, Polk sent in a request for the needed millions to "make peace with Mexico."

This message arrived on Saturday, August 8, 1846. It was hot, hot as only Washington can be hot. Some on that day may have anticipated a thunderstorm, but none perhaps realized that there would be loosed a verbal thunderbolt so shattering that its effects are still felt. No sooner were the words of this message read than a number sensed its meaning: Polk was seeking to increase the area of slavery.

In the stifling heat a flood of pent-up frustration burst forth. Eastern manufacturing representatives, disgruntled at the repeal of protection, Western advocates of acquiring the whole of Oregon who felt defrauded, those who feared a veto of the Rivers and Harbors bill, those who opposed slavery and chafed at the power of the South, and a strong phalanx of Northern Democrats who were about to seek re-election with their hands empty—from among all of these came a new resolve.

When the House adjourned at three for dinner, one little knot discussed the possibility. These met others on the way back to the Capitol and when the session resumed at five, and while a quorum was gathering, they put their pens to paper. The work of David Wilmot, Democrat from protectionist Pennsylvania, seemed best to fit the need and, at about seven, he obtained the floor. At the conclusion of his remarks he offered the famous Wilmot Proviso.

In the terms of the famed Northwest Ordinance of 1787, he proposed that in any territory to be acquired by any treaty with

Mexico, or from the use of the moneys for which Polk asked, "neither slavery nor involuntary servitude shall ever exist in any part of said territory, except for crime whereof the party shall first be duly convicted."

The time proved too short to enact this proviso or to answer it before Congress adjourned. But when the next session assembled in December 1846, the proviso was reintroduced and Calhoun answered it by introducing a set of resolutions maintaining that slaves were property and could not be excluded from any of the territories. Neither of these two proposals was ever adopted but they came to be rallying points, South and North. The South was becoming more determined that it must maintain control of the Federal government, the North that such control must be ended. The irresistible force was approaching the immovable object.

2

A New Balance

PRESIDENT POLK, as commander in chief of the armed forces, chose to conduct two wars for the price of one. Not only was he to fight the Mexicans, but his duty as party leader impelled him to give battle to the Whigs. In carrying on both of these contests he seemed almost oblivious to the implications of the sectional rivalry for power. He was something of an ostrich.

All during the summer of 1846 volunteers had been assembling at Taylor's rendezvous on the Rio Grande. By June he had a force of 8,000 and could carry out the plans for invasion which, in his usual blundering fashion, he had been failing to perfect. Early in July he began an advance designed to assemble his army at Camargo in preparation for an attack on Monterrey, the metropolis of northern central Mexico. Camargo was probably the worst place that could be imagined to mobilize a force as it was peculiarly unhealthy. But Taylor was developing a positive talent for blunders that rarely hindered success.

Rough and Ready spent the summer in making his approach to Monterrey. This city was in hilly country, well fortified and formidable. It was garrisoned by a Mexican army of 9,000, half again as large as Taylor's available fighting force. But by a series of attacks over six days, September 20-25, the Mexicans were beaten; the defeated lost some 400, the victors presumably twice

as many. Taylor's own army was so exhausted and disorganized
by the effort that he did not dare risk the all-out assault necessary
to bag the Mexicans. Instead he signed an armistice allowing
them to depart for the farther interior. This aroused Polk to anger
but the nation rejoiced in the great victory and Taylor was more
frequently than ever mentioned for the Presidency.

While Taylor was invading Northern Mexico, the War Department had sent an expedition into the farther reaches. Colonel Stephen W. Kearney had been ordered to lead a column
into the provinces of New Mexico and California. Starting
from Fort Leavenworth at the end of June he had followed the
Santa Fe Trail and taken over New Mexico in August. A month
later he set out for California where he arrived in December.
On the way he learned that much had been happening on
the Pacific shore.

During the preceding summer, an American exploring expedition had been seeking a more direct way to California than the
Oregon Trail. Colonel John C. Frémont, the so-called "pathfinder," was in command of this project and had completed it,
crossing the Rockies into California during the winter of 1845-46.
He had gotten into a quarrel with the Mexican commander
who had ordered him out of the province during the spring. The
local settlers from the United States had likewise been at odds
with the Mexicans and now undertook to declare California's
independence, setting up the Bear Flag Republic. Frémont before long added his explorers to their force. In the midst of this
revolution the American consul at Monterrey summoned the
navy, and Commodore Sloat brought a warship. By that time,
July 1846, news had come that the United States was at war
with Mexico and when, shortly thereafter, Sloat was relieved
by Commodore Stockton, the latter swore in Frémont and the
Bear Flag Republic's army. The combined naval and volunteer
force proceeded to complete the conquest of California. Colonel
Kearney arrived just in time to help in the final mopping up,

and together these various forces gained control of the Pacific shore province.

While these campaigns were in progress on distant fronts, Polk was embroiled on the home front of domestic politics. The difficulty originated in the fact that the Regular Army was so small, only 7,200 at the commencement of hostilities, too small to cope with the Mexican force five times that large. At first President and Congress had expected to depend on volunteers; but in the winter of 1846-47 measures were passed to add brigades and regiments to the Regular Army. It therefore became Polk's responsibility to appoint scores of officers, from major generals down, to command these troops. The Chief Magistrate was all too conscious of the fact that his two top commanders, Scott and Taylor, were possible assets to the Whigs. Scott had already been an avowed candidate of that party since 1840, and Taylor's victories had been giving Whig operators ideas, although Old Rough and Ready had no political experience. To Polk, this was galling.

The President now undertook to offset this Whig advantage by making a number of Democratic generals, hoping that from their number would emerge one with enough valor to rival Scott or Taylor. He himself was a convinced one-term President, but he was anxious to turn over his office to a fellow Democrat. He thereupon proceeded to name numerous Democrats to command the new divisions and brigades. He made William O. Butler of Kentucky a major general and then appointed four other very obvious Democrats as brigadier generals, Joseph Lane of Indiana, James Shields of Illinois, his own law partner, Gideon J. Pillow of Tennessee, and John A. Quitman of Mississippi. Before long Pillow and Quitman were made major generals and two more deserving Democrats, Franklin Pierce of New Hampshire and Caleb Cushing of Massachusetts, became brigadiers. The names of these seven men were to appear many times in the political annals of the next twenty years.

On the military front, Polk was becoming impatient. Despite

his victory at Monterrey, Taylor seemed nowhere near enforcing a peace. The President consequently turned to the idea of an
invasion of the seacoast and a campaign to capture the capital, the
City of Mexico. In planning this maneuver he was forced to rely on
Scott, much as he disliked him, so on November 19 he called
him in and offered him the command of the new expedition.
At the same time he immobilized Taylor in northern Mexico,
authorizing Scott to transfer his best troops to the new campaign.

Polk continued to be troubled by Scott's Whiggery and that
general was dispatched to Vera Cruz, literally surrounded by
Democratic brigade commanders and three Democratic major
generals. If these Democrats had any Whig associates among
the general officers other than Scott their names were never
revealed in the political headlines. These Democratic generals
were undoubtedly never instructed to make it as difficult as
possible for their commander but they knew their politics. Also,
Scott was probably the most difficult military prima donna the
nation has ever produced, and he proceeded to quarrel with his
Democratic associates.

Even this flock of Democratic generals did not erase Polk's
fears. After he had committed the command to Scott he considered giving the top authority to a civilian. He wanted to commission Senator Thomas Hart Benton a lieutenant general,
and give him over-all command of making war and making
peace. This bizarre move fortunately was not consummated because Congress would not agree to Benton's terms. Scott, however, learned about it and sailed south on his mission more
than ever apprehensive of what he once called "firing on his
rear."

While Scott's preparations were in the making the War
Department's unbelievable carelessness enabled the Mexican
forces to learn all about the plans for the invasion and they
proceeded to use this information to their advantage. Polk's so-
called political shrewdness began to bear bitter fruit. His hopes
that Santa Anna would make peace were blossoming in reverse.

That military politician used the opportunity Polk gave him to maneuver himself into command of the Mexican army at about the time Taylor captured Monterrey. He had built up an enormous force of 20,000 and during the winter he planned to overwhelm Taylor before Scott could get going and end the war. The fact that Scott had been taking some of Taylor's best troops seemed to ensure the success of his plan.

Taylor recognized his danger. In defiance of orders designed, he believed, to ruin him, he extended himself from Monterrey to a point where he could control the road from Mexico City to the north of Mexico, and disposed his fewer than 5,000 men as best he could. Santa Anna brought some 17,000 men against him and sought to annihilate him in a rocky area called Buena Vista. Santa Anna caught and routed an outpost, and Taylor arrived in time to see his army defeated twice more on that February 23, 1847. Still, the redoubtable if unconventional soldier sat imperturbable on Old Whitey and so directed the battle that when his army was on the run for the third time, he caught the pursuing Mexicans in a narrow defile where they then were massacred by his artillery until the survivors fled. The Americans had lost about 700 men and a large number of officers, but more than twice as many Mexicans had been killed. Santa Anna was thus forced to leave Taylor, and turned to stop Scott who by this time was approaching Vera Cruz. Taylor was more than ever a hero and his sense of grievance against Polk made him now a candidate receptive of Whig blandishments.

Scott was a careful soldier, quite a contrast to Taylor who never seemed to plan anything. "Old Fuss and Feathers" had first gone to New Orleans to superintend the assembling of a great flotilla to carry 10,000 troops, and to make sure he would get Taylor's best men. At length, by early March, he was off Vera Cruz where he landed successfully on the ninth. Instead of organizing an assault costly in lives, he massed batteries of guns heavy enough to blast the citadel, and in less than three weeks he had captured it. As the terrific summer heat was approaching, and tropical diseases could easily lay an army low, Scott lost no time in sending the troops inland to higher ground. In less than a fortnight they were off. They were not to be unopposed.

Santa Anna had quickly recovered from his failure to annihilate Taylor at Buena Vista. In fact, he persuaded the people that he had won the battle and on the strength of this victory secured the Presidency for himself. Now he would make a vigorous attempt to stop Scott. But his efforts were in vain. Scott's march was slow but irresistible. Between April 17 and August 23 he fought and won seven battles and was at the gates of Mexico City. Here an armistice was agreed upon to allow peace negotiations, but they failed on September 6 and fighting resumed. After another series of engagements which culminated in the gallant assault on the Castle of Chapultepec, the city capitulated on September 14, 1847. The fighting was over. But the problem of peace-making was still to be solved.

During the months of garrison duty the climate of Mexico City proved very trying. The altitude was very wearing on the nerves and tempers were frayed. The men, and particularly the officers, had relatively little to do. Scott made enemies of several politicians among them, particularly of Polk's law partner, Major General Gideon J. Pillow, who claimed he had made Polk President. These officers and numerous others, who were later to meet on the battlefields of national party conventions and in the bloodier contests of 1861-1865, formed an Aztec Club in Mexico City and swore eternal, and sometimes spirituously exuberant, friendship.

During this period of bad temper and idleness, a peace was made. Santa Anna was out of the picture and it was hard to find anyone who would sign a treaty such as Polk demanded. However, it was finally done. The United States returned to Mexico her central states but retained California, New Mexico, and Utah. For these Polk paid $15,000,000. But the new glory had already cost the nation 1,550 killed and 3,500 wounded out of 90,000 under arms, and $100,000,000. The nation added more than half a million square miles to its estate, thereby increasing it by approximately one fifth, and again opening a political Pandora's box.

The first political fruit of these military operations was garnered in the Presidential campaign of 1848. No sooner had Zachary Taylor won his first battles in May 1846 than Whig managers began to see in him another military hero such as Andrew Jackson or Willam Henry Harrison, whom they could expect to lead them to political victory. The General became increasingly convinced that Polk was determined to break him and within a few months he was receptive to Whig overtures. Finally, in 1848, the Southern Whigs, who had come to distrust both Henry Clay and Winfield Scott, rallied behind Taylor both as a hero and as a Virginia-born Louisiana planter and slaveholder. Certain Northern Whigs like Truman Smith and Abbott Lawrence joined them and Taylor was nominated without a platform.

The Mexican War had not brought the Democratic party that had waged it a successful general to promote its fortunes. On the contrary, the conflict had precipitated an internal party schism which was to prove immediately disastrous, and to have consequences of major effect in the destruction to follow.

Polk had been nominated originally because he was a compromise candidate from among Van Buren's enemies whom the Van Buren men would accept. The new President realized that he must re-form the party and get the Calhoun and Van Buren supporters into the same tent. He tried to do this by appointing their friends to office, but he and the Van Burenites could not agree on the places they should have and he finally gave up trying to satisfy them. He and his New York appointees undertook to wrest the party management in that state from the Van Buren faction. This struggle split the party and gave New York to the Whigs. The two halves of the Empire State Democrats refused to meet in the same state convention, and each sent a full delegation to the Democratic National Convention in 1848.

This national body was under the control of the same combination which had defeated Van Buren four years before. They proposed now to seat both the Van Buren and Polk delegations, giving them each half the vote of New York. This arrangement the Van Burenites spurned and walked out of the convention. General Lewis Cass of Michigan was then nominated, the favorite of the opponents of Van Buren in 1844, together with one of Polk's major generals, William O. Butler of Kentucky.

Then came the calamity marking another step toward destruction. The bolting Van Burenites refused to accept Cass, and in the course of a few weeks joined forces with the Liberty party, organizing a new Free Soil party pledged to prevent the spread of slavery into the territories or to admit new slave states. They nominated Martin Van Buren for President. Their action, attracting nearly 300,000 votes, presumably lost Cass the election; under the Mexican War hero, General Zachary Taylor, the Whigs were back in power. Here was disturbing evidence of the growing incompatibility of Northern and Southern political collaborators in operating the Federal system.

Another effect of the Mexican War upon the nation's stability arose from the terms of the treaty of 1848, by which the United States had acquired California, New Mexico, and Utah. California and New Mexico were two huge but very sparsely settled Mexican territories. Utah was a small colony of Mormons with headquarters in the vicinity of the Great Salt Lake. These three territories, together with the southern half of Oregon below 49° which Great Britain had just acknowledged to be part of the Republic, must now be given political status by Congress. Both California and New Mexico had the governmental organization, such as it was, under which they had lived as parts of Mexico. Now they were governed by the military officers who had led the troops which had taken them over. Utah had an ecclesiastical government of its own creation, and Oregon likewise had contrived a frontier pattern of its own.

Congress had to deal with various complicating factors. The most difficult was the slavery question. Under Mexican law, California and New Mexico were free. A majority of the national

House of Representatives was prepared to try to keep them that way by enacting the Wilmot Proviso. This the Senate would resist. A further complication arose because Texas claimed half of New Mexico and was preparing to take it over by military force and thus make it slave.

What might have been the outcome had the normal course of events been followed will never be known. Ordinarily, the fact that all these regions were so far away and so sparsely settled might have meant that any question of admission to statehood and consequent alteration of the balance in Congress and the National Conventions would be far in the future—but the unexpected happened and the whole face of things was changed.

In January 1848, scarcely a fortnight before the treaty of peace was signed, a channel was dug to divert the water from the American River at Coloma, California, in the course of constructing a sawmill at the south fork of the river for a John Augustus Sutter. James W. Marshall, in charge of the work, saw something bright along this newly dug mill race. It was gold!

By May a local gold rush was on, and the news was traveling east. By the end of summer countless imaginations had gotten to work and that winter many a plan was laid to go in search of El Dorado. So it was that 1849 became the year of the Gold Rush. By that year's end the ten or twelve thousand inhabitants in California had increased to nearly 100,000.

The influx of population into California changed what might have been a distant issue into an immediate one. The rush of adventurers caused a social breakdown in California, a collapse of government which had to be considered in Washington. Likewise, the flow of population opened up an overland route of travel which placed Mormon Utah on the highroad. Instead of a hidden enclave almost lost in the desert, it was now a community which must deal daily with the Gentiles rushing, they hoped, to fortune but finding the city by the Great Salt Lake an oasis both alluring and repelling. New Mexico too came into the public eye because of the warlike moves by Texas to secure territory which the New Mexican military government felt bound to resist.

Such was the general situation when Congress met in November 1848, immediately after Taylor's election. Congress, though it provided no government for either California, New Mexico, or Utah, admitted the state of Wisconsin, which made the Northern and Southern Senators evenly balanced. Oregon had previously been organized as an antislavery territory. The debates in this short session showed that there was going to be a bitter struggle over California, New Mexico, and Utah.

Public opinion was beginning to focus on five points of view which had been previously formulated. The nucleus of Northern Congressmen who in August 1846 had formulated the Wilmot Proviso had attracted a host of followers who agreed that there should be no more slave territory. Calhoun had launched his counterblast in a series of resolutions demanding that slave property be permitted anywhere in the common territory. Between these two extremes, three compromises had proved attractive. The most obvious one was to extend the Missouri Compromise line of 36°30', established in 1820, to the coast and thus divide the territory. A second was to be known as "popular sovereignty"; it would let the people of the territories make their own decisions as to whether they would permit slavery. This had been General Cass' solution when he ran in 1848. Finally, there were those who would leave the question of the legality of slave property in the territories to the Supreme Court. President Polk who favored the Missouri Line extension could not persuade Congress to any action. So the problem must await the Taylor regime.

Inauguration Day 1849 brought General Taylor to the White House. Believing the people of these distant regions should frame their own state governments, and be accepted into the Union, he proposed this as his solution to the problem of assimilating the new lands and avoiding a slavery quarrel. Being a man of action he sent T. Butler King, a Georgian, to California to make known to all and sundry that the President was urging that they

organize themselves into a state as quickly as possible. He likewise looked with jaundiced eye on Texas' claims to so much of
New Mexico, and made known his belief that the best way New
Mexico could protect herself was to seek statehood. If she were
successful, the Supreme Court could then adjudicate her boundary.

As Taylor undertook to put his California-New Mexico program into effect he was under heavy handicap. Politically inexperienced, he had no idea of Congressional procedures. He had
naively appointed a Cabinet of men who could be of no political
help to him, in fact, quite the reverse. He had a hostile and confused Congress with no administration leadership to marshal
forces for him. There were men of great reputation in his own
party who had little real sympathy for him and who would probably seek to take advantage of his inexperience. His newspaper
support was half-hearted and ineffective.

When the new Congress assembled in December 1849, it had
before it a confused series of problems. California and Utah had
organized state governments and New Mexico had elected a delegate. California was sending two Senators eastward, one of
whom was Senator Benton's son-in-law, John C. Frémont, together with two Representatives. Utah's constitution as the State of
Deseret had been forwarded. Texas was threatening to send troops
into New Mexico to seize most of its populated area. Besides,
fugitive slaves were making their way northward, aided by an
organized "underground," and free states not only refused to recognize the constitutional rights of slave-owners to aid in recover-
ing their property, but often encouraged the fugitives. Finally,
slavery was permitted in the nation's capital city; slave markets
were operated almost under the eaves of the Capitol, making a
mockery of the basic doctrines of liberty which the Republic daily
proclaimed.

The President's leadership could have little influence in solving
these problems. They were in the hands of Congress and it was
an unusual Congress. The Senate was particularly notable.

Thomas Hart Benton, pompous and polysyllabled, had been in the body for thirty years. He was a man with an ego so large that it deprived him of the Presidency which Jackson had hoped to bestow upon him after Van Buren had served his term. He had been at first Polk's great hope, and then one of the many thorns in his flesh. Polk had been willing to give him command of the Army, but then Benton had quarreled with the President when he would not favor the Senator's son-in-law, Frémont, whose free-lance activities in California had gotten him into trouble with the military authorities. Lesser men had taken to goading the old lion, and in the Senate's tumultuous debates he could be exasperated past all endurance by little Senator Henry S. Foote of Mississippi who delighted in baiting him. One day the giant at last turned on his small tormentor with such apparent ferocity that Foote pulled a gun. Whereupon Benton tore aside his waistcoat and shouted, "Shoot, assassin, shoot!" There was no shooting.

Calhoun and Clay were still on the scene though Calhoun was wasting away in the last stages of illness. Clay, almost convinced that he could never be President, was returning to promote for the last time a healing compromise.

Most impressive of all was the imposing Webster. "No man was ever as great as Webster looked." He was planning to take on the nation once more as his client with Boston businessmen again supplying his substantial retaining fee. He made the Seventh of March a famous day by pleading the nation's cause. God had marked the bounds of slavery. Why would the South continue to demand the impossible, slavery everywhere? Why not sit down and work out a reasonable compromise?

Then there was a new and much younger figure, Stephen A. Douglas, who had just been elected Senator from Illinois. He was a man with a large head, a mighty voice and very short legs. He had the exaggerated aggressiveness of many men of small stature and the ensemble gained him the title of "The Little Giant." He thought of the West as his province and he was determined to develop it as fast as possible.

When these men came to legislate they found the South to be difficult. For the leaders from this section felt it would be humiliating if the property of migrating Southerners would be excluded from territories which many of their fellows had fought and died to secure. Likewise they resented the proposed denial of their property rights, namely, the abolition of slavery, in the nation's capital. They saw their neighbors in the North willfully and self-righteously attempting to deprive them of their Constitutional privilege of regaining their fugitive human property. They saw the admission of a new series of free states enforcing upon them a minority status which would leave them helpless. Southern anxiety had already caused Mississippi to call a Southern Convention to meet in Nashville in June 1850 to consider united action to stop Northern aggression. With such attitudes becoming more dominant in the section, it was evident that somehow the South must be placated, otherwise California and the rest of the Cession would either continue as military provinces or be left to set up for themselves—and what would become of the gold and the Pacific coast trade? Some Southerners undoubtedly would prefer to part with the new acquisitions rather than lose their veto power in the Senate.

It was at this point, in January 1850, that the veteran statesman, Henry Clay, saw his chance. He had returned to the Senate, he said, to aid Taylor and his fellow Whigs in promoting a program and in bolstering the fortunes of his party. But Taylor did not give him his confidence, nor did his fellow Whigs seem particularly eager to encourage what some still believed to be his insatiable desire for the Presidency. So he must, he believed, take over in a spectacular coup. This he did by returning to his ancient role of compromiser. He gathered a group of bills already introduced into Congress and presented them as a package which he would try to persuade the South to accept.

His main offerings were not territorial; they could not be, for there were no possible slave states to offer in compensation for the admission of California as a free state. But he would offer the

South dignity, security in their property and the assurance of no stigma in the laws. The territories should be organized without exclusion of slavery; the people settling there could decide for themselves. Texas and her creditors, who included a number of influential speculators in the Texas debt, should be well paid for the redrawing of her boundaries in favor of New Mexico. An effective fugitive-slave law placing enforcement in Federal hands should be passed. Congress should declare that it had no power to interfere with the interstate slave trade. Slavery should be continued in the District of Columbia, but the sale of slaves there should be prohibited and a promise made that slavery would not be abolished in the District without the approval of its inhabitants and the citizens of Maryland.

Clay offered this program to the President and his faction, and to the moderate men, South and North. After weeks of Congressional maneuvering, a select committee headed by Clay produced a Compromise package of three bills. One, called the Omnibus, would admit California under the free state constitution she had just made, organize New Mexico and Utah with freedom to decide about slavery, and adjust the boundary dispute between Texas and New Mexico in favor of the latter with financial compensation to the former; the second measure was a fugitive-slave bill, and the third a proposed statute abolishing the slave trade in the District of Columbia.

Taylor, certain Democrats who were enemies of Clay, and numerous others opposed this package deal, and Calhoun rose from his deathbed to make his last speech against it. Even the eloquent speech of Webster, delivered in its favor on March 7, had little effect. Taylor stigmatized the foes of California admission as traitors and even spoke of leading troops there himself to ensure statehood. His opponents threatened to impeach him. The whole program appeared in danger and an impasse seemed again impending. But Calhoun died. The ill-assorted Nashville convention of delegates from Southern states called by Mississippi contented itself with issuing a warning and adjourned without action; it would wait to see if Congress heeded its admonition to accept Southern demands. In July Taylor passed away. His successor, Millard Fillmore, was more tractable and favored the Compromise, but still Clay and Fillmore together could not muster enough votes for the package. Clay, old and worn out, relinquished leadership and went to Newport to restore his strength by the sea. At that point, command was taken over by the Democratic managers who, under Douglas' direction, split the package into six bills, for California, Utah, Texas, New Mexico, fugitive slaves, and the District of Columbia. In this separate form, enough votes could be found to pass them finally as five separate bills although a majority could never be found to pass them in a package. The fact that millions were to be appropriated to redeem scattered masses of depreciated Texas paper insured a certain persistent lobby support, and the fact that in the House the Texas boundary bill and the New Mexico bill were united into one bill, and passed first, may have ensured the success of the Compromise. People who were politically active in both parties and in all sections profited by this measure.

The great point in the Compromise was that the Northern interests surrendered the Wilmot Proviso, and the Southern extremists the concept that citizens could take their slave property anywhere as a Constitutional right. In place of these principles was substituted popular sovereignty: the people in new units could create their own institutional and property patterns. The territorial legislatures were given power to legislate on slavery. If these legislatures should prohibit slavery, and if their acts should be questioned in court, appeals could be taken to the Supreme Court which was Southern in composition. A promise was made that the territories should not be refused admittance to the Union because they either permitted or prohibited slavery. Finally, nothing in the acts either "pronounced or even implied a moral judgment against slavery." The South could accept these laws with dignity if not with satisfaction. The Federal enforcement of the new fugitive-slave law was a recognition of Southern Constitutional rights and the obligation of the Federal government to protect them. The mere discontinuance of the slave trade in the District without interfering with the existence there of slavery also left the South in a dignified position, that is, undiscriminated against in the national capital.

The actual significance of these laws did not appear immediately, but when it did it was somewhat different from that anticipated. California was admitted as a free state and theoretically the South was at last placed in a minority position in the Senate. This turned out not to mean anything because during the entire decade of the 1850's, California sent either one or two Senators of Southern loyalty. The size of the slave state, Texas, was reduced, but it lost no Congressman thereby, nor did the separated area contribute to the size of the free labor phalanx because New Mexico was not admitted for sixty years. The Fugitive Slave Law was practically unenforceable and contributed nothing to Southern advantage, and the discontinuance of slave trading in the District provided only a minor inconvenience. Slaves could be purchased nearby.

So far as political or even material advantage was concerned the much-vaunted Compromise probably profited nobody save the citizens of California and the Texas bondholders. It settled no disputed questions in any permanent fashion. It left a distinct feeling of grievance in the South; their basic right to carry their property anywhere in the Union had been sold for a mess of pottage. To this extent it may be said that the whole thing was a failure.

It was more than ever obvious that the nation was to grow and that its new areas were to be free soil if the nation stayed within the limits of territorial expansion achieved in 1850. The South in 1850 was not mobilized and helplessly divided. Georgia, for example, sounded a warning in convention where she solemnly resolved to abide by this Compromise but vowed she would never yield anything more. Had the South been defied it probably was not sufficiently aroused or united to have retaliated. It might

have been disabused of any sense of that effective mass resistance
which was carefully cherished in the 1850's and then unsuccessfully tried in 1860-61. As it was, during the 1850's Southern leadership could look back upon the Compromise as one that they had
exacted in the parlous year of 1850. Yet the magic of Compromise
had not dispelled a cancerous sense of grievance. What avail were
rights and guarantees in the face of a growth in population and
power so unequally distributed? But for the moment a new
balance had been achieved.

3

Dreams and Delusions

TWICE NOW a political decade had been ushered in by a funeral dirge. On an April day in 1841 muffled drums and muted trumpets had preceded the body of President William Henry Harrison down Pennsylvania Avenue. Now in July 1850 the slow cadences once again sounded along that historic thoroughfare as President Zachary Taylor's cortege left the White House to escort his body to its final resting place. The nation's emotions were deeply stirred by this repetition of tragedy. Today we can see that it marked in a sense the true character of the era, ominous of coming sorrow and bereavement.

These were not years of calm and quiet. The decade had indeed been boisterous. War, two Presidential campaigns, threats, defiance, fear, real or simulated, anger and resentment, and extravagant dreams of wealth had allowed little peace. To many it seemed as though the Republic might collapse. Did anyone then realize how much attitudes toward public events, judgments about standards of conduct, feelings toward popular leaders, concepts about the meaning of events—how these influence and control human behavior and the life of the community? Who understood that a large proportion of the basic determinants in the operation of democracy are emotional and depend not on the reason so much as upon the imagination?

The forties and fifties were years in which American imaginations were highly active; it was a romantic age. This was not solely an American phenomenon; it was part of a psychological situation characteristic of Western civilization. The United States shared with Europe this glowing epoch. This emotional activity, with its violent fluctuations between high hope and deep sorrow, had much to do with the crises and conflict. Yet, for a time, there seemed to be a season of peace. Sorrow at the death of Taylor gave way to relief at the successful passing of the political crisis. The achievement of the Compromise of 1850 seemed an evidence of security regained. Few realized that it was but a calm before a storm.

There were reasons, then obscure but now more obvious, why there could be little hope of permanent peace. Romantic ages are times when men and women are less willing to face reality, when they are less inclined to count the cost of their emotions. It was a period when Europe had been embroiled in revolution, particularly in the feverish revolutionary year of 1848, when thrones tottered, though many did not fall, and when France, Germany, Austria, and even England had to cope with uprising and violence in the streets. The American imagination, volatile and easily stirred, saw in European turmoil new evidence of the strength of republican ideals.

The new Republic now had cause to rejoice in its cultural as well as its political independence, and was seeking means to express its faith in a manner much more vivid and colorful than that in vogue in the classically conditioned eighteenth century. Had this expression had the rational uniformity of the preceding century it would have been less combustible, but there was a growing divergence in interpreting America's mission, and the meaning of its culture, which boded ill for continued peace. For a very vocal group was evolving a definition of American ideals which was to provoke bitter controversy.

Certain gifted Americans were busy formulating ideas and devising ways of communicating them. A group of literati were flourishing in New England and were busily putting pen to paper.

Emerson, Hawthorne, Whittier, Lowell, Holmes, Longfellow, and Thoreau, among many lesser lights, were rejoicing in the beauties of American nature, were glorying in the patriotic achievements of their forebears and were seeking to perfect the free society of which they essayed to be the spokesmen. To some of these writers, and to many of their readers, as well as to certain clergymen and publicists such as Theodore Parker and William Lloyd Garrison, a moral sense clearly defined right and wrong. Virtue was exalted. The good triumphed, while villains were shamed and punished. People did not admit publicly that sex complicated existence. It was truly an age of good and evil, black and white; no one seemed to see any indeterminate gray areas in which to become confused.

Therefore, when these literati sounded their message that the nation was harboring evil, that slavery was wicked and must go, their judgment was not allowed to go unchallenged. A group of lesser men in measure of talent, if not in vehemence—editors, educators, clergymen, lawyers, and literary men—formulated a Proslavery Argument. Citing the Bible, ancient literature, and a sociology of their own creation, they proclaimed slavery a positive good. Heathens from darkest Africa, doomed to die without benefit of Christianity, were brought to America, fed, clothed, and otherwise cared for, then given a chance to hear the Gospel and attain salvation. This enlightened institution enabled the masters to devote themselves not to backbreaking toil but to statesmanlike endeavor to put the great wealth of America to the best uses of mankind. Naturally the philosphers of the antislavery movement and the proslavery defense were miles apart and, in a fiery, romantic age, were bound to stir up conflict. For they were arguing about sin.

This was an intensely religious age and sin bulked large in the anxieties of men. The old, somewhat hopeless determinism of Calvinism, and the complacency of Deism, had given way before a vivid surge of religious revival which was another mark of this emotional, romantic age. An Arminian Revolution had come into being, swept onward by a flood of revivalism. The old concept of Calvinistic predestination, which left the individual helpless, was giving way to an Arminian concept of free will. Man could choose and, to all who would, salvation was free. This democracy of salvation was much more typically American than was the aristocratic Calvinism with its elite of the predestined saved.

Also, this was a period when new faiths were coming into being, such as those of the Mormons, the Millerites and the Campbellites. Unfortunately, it was also a period of religious rivalries. Various Protestant sects vied with one another. The Presbyterians split into old and new schools, and the Methodists and Baptists divided into Northern and Southern churches. Ancient antagonism between Catholic and Protestant flared up, particularly after the immigration of large numbers of Catholic Irish in the wake of the Irish famine of the mid-forties.

The determinism of Calvinism, the revivals, the romantic concept of virtue and vice combined to make people sin-conscious. Church attendance was high; most churches had at least two services on Sunday and often two prayer services on week nights. Many were constantly listening to sermons, and in periods of revival this preaching was perfervid. The punishment of sin was described in highly emotional terms, and hatred and fear of sin became very real. This heightened sectional controversy. To many in the North the South seemed steeped in sin. This the South, likewise very religious, would not for a moment admit.

The rapid changes taking place in these crowded years intensified the moral conflict. Many people were crowding into sprawling factory towns. Workers lived huddled together in squalor. Many were foreign immigrants used to a lower standard of living and ignorant of American ways. Their lives were hard and their suffering often too obvious, particularly when they became diseased or fell victim to drunkenness. At the same time settlement was advancing in the Lower South, new farms opening up. This meant more slaves had to be secured. They were brought in illegally from Africa or the West Indies, or bought in the Upper

South where the natural increase could not be put to work in the limited fields under cultivation. This traffic in human flesh, like the exploitation of the factory workers, stirred the emotions and roused the consciences of the sensitive. These conditions seemed so at variance with republican ideals of liberty and equality.

The slave and the drunkard were not the only unfortunates who attracted sympathy in this romantic age. The plight of the poverty-stricken, the sick, the deaf and dumb, and the insane aroused concern. These unfortunates had by and large been looked upon as individuals who must be cared for, if at all, by their relatives or by charitable citizens; their welfare was not a public charge. Now there developed a greater interest in public and private institutions for their care. Poorhouses, hospitals, and asylums were advocated and established, supported by private donation and tax money. More enlightened interest was displayed in the criminal, and better jails and less barbarous penology were supported by many who were interested in these reforms. There was an interest not only in these unfortunates—slaves, drunkards, the sick, insane, and criminal—but the high-minded cherished hopes for recognition of the rights of wage workers as evidenced by support for labor organization. Some also championed the rights of women, at least to the extent of permitting them to control property, and freeing them from the degrading legal status of being the chattels of their husbands.

These situations aroused feeling in various sections of the Republic. The religious absorption of so many people and the nature of their religion, in demanding perfectionism and waging a persistent war on sin, quickened the individual conscience, meant that they would fight certain of these evils. They would fear the sin of slavery and the sin of drinking. As Northern zealots stepped up their attacks on slavery, equally zealous Southerners launched counterattacks upon the wage slavery imposed on the factory workers who were kept in a helpless bondage worse than rural slavery where the owners were at least presumed to be interested in the welfare of their property. These reformers conducted veritable crusades to abolish the sin of slavery and the sin of intemperance. They preached abolition and prohibition.

These demands for the suppression of sin were reflected in literature, journalism, politics, and the pulpit. Novelists, editors and orators joined clergymen in warning and admonishing, calling people to repentance. The recently established free schools, and the multiplying number of teachers and school children, sent into society increasing numbers of those who could read and understand their pleas. The number of newspapers, magazines, and books that were published increased, in part, because the population was growing, and in part because improvements in the technical processes of printing made large, cheap publication practical. To this was added ease in distribution.

The expansion of railroad communication meant that the distribution of printed matter and letter mail was facilitated. Improved postal service meant that newspapers could be more efficiently and more widely distributed. Postage was made cheaper, and postage stamps were introduced in 1847. People became more frequent letter writers, and personal communication and exchange of ideas increased. The invention of the telegraph increased the speed of communication. Individuals could keep in closer touch with one another. Also, as so much news was now telegraphed to the newspapers, their coverage brought the world that much nearer to people heretofore isolated by distance. Thousands who now read could feel much closer to events and distant happenings. A new comprehension of the world was at hand.

The romantic, emotional, and religious attitudes that prevailed gave certain journalists and authors a vogue and an influence that was to be highly dynamic. Several examples may be cited. The attack on slavery was given renewed impulse by such papers as Benjamin Lundy's *Genius of Universal Emancipation* and, more particularly, William Lloyd Garrison's *Liberator*. Horace Greeley's New York *Tribune* sponsored many reforms and its attacks upon Southern slaveholding were widely read. This paper proved particularly influential because of its weekly edition which had a

very wide circulation among a far-flung army of rural sub-
scribers. Many of them read only the Bible and the *Tribune,* and
the latter may be said to have had the added appeal of greater
novelty. Southern journalists like Robert B. Rhett in the Charleston *Mercury* introduced a counterattack upon Yankee greed and
cruelty which exploited human beings ruthlessly. These journalists
maintained that definition of rights and liberties must be the
responsibility of the several states, based upon how they judged
the needs of their societies.

The climax of this literary emotionalism came in 1852. In that
year the daughter of a vigorous revivalist and evangelist wrote a
book which proved to be a firebrand thrown into shavings.
Harriet Beecher Stowe published *Uncle Tom's Cabin, or Life
Among the Lowly.* In highly romantic and most popular fashion,
this lady spun a tale that ran the gamut of human emotions, pointing out the cruelty of slavery, its debauching influence upon the
society which tolerated it, and the saving influence of religion
upon those suffering most cruelly. Literally hundreds of thousands
read and cried over this heart-rending story. For countless people
this was the truth about slavery, this great national sin. Southerners were hardened sinners, cruel, lustful, and rapacious. The
Slave Power which dominated the Federal Government must be
thrown from its place of control in the nation's capital.

Added elements which contributed to this tendency to emotionalism were certain changes in the nation's way of life. As
people came more and more to congregate in cities and in slums,
the incidence of ill health increased. In earlier days, the majority
had lived their lives out-of-doors, with a great deal of vigorous
muscular exercise. They ate heavily of starchy foods, with a good
deal of sugar, and then worked off the surfeit in hard labor in the
open air. Also, if men and women were out in the open a great
deal during the day, the fact that they slept in airless rooms at
night was not too dangerous. But more and more people were
living indoors, engaged in work that required a minimum of
muscular effort. Likewise they had little oxygen during the day

and none at night. Many lived in crowded squalor with a minimum of sanitation. All this added up to improper food, multiplying germs and too little fresh air. The result was much digestive disease and tuberculosis. Plagues like cholera and yellow fever spread through cities, and death stalked. Malaria was prevalent in many sections along river banks. Social diseases were common in the slums.

Untimely death was frequent. The mortality rate among children was high and many survived the hazards of childhood sickness only to die in their twenties and thirties of wasting diseases. Death in childbirth, too, was prevalent. In large families death was almost a routine occurrence. Sorrow, tears, mourning were ever present in the community. Love, parting, grief, all highly moving to the emotions, kept people tense, apprehensive, or sentimental and tearful. Comfort was sought in the churches, in thoughts of life in the hereafter, of mercy and punishment, and of the inscrutable will of God who decreed these sufferings in his infinite wisdom as a part of his great program for man's salvation. Tears came easily, pity was often aroused, and conscience made uneasy. Anger and resentment, too, could flash out sharply, and it was easy to resort to tongue-lashing and to blows. Duels were still not wholly obsolete and human life could be accounted cheap.

Another factor, less tangible but significant, was the changing status of women in the growing cities. Expanding wealth, the plentiful supply of servants available, particularly as the number of immigrants increased, some few housekeeping conveniences like gas and plumbing, all these meant less absorption with household duties. Married couples in cities more frequently did not establish homes but lived in hotels and boarding houses. New knowledge enabled them to avoid having children. These situations meant that a number of women were free to take up new interests. Thus, when clergymen, publicists and other apostles of reform began to preach crusades against evils, women were able to turn some of their great energy to the promotion of good causes and to the waging of warfare against evil.

Another element which added to the romantic flavor of the age and increased the power available to raise its dynamic potential was the cumulative effect of man's inventive genius. The tide of this creative activity gave man not only a greater use of machinery but harnessed increasing amounts of steam power to these mechanisms. Thus these advances had brought Americans an ever greater capacity to work and, viewing their mounting production, a greater confidence in the fabulous character of their power.

This industrial advance and the ever increasing rise of machines and engines was mechanizing many processes. Textile factories, smelting works, blast furnaces, and rolling mills increased in number. Coal mining provided new fuel, and the smoke of furnaces begrimed many an industrial town. Mechanical and human power were crowded together where once there had been a fair landscape. Wealth was spun on the spindles, rolled off the looms, drawn molten from the furnaces. The machines and steam power were performing miracles.

Machinery and steam power were likewise revolutionizing transportation on land and lakes, on rivers and oceans. New speeds developed. The steamboat had come first on the rivers and lakes. Then the steam locomotive on rails began to be projected in all directions. In the decade of the Mexican War some 3,300 miles were constructed, and the noise of bell and whistle, and the clatter of wheels on rails began to be heard more often up and down the land. But, as yet, these roads were generally short, built according to the capacity and interest of local capital.

The sea likewise was submitting to steam mastery. So far as American mariners were concerned, their use of the new power was reluctant. Yankee captains rejoiced in sails and the force of the wind, and when American genius invented the swift-sailing clipper ship, to many this was the climax. But the steady-ploughing coal-burning steam vessel cut new paths through the sea, and by 1850 some American shippers had waked up to the fact that the British were achieving ocean supremacy with their steam packets. At length United States capitalists responded, and Vanderbilt and Collins undertook to rival the British Cunard in the struggle to control Atlantic traffic. The time of crossing was cut down to less than two weeks.

Further evidence of man's power was the invention of the prairie plow and the horse-drawn reaper. Now, as Americans were settling the vast treeless prairies cloaked with thick grass, they found first a tool strong enough to break the deeply root-matted sod, and then a machine to reap the great acreage. Southern cotton planters worried because of the farmers' swift advance, much of it immigrant, into the West. Would not these pioneers create free labor territories and states, sure to outvote them eventually?

One of the evidences of the romantic and emotional set of the American attitude toward existence was the oft-expressed belief in the Republic's preferred place in the world, its Manifest Destiny. It was a society superior to the effete monarchies of the Old World, charged with a mission to promote freedom. Part of this feeling embraced a concept of the elasticity of the nation's natural boundaries and influence which seemed to permit of indefinite expansion, certainly to the Pacific and perhaps beyond. This belief in destiny was closely associated with another fixed idea, distrust and hatred of Great Britain, and a more recently acquired suspicion of France, particularly after the Third Napoleon had scuttled the Republic of 1848 and turned toward empire.

The tendency to think in terms of Manifest Destiny had, of course, been quickened into vigor by the enthusiasm for Texas and Oregon. It had reached its climax when, during the Mexican War, the march to the Halls of the Montezumas had ended in the acquisition of California, that prize which so instantly had turned out to be El Dorado. To many who had served in the Mexican War, and had "rushed" to the gold fields of California, the experience had been a renewed stimulant to high-flown thoughts of a greater and more glorious future.

The fair island of Cuba had been a stopping place for various warriors on their way to or from the Mexican Crusade. Cubans were suffering under Spanish tyrants. Should they not be freed? The need for a quicker route than was possible around the Horn or across the interminable American desert was obvious. There were the narrow isthmuses from Panama north to Tehuantepec. Should not transit by road, railroad, or canal be organized across Panama, Nicaragua, Honduras, or Mexico? Then, too, transcontinental railroads began to be dreamed of. One possible route could pass through the Gila River Valley in northern Mexico. Should not more territory be sought from that republic?

All of these areas were in the tropics or semitropics, and were regions where presumably Negro slavery could flourish. Now, at this time, when the "natural limits" of slave extension were believed by some to have been reached, Manifest Destiny took on new meaning. Certain Southern opinion, apprehensive of what might happen when Northern population growth gave control of the Congress and national party conventions over to that section, could see in Manifest Destiny a means of protection. If new possessions were acquired to the southward, here might be new Southern states which would maintain the balance in the Union.

An interesting variety of individuals began to work toward realizing these dreams, diplomats, politicians, promoters, steamship operators, adventurers, Army officers, and discharged soldiers. Several groups of capitalists were thinking in terms of transit across the several Central American isthmuses. A motley group of adventurers conceived of a filibustering expedition to free the Cubans from the yoke of Spanish tyranny. Fevered relations with Great Britain were featured, particularly as England had interests in these regions. She was obviously active in the West Indies and in Central America, where she had abolished slavery in her island colonies and in her "protectorate" within Nicaragua, adjacent to her colony of British Honduras.

The diplomats and the filibusterers were very busy. Americans sought to advance their interests in the isthmus areas, knowing that the republics of that region were fearful of Britain's designs. So treaties were negotiated at various tropical capitals, only one of which was ratified, that whereby Colombia gave the United States a canal right of way across Panama. A greater feat of diplomacy was the signing of the Clayton-Bulwer treaty with Great Britain whereby the United States and that nation forswore any extension of property rights in Central America, and agreed that any canal built across an isthmus should be a joint venture. No capital could be found for canal projects though Britons and Americans did pool their funds in a project to build a railroad across Panama.

This slow motion was very disappointing to a group of younger men who protested against the feeble action of the "Old Fogies." They in turn boasted of their own prowess and demanded that "Young America" be listened to and entrusted with the nation's interests. Some of these irrepressible spirits had been fired by the revolutionary movements in Europe in 1848, and had since been inspired by those who had then fled hither from Europe. The most dynamic was Louis Kossuth, the Hungarian leader, whose gallant attempt against the Hapsburg Monarchy had failed. He was given asylum in the United States and toured the country in 1851-1852 in the interest of spreading republicanism in Europe. He collected $90,000, but also stirred up a certain amount of Southern apprehension at this enthusiasm for the liberation of his people. In these years of enthusiasm, "Young America" was very vocal and the American Eagle on occasion was made to scream.

In domestic affairs the period between 1850 and 1854, while outwardly calm, was marked by some developments which were to have later significance. The operation of the new Fugitive Slave Act aroused Northern ire. All proceedings were now handled by Federal officials, commissioners, and marshals. The affidavit of a reputed slave-owner was all that was necessary to secure the arrest of a Negro. The alleged fugitive could not testify, nor summon witnesses, nor have a trial by jury. If the owner satisfied the commissioner, the Negro might be delivered up and from this decision there was no appeal. Anyone seeking to hinder this process might be fined $1,000 or imprisoned for six months. If the marshal suffered an escape, he might be fined $1,000 and be liable for a civil suit by the owner

This system met with resistance from the beginning. Citizens sought to rescue and protect fugitives. In some instances there was violence and rioting. Indignation meetings were organized, protective organizations formed, and vigilance committees put on the watch. The operation of the "Underground Railroad" was improved. Under these circumstances it soon became evident that it would be no easy thing to secure many fugitives and return them to servitude. Every attempt aroused new Northern indignation and resentment against Southern "slave stealers." Thousands of readers of *Uncle Tom's Cabin* were in a mood to protest, even to resist police. This frame of mind and form of action reinforced Southern belief that the Compromise of 1850 was a sham from which they received worse than nothing. The Yankees did not play fair. Their truculence was wrecking the only real concession made to the South. Confidence in good faith was failing.

In this uncertain but still predominantly peaceful interlude, the game of politics went on. In the Congress, the business of lawmaking and President-making, in preparation for 1852, was carried on incessantly. Here a bipartisan group was endeavoring to create a bloc committed to the idea of abiding by the compromise measures of 1850, and eschewing further sectional controversy. An effort was made to get an agreement signed by many members of the Senate and House to support no candidate in 1852 who would not forswear sectional conflict. A relatively small number signed and they were mostly Whigs. This idea was held to be an Old Fogy one and the younger members, and those attached to the growing Southern Rights movement, would have none of it. The fact of the matter was that there was something akin to Southern nationalism developing, a move working to organize a united South. But though many Congressmen might not sign an agreement to forget sectionalism, there was a large uncounted portion of the population determined that there should be no more strife. In the meantime the process of President-making picked up momentum.

As in 1848 so in 1852 the influence of the Mexican War was to be a major factor. General Winfield Scott had been thought of as a possible Presidential candidate as far back as 1840, and the laurels gained in the conquest of Mexico City had added to his availability. He was able to crowd President Fillmore and the ever-hopeful Daniel Webster out of the running for the Whig nomination. Taylor's success might be followed by a similar victory for a second hero. But Scott was now to gather some of the fruit of his quarrels with his Democratic brigadiers.

No small factor in the defeat of the Democrats in 1848 had been the secession of the Free Soilers. Could that rift be healed? A cure had been achieved very quickly in New York because only by union could the Empire State Democrats return to power. In the meantime the logical candidate for the Presidency was assumed to be Lewis Cass who had been defeated by the split; it would only be fair to give him this opportunity for vindication. But he was elderly, an Old Fogy. Also, many were not so sure that he could win even with a united party; a new face was needed, one who could make surer the necessary unity. Many who had refused to vote for Cass in 1848 would not be attracted by him now.

Various Barkises were willing, among them some who were not so young. The Mexican War still exercised an important behind-the-scenes influence on the welter of candidates. Many politicos, including the "wiser" Democrats, were well aware that Scott might be the Whig candidate. This aroused one of the Democrats in particular, namely Major General Gideon J. Pillow of Tennessee. Pillow had quarreled violently with Scott during the Mexican War and been court-martialed by him. He and other of his Democratic military associates at the Aztec Club had the same idea: they must work together to beat Scott. At first they took heart when one of their number, General William O. Butler of Kentucky, seemed promising; but when his chances collapsed they bestirred themselves to find another candidate.

Pillow undoubtedly had ambitions himself and was actually looking for a running mate. He corresponded with some of his fellow generals, and made a trip north. There he found that a group of New England politicos were grooming a comrade, Brigadier General Franklin Pierce of New Hampshire, and that some of his Aztec Club brothers, such as Brigadier General Caleb Cushing of Massachusetts and Colonel Thomas H. Seymour of Connecticut, were joining with these civilians. Pillow was attracted by the idea of a Pillow and Pierce or Pierce and Pillow ticket. With other of the generals, he proceeded to exploit the situation which had developed: major Democratic contenders had become so numerous as to prevent any of them securing the needed two-thirds vote at the Convention. A dark horse was indicated— and why not Pierce?

At the Democratic national gathering, the anticipated deadlock developed. The dominant Southern bloc, which as usual held the balance, accordingly decided to try out various dark horses. It was then that the plan of the New Englanders and the Mexican War generals bore fruit; Pierce was nominated almost by acclamation. But then the managers took over; Pillow was forgotten and one of the Southern Senators, William R. King of Alabama, received the nomination for Vice-President.

When the Whigs met, President Fillmore was pushed aside with little ceremony, and Winfield Scott put on the track. In both parties the experienced and safe managers wrote the platform; sectionalism was eschewed, and all agreed to abide by the Compromise of 1850. The only issue left was the relative military prowess of the two candidates. Scott failed to attract popular support, despite his laurels, and a normal vote gave the Democrats their usual edge. A second dark horse took up residence in the White House.

Such a colorless election seemed to be an earnest that the Compromise of 1850 had solved the problem of sectional conflict, particularly as the California Senators turned out to be loyal Democrats, one of the two actually being Southern in heritage. The usual Democratic Congressional leaders, predominantly Southern, were in control of the Congress, and the new President was unsympathetic with Northern schemes or hostile emotions. Yet there were signs of anything but peace.

Fugitive slaves continued to be rescued. There were increasing instances of resistance to the law, and captives were being spirited away from jails. Restless souls were looking with longing eyes on Cuba, and unsuccessful filibustering expeditions had already cost American lives. American steamers were having trouble in Cuban ports, and anti-Spanish feeling had broken out in New Orleans, causing the destruction of the Spanish consulate and the looting of business places kept by Spaniards. Cornelius Vanderbilt was trying to set up a transit route across Nicaragua, and was getting into trouble with local authorities there. The Navy was alerted.

Consciences were quickening. Various efforts to stamp out the shame of intemperance had come to climax in 1851 when the state of Maine prohibited the sale of liquor. The number of readers of *Uncle Tom's Cabin* was constantly mounting. Hatred of slavery and slaveholders was rising as the cruelty of Simon Legree and the heroic faith of Uncle Tom entered more actively into the imaginations of an indignant public. In the South, the portrayal was bitterly resented as unfair, overdrawn, and wickedly misrepresentative of an institution which was felt to be humane and Christian. Despite these differences, however, dreams of destiny were uniting the American people in the hope of greater possessions, power, and glory. Their visions blinded them to the dark clouds lurking on not very distant horizons.

4

A Sectional Party Is Born

FROM CALIFORNIA and Oregon citizens of the Republic could now scan the Pacific horizon and face a new world orientation. Beyond this horizon was the Far East, and Americans were invited to new trade and adventurous voyaging in the South Seas. But there were other attractive opportunities between the Mississippi and the Pacific. The West lured a restless, migratory people to search for treasure, or to found new settlements. The generous response to all of these raised problems in transportation, diplomacy, and politics of such magnitude as to bring threats of foreign war and internal strife.

The United States government responded to these challenges to peace and stability with growing concern as the fifties advanced. The Democrats returning to power in 1853 undertook to use as their principal operative device a flamboyant diplomacy quite in contrast to the stodgy policy of the Whigs. Political expediency guided the Pierce regime in shaping its brand of diplomacy. The Democratic party was almost completely dominated by its Southern Congressional leaders, who had consistently thwarted the demands of Northern interests for protective tariffs and various forms of subsidy, and thereby cost the party much support in the free states. For this the Democratic leadership sought to compensate by a spread-eagle foreign policy aimed at promoting American interests abroad. Such a policy had worked during Polk's regime, and they believed it would work again under Pierce.

The new President, under the influence of some exuberant "Young Americans," sought to push American interests ahead fast. A strange company of amateur diplomats was sent out to promote these ends, sometimes in highly unorthodox fashion. Some of their most bizarre activities were in response to the demands of rival American businessmen who wanted to secure wealth from the Pacific Coast transportation business. While one group of capitalists was getting the Panama railroad into operation, others sought to develop competing lines. The steamboat operator, Cornelius Vanderbilt, undertook to exploit a possible isthmian crossing in Nicaragua by a combination of river and lake steamers and an overland coach, while a New Orleans enterpriser sought to build a plank road, and perhaps a railroad, across the Tehuantepec Isthmus in Mexico. Vanderbilt, his enemies, and local Nicaraguan politicos produced such chaos and civil war in that unstable republic, all of it complicated by the invasion of an American filibusterer, William Walker, that the whole enterprise broke down. At one point there was a naval bombardment and danger of war with Great Britain. The Mexican enterprise was more peaceful but it proved too expensive, and when its mail-carrying subsidy was withdrawn by an economy-minded Postmaster General, that too faded. In these operations American diplomats were busily engaged promoting one interest or another, and negotiating treaties which were either never ratified, or not carried out.

Efforts were likewise made to get more territory from Mexico, to lease a coaling station from the Republic of Santo Domingo, and to persuade Spain to sell Cuba. The jealous concern of Great Britain and France, who did not wish the United States to control Caribbean and Pacific approaches, probably nipped West Indian advances in the bud; and the Cuban project fell afoul of sectional rivalry and the unbelievable comedy which was the product of our naive diplomacy. Such seasoned diplomats and shrewd financiers as James Buchanan and August Belmont had an idea that bankrupt Spain might be pressured by her creditors to sell Cuba

so that her finances might be bolstered, but a group of gasconad-
ing amateur diplomats gave the game away by their ludicrous
irresponsible behavior. A small group of these diplomats met at
Ostend in October 1854 and prepared a cautiously worded proposal to the President that he seek to purchase Cuba. This report
recommended that he watch the situation, for there were reports
that the Negro slaves might take over Cuba. If this happened the
United States, in self-defense, would have to intervene. Called
the Ostend Manifesto, some American newspapers interpreted it
as a threat to Spain to sell Cuba to the United States, or face its
seizure. All this fanfare scared the Spanish, and aroused antislavery indignation in the United States. But the hope of securing
Cuba, if necessary by force, still burned in the breasts of some
"Young Americans."

In this expansive era there were numerous other projects for
acquiring more empire. But they came to little. Whatever thought
there may have been of annexing Canada got no further than an
agreement with Great Britain for reciprocal trade and fishing
rights off the shores of that province. Projects for annexing
Alaska and the Hawaiian Islands, though discussed and even
drafted, had to wait many years for fulfillment. In the end, these
efforts brought a minimum of success. Pierce was pleased to
report that a naval expedition sent to Japan by Fillmore had succeeded in securing a treaty opening that "hidden kingdom" to
limited American access. Mexico was persuaded to agree to the
Gadsden Purchase by which the United States acquired the Gila
River Valley in southern Arizona, where a route for a southern
transcontinental railroad had been recommended by the War
Department surveyors. In the Panama region, British and American capitalists put a railroad in operation in 1855. The only
acquisitions of territory, beyond the continental limits of the
United States, were one guano island, or bird rookery, in the
Caribbean, and three similar islands in Polynesia, from which
could be secured fertilizer for exhausted Southern acres.

During this vibrant decade the American imagination was constantly urged into political as well as diplomatic action by the new possessions on the Pacific shore in such a way as to threaten the internal security of the Republic. Much as the Democrats attempted to divert attention from domestic danger by spread-eagle diplomacy, sectional rivalry would not down. Any expanse of unoccupied frontier land had always been an invitation to adventurous Americans, but the discovery of gold on the Pacific shore had written a tremendous exclamation point at the end of the phrase *Westward Ho!* Subsidiary opportunities followed in the wake of the westward trek—opportunities in organizing public transportation, developing real estate, and reaping political advantage from activity in new territories and states. The map of the United States visually spelled out these opportunities in the huge area north of the Red River, between the great Missouri and the Rockies.

Within this huge area there was ever greater pressure for transcontinental transportation and communication. Whether by coach, horseback, or railroad, transportation was made extremely difficult by a geography which imposed great capital expenditure and provoked sectional animosity. The more enterprising realized that the government would have to share the responsibility. The first real step taken toward solving the problem was Congressional action directing surveys to be made of possible rail routes under the direction of the War Department. These were made in 1853 and 1854, and numbered five. When the results were published, a contest ensued whether a northern, a southern or a central road should be authorized. Northern and Southern interests fought back and forth, while some advocated two, and even three, roads in the hope that the sectional rivalries might be placated.

Between the Missouri and the Rockies there was no political organization; the region was vaguely dedicated to the Indians who either roamed the plains or occupied the "Indian territory" they had taken over after being dispossessed from the more easterly lands they had once inhabited. The occupation of Oregon, the Mexican cession, and the gold rush had accelerated the activity of explorers, trappers, and traders in marking out routes of travel. To the older Santa Fe and Oregon trails was added the central route, the California trail to San Francisco and the gold fields. These trails were long, difficult, and dangerous, but they passed through a country which inspired ideas in those who traveled them. In these prairies and mountain ranges were to be found opportunities in real estate, mining, transportation, and politics, when government could be established therein. Officers would be appointed, legislatures elected, defense organized, land patented, franchises voted, towns built, railroads constructed, economic and political fortunes created. None of these opportunities could be realized so long as this vast range of wood, plain, and mountain was left to the Indians.

The westward population push thus made pressure for the establishment of government inevitable. The adventurers, whether interested in mere wandering, fortune hunting, mining, real estate, railroad building, or politics, were importunate. Bills were drawn to organize territorial government in the region, to give homesteads to settlers, to establish post routes, to build military roads and to subsidize railroad construction. But the principal question was not whether these things should be done, but by whom, and this depended to some extent upon whether Northern or Southern settlers should create the new communities.

By law, all the region north of the Red River, save the small strip between it and 36° 30′, had been dedicated to free-state status by the Missouri Compromise of 1820, and no change in this had been made in 1850. Some did argue that, by refusing to extend 36° 30′ to the Pacific, the nation had abandoned the idea of a set boundary line between slave and free territory, and that the principle of Popular Sovereignty had been substituted, by admitting California and by advising Utah and New Mexico that they could be admitted on terms of their own devising. But this was only argument; the law still prescribed that this empire be dedicated to freedom.

Such a limitation had an aggravating influence on a number of Southern people, particularly on the political operators. Despite the admission of California, which gave the free states a theoretical majority in the Senate, the Southern influence had remained predominant. Members from the South were retained in their places longer by their stable constituencies, and thus gained seniority and, with it, control of the important Congressional committees. By the same token, they were dominant in the Democratic national conventions; theirs was the voice that controlled the platforms and nominations in the quadrennial Presidential contests. But the number of people and the spirit of enterprise were mounting, and more individuals were dissatisfied with Southern rule because of its negativism. Southern leaders saw nothing in tariffs, public improvements, and subsidies but expense to their constituencies, and as strength contributed to the very people who wished to diminish their power and even destroy their society. Too many people were finding this power frustrating. And such frustration was bound to make an explosion of some sort inevitable.

Congress felt a constant pressure urging the organization of territories and states in this vast western enclave. Bills had been repeatedly introduced into Congress for ten years before 1853. Now real estate and railroad interests, anxious for Indian lands and rights of way, renewed their efforts, backed by a restless tide of population and a myriad of small-time, adventurous and speculating rovers. Would Southern leadership still say no?

The Southern Congressional leaders were also faced with threats to their power from within Congress. The Western states shared in these desires, and their Congressmen were demanding a greater share of control. Typical of this new force were Senators from Ohio, Illinois, Indiana, Missouri, Texas, Michigan, Iowa, and Wisconsin, sixteen of the sixty-two, who demanded their share of authority. Their most effective spokesmen were men like Douglas—men with whom the South must come to terms, must in some way reckon.

Douglas was chairman of the Senate committee on territories, the only Northern Senator to hold an important Senate committee chairmanship. He was also a man with many business interests, particularly real estate and railroads. Most important, he had his eye on the Presidency. He had been working hard for a decade to organize the Kansas-Nebraska region so that population might enter and buy land, so that a transcontinental railroad might be built to the Pacific coast, and so that new Western states might be admitted which would support Western measures, and perhaps help him to the White House.

After a complicated series of maneuvers, Douglas piloted an act through Congress in 1854 giving territorial government to the great unorganized balance of the Louisiana Purchase. This Kansas-Nebraska Bill was passed by a bipartisan combination of Southern Democrats and Whigs, with such reluctant Northern Democratic support as could be whipped into line by Douglas and the Pierce administration. Douglas had hoped to open this territory without raising the slavery issue, assuming that the same phraseology used in the Compromise of 1850 would be acceptable. By this act, these territories would be admitted as states "with or without slavery, as their constitutions may prescribe at the time of their admission," and the question of whether slaves could be taken into the territory would be left to the courts as likewise prescribed by the acts of 1850.

But the complex exigencies of senatorial politics were such that Douglas' rivals in that body forced into the bill a specific repeal of the Missouri Compromise, thus opening the territory, divided by the bill into two, to those who wished to carry slave property into it. Douglas and his Southern Senatorial colleagues who dominated the Democratic party then were able to persuade President Pierce to make it an Administration measure: he needed their support for his policies, domestic and, particularly, foreign.

The repeal of the exclusion of slavery, hallowed by thirty-four years of existence, fanned an indignation which the politically

minded were quick to use to their advantage. The opponents of
the "Slave Power" felt that their surest means of destroying it was
to defeat the Northern Democrats. The Whigs had seldom been
able to achieve this, and it seemed as though it could not be done
unless a new issue were contrived with special appeal to Northern
voters. This the Kansas-Nebraska Bill, by favoring slave interests,
seemed to provide.

The advantage was seized immediately. A small group of
Northern Senators and Representatives was led by Salmon P.
Chase and Charles Sumner, two Senators elected by strategically
placed free soilers holding the balance of power in the legislatures
of Ohio and Massachusetts. They badly needed a strong anti-
Southern party, and they called upon the Northern voters to
rally against this repeal of a "sacred compact." They sounded an
alarm: the bill was "a gross violation of a sacred pledge; . . . a
criminal betrayal of precious rights; . . . part and parcel of an
atrocious plot."

This tocsin boomed out in a year of Congressional elections
when all the House members must resubmit their fortunes to the
voters. If anti-Southern opposition could be mobilized in the
Northern states, it might well go hard with those Northern
Congressmen who followed Douglas and the Pierce Administration in supporting the measure.

The "appeal" struck attentive ears, and probably was the final
push needed to project a political regrouping. Such a regroup-
ment would be dictated in part by circumstances which had nothing to do with the sectional divisions in the nation or with
the indignation aroused by the Kansas-Nebraska Act. Some element in our history appears to have decreed that a series of
twenty-year cycles would shape the pattern of nineteenth-century
American politics. Every double decade produced some sort of
political reshuffling. The Whigs and Democrats had been bat-
tling it out for twenty years, and a fundamental change was due.
The time was ripe.

The Democratic party, in power for more than twenty years

with slight intermissions, was now plagued by rivalries and factions. Although nominally loyal to President Pierce, Senator Douglas itched to be its leader. The party leadership, predominantly Southern, was officially supporting Pierce but some of its members were covertly "looking around," and James Buchanan, recently Minister to England, was, as usual, available. Antagonism was latent between Northern and Southern elements in the party. At the same time the Whig party appeared disorganized, leaderless, and without any reason for being beyond that of opposing the reigning Democrats.

The fullness of time was at hand for a new party; the question was what shape it would take. There were several significant trends which might draw the pattern of politics to come. One of the features of the expanding population was the great increase of European immigration. During the 1840's famine and revolution had sent thousands to America in search of better fortune and greater freedom. The bulk of these had come from Ireland and Germany. The first group was largely Catholic, and brought with it the seeds of religious dissension; the second group contained many who had suffered in the cause of liberty and were unalterably opposed to slavery. Both groups brought strange speech and customs. The Catholic immigrants, on their part, intensified the antagonism, as old as the Reformation, between those of their faith and the Protestants.

Immigration had been fomenting political strife at intervals. In 1849 a secret organization, the Order of the Star Spangled Banner, was formed. It had all the attraction of mystery and ritual, and fitted into a pattern of secret organizations copied to some extent from the Masonic order.

In the early fifties, nativist political tickets had been supported in New York, Pennsylvania, and New Jersey. As the Whig party seemed to be declining as an effective instrument to oppose the Democrats, some felt that Native Americanism could be used to take the place of Whiggery. It became evident that such a party was mobilizing in secret, and its members, because of their refusal to impart any information, were derided as "Know-Nothings." In the spring elections of 1854, while the Kansas-Nebraska Act was under debate, this new political organization was discovered in action when in certain municipalities in New York citizens, who had made no campaign and indeed had not been announced as candidates, received majorities at the polls.

At the same time the revulsion in the Northern states against the repeal of the Missouri Compromise was demonstrated when, in the President's own rock-ribbed Democratic New Hampshire, the Democrats lost the lower house of the legislature in March, even before the Nebraska bill was passed. In April, a combination of Whigs and temperance voters carried Rhode Island and Connecticut. In the west, in Wisconsin and Michigan, coalitions of Whigs, anti-Nebraska Democrats, Know-Nothings, and Free Soil men were shaping a pattern which would be followed in most of the other trans-Appalachian states. In the East there was a similar fusion in Vermont and Maine, and a partial union in New York; in Pennsylvania and New Jersey the combination was between Whigs and Know-Nothings.

The trend, indicated in the spring elections, was unmistakable in the fall. Iowa in August, Maine and Vermont in September, Ohio, Indiana and Pennsylvania in October and in November, all seven voting states went against the Democrats. A number of these fusion parties adopted the name "Republican," indicating that a new party was rising, reminiscent of Jefferson's old Republican lovers of liberty. But in Massachusetts and Delaware the Know-Nothings won, and they were an important element in several of the fusions, particularly, as noted, in Pennsylvania and New Jersey; their numbers were also impressive in New York.

At the conclusion of the elections in 1854 it was certain that the Democrats had lost the House, but it was by no means clear who would control the next Congress. If there could be a coalition of anti-Nebraska, Whig, and "American" (the party name assumed by the Know-Nothings) forces, the House management would be theirs. Also, to those who were looking ahead to 1856, there was another possibility. Could such a combination be formed to defeat the Democrats in a Presidential contest? The elections of 1854 and 1855 had indicated two possibilities. One was an anti-Southern, antislavery combination, frequently called Republican. The other was a Know-Nothing, or American, opposition. The great advantage of the latter, as many viewed it in 1855, was the fact that it had a national appeal. On the face of things the Republicans could not expect to carry any Southern states, while 100-per-cent American, anti-foreign and anti-Catholic sentiments might be very popular below the Mason-Dixon line. Which way would the anti-Democratic trend take? As 1856 approached there was no clear indication.

Direction was to be found on the plains of Kansas as Popular Sovereignty began its work. Before the Nebraska bill had been signed into law, plans for settlement had been formulated in an unusual way. Normally, the new territory would have been settled from Missouri and Iowa, and the states in the Ohio Valley, and would have been made up largely of people who had some experience with frontier conditions. But now romantic enthusiasts wished to alter the pattern. Zealous antislavery, anti-Southern protagonists in New England believed that only true antislavery immigrants from the east coast could be trusted to vote against establishing slavery in Kansas. So, even before the passage of the Nebraska bill, New England's promoters got busy. A New England Emigrant Aid Society was chartered with authorization to secure capital up to $5,000,000. News of this incorporation stirred much emotion. In Missouri, and in other slave states, it was interpreted as a Yankee plan to send out free-soil voters at a cost of millions to erect a free community next door to Missouri.

The settlement of Kansas began, therefore, not as a haphazard migration of an assorted number of individuals and families, but with an unusual degree of organization. Even more unusual, in fact unique, was the appearance of rival, even hostile, organized groups. The first comers in the Southern, or Kansas, territory were of Missouri origin, and they had spread out from the vicinity of Fort Leavenworth on the Missouri River, a long-established Army post. When the first contingent from New England arrived in August 1854, and began building the town of Lawrence, a little to the westward on a Missouri tributary, the Kansas River, the Missourians bestirred themselves to develop a rival town, called Leavenworth, not far from the Fort. In Missouri protective organizations were formed to save the region from Yankee "slave stealers." Efforts were made to organize emigrant parties in the Lower South, and several did enter the territory. However, the distances from New England and the Gulf states were too great. The New England Emigrant Aid Society probably sent fewer than 2,000 settlers, many of whom did not stay. Their significance lay in the advertisement their effort received which aroused Southern ire. The bulk of the migrants in the end came from the Ohio Valley.

After some delay in Washington the newly appointed territorial officials came to their posts. President Pierce, desiring to be neutral, had appointed a Northerner Governor of Kansas and a Southerner Governor of Nebraska. Governor Reeder of Kansas was a man with political and real estate ambitions who believed in Squatter Sovereignty, and wanted to see that it was fairly operated. His late arrival in the territory meant that no census could be ready upon which to base a legislative apportionment until spring. Also, bureaucracy was slow in making land surveys and in providing the section maps which were necessary before land titles could be located and registered. Thus, in respect to government and property, everything remained uncertain for more than a year after the Kansas-Nebraska Act had been passed.

The spring election was an invitation to violence. Organized groups came over from Missouri to vote as landowners and taxpayers, and the legislators who secured certificates of election were in large proportion favorable to introducing slavery into the territory. The Governor, somewhat overawed by this show of force which he had no power to resist, particularly as the Federal courts and law officers in the territory were largely in sympathy with it, felt he must accept this result. He attempted, however, to move the new government far from Missouri influence, and at the same time promote some real estate operations in which he was interested, by setting up the capital of the territory and the meeting place of the legislature on the Kansas River at a place to be called Pawnee City in the center of what is now the state of Kansas, near Fort Riley.

In the meantime, the legislature was developing ideas of its own. It went to Pawnee City as directed by the Governor but almost immediately voted to recess and resume its meetings near the Missouri border at Shawnee Mission. Despite the Governor's steps to prevent it, the legislature met at Shawnee Mission and enacted laws favorable to the slavery interest. The free-state men declared this legislature to be bogus, because the election had been decided by a force of invaders, and that all its acts were fraudulent. Many from the free states, particularly those who had come from distant New England, organized a boycott of this territorial government. Largely on Southern demand, Governor Reeder was removed by the President, ostensibly for illegal land dealings with Indians, and he joined the Free State party in organizing a "state government" for Kansas. In October 1855, the Free State party held a convention which drew up a state constitution and elected a state government. Ex-Governor Reeder was chosen as delegate to Congress to present this constitution as Kansas' application for admission to the Union as a free state.

Thus, two governments were in being. Washington recognized the territorial government headed by Reeder's successor and the generally proslavery legislature. But the Free State government, chosen by the Free State voters, was likewise attempting to act. As the surveys were still incomplete, and all land titles still uncertain, guerrilla warfare broke out, sometimes over real estate thefts by claim jumpers. Bloodshed made it necessary to call out troops. Eastern newspapers, particularly the Free Soil New York

Tribune, were carrying much news about "Bleeding Kansas."
Squatter Sovereignty seemed to have broken down.

When Congress met in December 1855, on the eve of the Presidential campaign of 1856, it was in a state of dangerous disorganization. It took two months of angry debate and delay before a Northern coalition was worked out on February 1 which chose a Massachusetts American, Nathaniel P. Banks, the Waltham Bobbin-Boy, as Speaker. During this period there was continued trouble in Kansas. As soon as the House organized, it received the petition that Kansas be admitted as a free state, and after prolonged debate passed an act of admission which the Democratic Senate would not accept.

Kansas continued to lead. A proslavery sheriff started a move to discipline the free-state town of Lawrence, which resulted in his being shot and the town "sacked." An antislavery zealot gained notoriety by a ferocious assault. One of the contingents which sought to make Kansas free was a dedicated family of Browns. John Brown, Sr., a wandering cattle drover, unsuccessful in business, twice married, had established a family of twenty children. He had also acquired a great concern to free Negroes held in bondage. He came to believe himself an agent of the Lord, duly appointed to liberate the enslaved. When Kansas was opened, several of his sons went out to aid the cause of freedom and to secure real estate. As trouble developed in the summer of 1855 between proslavery and free-state protagonists, they sent for their father who brought out a load of arms. So aroused was he by the situation that he and a small party, which included four of his sons, resorted to terrorism and in this tumultuous May of 1856 massacred five proslavery men in the Pottawatomie region. Retaliation resulted in the killing of one of the sons. Almost at this same time, Senator Charles Sumner delivered a speech in the Senate on "The Crime Against Kansas." This speech alluded to several Senators in such terms that a Southern Congressman, who was a relative of one of them, beat Sumner over the head with a cane right in the Senate, and kept Sumner from his seat for more than three years. All this was useful political propaganda for the new Republican party just going into its first campaign.

The two forces, Republican and American, were mobilizing to drive the Democrats from the White House, each hoping to be the dominant anti-Democratic organization. But Bleeding Kansas tipped the scale because the warfare stirred so much anti-Southern indignation in the North. The Americans tried to keep sectionalism out of their councils; but when the party managers attempted to avoid the issue in February 1856, the Northern wing felt they could not afford to join in ignoring it. When their demand for denunciation of the repeal of the Missouri Compromise was refused, they broke up the party. This disruption contrasted with the enthusiastic Republican meeting that same month which succeeded in creating a vigorous Northern party, and in arranging for a national nominating convention to meet in June.

The opposition to the Democrats was therefore to be marshalled largely under the standard of the new Republican party. At its nominating convention a romantic expedient was adopted. Colonel John C. Frémont, the Pathfinder, was chosen as the nominee. An explorer and an Army officer, he had political connections in the Southwest, particularly in Missouri. He was nominated on a platform dedicated to preventing the further extension of slavery and to subsidizing a great Pacific Railroad. The Americans made a coalition with some Whig remnants and nominated ex-President Fillmore, but the Northern Americans refused to support this ticket. They eventually fused with the new Republicans. The Democrats, realizing something of their danger, abandoned Pierce, refused to accept Douglas, and sought victory with the experienced James Buchanan of the pivotal state of Pennsylvania. He had been Minister to England during the Pierce Administration, and thus had avoided any involvement in Kansas-Nebraska.

The battle of 1856 was a close one. Frémont had the appeal that had been anticipated, and carried all but five northern states— Pennsylvania, New Jersey, Indiana, Illinois, and California. In

1852 the Republican party had not existed, was hardly dreamed of; now, four years later, its candidate received 114 electoral votes. One thing was plain: if in 1860 the new party could capture Pennsylvania, and either Indiana or Illinois, it would win. Buchanan had succeeded by only a hair's-breadth, and Fillmore had carried but one state, Maryland. This result had been watched with apprehension in the South. At least one Governor, Wise of Virginia, was thinking of secession, if Frémont won. How general such thoughts were cannot be said. But they were there, and the election of Buchanan was welcomed by many, North and South, with relief. A danger had been averted. But what of 1860? Two states were but a slim line of defense.

In the North, a new militancy was abroad. Opposition to Southern control of national policy was rising. Of all the measures advocated by Northern enterprise—protection, appropriations, subsidies, opening of new areas for settlement, organization and development—all had failed save one. Nebraska had been thrown open, but at the price of division into two territories and of the repeal of the Missouri Compromise. Frustration and indignation were accumulating.

5

Impending Danger

THE QUICK GROWTH in power of the new Republican party was bound to increase the tension between the sections. The trend of migration was to the northwest. These migrants were destined to carry "freedom" on their banners. The South could not fail to realize how narrow had been the Democratic victory in 1856. Already, some political prophets foresaw the probability of a Republican victory in 1860. Would the slave states acquiesce in such a result or was secession inevitable?

At first, the South received reassurance from a high authority. Hardly had Buchanan been inaugurated when the Supreme Court concluded extended deliberations on the legality of slavery in the territories. In the Dred Scott case, an opinion was concurred in by the majority of the Court that Congress could not interfere with slaveholding in the territories. In effect, they concurred in the view that the Missouri Compromise had been unconstitutional, and that the Republican platform, demanding the exclusion of slavery from the territories, was contrary to the fundamental guarantees protecting property rights.

This dictum of the highest court in the land not only reassured the South, and seemed to cut the ground out from under the Republicans, but it disturbed Senator Douglas and those who joined him in advocating Popular Sovereignty. For, if property rights were guaranteed everywhere, must they not be immune from interference by settlers in territories? Must not the "sovereigns" respect them too?

The South received reassurance from a second event, this time from a national calamity. Business was booming in 1857, but it was overexpanded and riding for a fall. The round of another business cycle was reaching a dizzy climax. Twenty years before, in 1837, there had been a smash; now there were signs of another. In 1854 there had been some failures, but now general disaster was impending. The flush 1850's had encouraged overproduction, overbuilding, overbuying, overextended borrowing on too-generous credit. Then the Crimean War had upset European finance and exchange. European capitalists could invest their money more profitably on their own continent. They therefore sold a good many of their American securities, dumping them on American exchanges, forcing prices down, and making it necessary to ship gold to Europe. This meant that American stocks and bonds, held as security for loans, particularly railroad issues, had lost much of their value, and that American gold, held as collateral for bank notes, was being drained away. The large supply of American bank notes became of uncertain value.

Also, the demand for American raw materials fell off. Americans had no way of selling sufficient of their produce to pay their debts. They were threatened with bankruptcy. Factories, unable to sell, closed down. Labor forces were out of work; they could neither buy what they needed, nor pay what they owed. Storekeepers and landlords were caught. In August 1857 banks began to discover that they had loaned too much cash and could not meet the demands of depositors. One after another failed, and by the middle of October the banks in most cities had closed their doors. Business was at a standstill. Firms of all sorts were failing right and left. Masses of unemployed faced starvation; the business world and the poor of the cities were threatened with chaos and dark night.

The climax came in the second week in October. The banks in Philadelphia and other centers had closed their doors by the end of September, but those in New York City had been holding on. Then, on October 13, panic seized Gotham where many determined to get their money out of the banks before it was too late. Wall Street that morning was densely crowded. A steady stream of people moved toward the counter of every bank and the depositors were calling for gold. One dignified banker addressed the crowd, assuring them that the sound banks were acting in concert and would not suspend. The crowd cheered but continued toward the counters. As an observer recorded the scene, for blocks the "sidewalks were densely packed with businessmen, capitalists, and operators. It was a most 'respectable' mob, good-natured and cheerful in its outward aspects but quivering and tingling with excitement. They laughed nervously, and I saw more than one crying." Next morning, all New York banks save one were closed.

Within a week this New York observer reported, "We are a very sick people just now. The outward and visible signs of disease . . . are many." Building construction was almost suspended. Walking down Broadway the passer-by could see expensive buildings started in the spring which had gone up two stories, now stopped. It was feared they might stand unfinished and desolate for years. "Almost every shop has its placards . . . announcing a great sacrifice, vast reduction of prices, sales at less than cost." Many of them had their goods out on the sidewalk with price tags conspicuously announcing their distress. The stores were kept open in the evenings in the hope of catching purchasers. "In Wall Street every man carries Pressure, Anxiety, Loss written on his forehead. This is far the worst period of public calamity and distress I've ever seen, and I fear it is but the beginning."

The observer was right. By November, the financial crisis had thrown thousands of the working class out of employment, and would make it a difficult matter to maintain peace and order through the winter. The Mayor of New York urged the Common Council to provide work in Central Park, and to buy flour for the poor. He stirred up class feeling by calling attention to the "rich who produce nothing and have everything and the poor who produce everything and have nothing." The poor staged "rather alarming demonstrations. They began marching in processions, holding meetings in Wall Street, proclaiming themselves entitled to work and demanding that they be given work," otherwise they would take food by force.

On November 10, a mob gathered at the City Hall and threatened to invade the Council chamber, but the presence of 300 police stopped them on the brink of vandalism. Soldiers and marines were brought in to guard the Custom House and the government treasure in the Assay Office. Fortunately, the mob spirit died down in a day or two. Relief measures were adopted, and fear abated. The banks were not basically unsound, more gold arrived from California, mills began to operate again. By mid-December the New York banks had reopened, and before midsummer 1858 banks throughout the country were again doing business.

These hardships, however, touched the agricultural South but lightly. Cotton continued to grow; the slave economy continued to produce the crop and Europe bought it. The money from cotton sales helped rescue the banks and commission merchants, and some rays of a new dawn began to shine. This situation caused many a Southern leader to draw an unwarranted conclusion. The South was stable, impervious to business fluctuation, her wealth and prosperity were secure. Only the North was weak and insecure. The South was necessary to the North, but the North contributed little to the South. Cotton was King! If relations between the sections got too bad, the South could set up for itself with plenty of resources. Its cotton crop would support it. The North, on the other hand, would perish without the South. The South therefore could contemplate independence with great confidence, could be careless in its demands with slight fear of evil consequences.

But these reassurances could hardly blind perceptive observers to contrary trends. Despite the opinion of the Supreme Court, the question of slavery in the territories was not settled. Trouble was flaring again in Kansas. During the campaign of 1856, President Pierce had sent a third Governor, John W. Geary, to the troubled territory. He was a frontiersman of sterner stuff than his two predecessors. Backed by Federal troops, he took decisive measures, and telegraphed, conveniently for the election: "Peace now reigns in Kansas." But not for long. During the winter trouble broke out again.

Buchanan came into office with a determination to send a Governor to Kansas of such importance and reputation that he could command the respect of both parties and bring them all into the June election for a Constitutional Convention. He chose no less a man that the great financier and promoter who had been with him in Polk's cabinet as Secretary of the Treasury, Robert J. Walker. Walker had a reputation for getting things done. Important speculative interests presumably had confidence in him, and his political contacts were significant. He was a man deemed by some to be of Presidential timber, one who might come back from Kansas as Senator. Walker exacted a promise from Buchanan that Washington would back him up in insisting on a fair vote on the slavery issue by the people of Kansas. At the same time, he worked in harmony with Douglas.

But the damage had been done before Buchanan and Walker took over. The Constitutional Convention election had been arranged at Lecompton by the "fraudulent" proslavery territorial government and, do what he might, Walker could not get the Free State people to participate in it. In June a unanimously proslavery convention was elected, and these delegates were determined to draft a proslavery constitution. This they planned to send directly to Congress without submission to the people. All that some of the agents of the Buchanan Administration could do was to contrive a weak compromise which provided for submission to the voters only the question of whether slaves should be admitted to Kansas in the future. Walker denounced this subterfuge which would have left slave property already in the

territory undisturbed, and would have prevented amendment to
the new state constitution for several years. Whichever way this
vote went the proslavery forces would remain in control of the
government and of the granting of franchises to enterprise. After
further efforts to stop frauds in territorial elections, Walker went
back to Washington to demand that Buchanan keep his pledges.

The President, on his part, felt that the country must be rid of
Kansas. The odds in 1860 appeared to be dubious and the Republicans must be deprived of any more campaign material from
the territory. Also, Southern pressure was on him to accept this
partial submission and have the constitution sent to Congress so
that the two houses, both Democratic, could dispose of the
question early and have the whole thing out of the way long before 1860. But Walker demanded that he reject this "fraud"; and,
more important, Douglas was even more emphatic.

When Buchanan had pledged support of Popular Sovereignty
Douglas, like Walker, thought that the President had undertaken
to ensure a fair vote. Instead, this proslavery gang was now attempting a subterfuge which was designed to ensure slave property in Kansas. Douglas felt this to be a travesty on Popular Sovereignty. He was coming up for re-election as Senator from Illinois
in 1858, and the Republicans were pressing him hard. He could
not accept this "fraud" and be re-elected in Illinois, and if he lost
in Illinois he would be eliminated as a Presidential possibility.
Furthermore, Buchanan had ignored him in patronage matters
and had, in a sense, insulted him. The "Little Giant" wouldn't
take it. There were bound to be fireworks when the national
legislature assembled, in a session which would resemble the
Nebraska Congress of four years before.

The Lecompton constitution was endorsed at an election in
which no free-state people participated. As the legal forms had
all been followed, Buchanan thereupon recommended to Congress that Kansas be admitted under the Lecompton constitution.
As leader of the Democrats, he ordered the Democratic houses of

Congress to accept this and take Kansas out of politics. Douglas and Walker had protested in vain.

The Republicans, a number of Americans, and some of the Northern Democrats, particularly followers of Douglas, now organized to defeat the admission of Kansas under this "fraud." So many defections occurred that after three months of bitter debate it became almost certain that the House would not obey the President's commands. The opponents of Lecompton demanded that the whole constitution be submitted to the people. A tortuous compromise finally was worked out by which the issue of admission, but not the question of slavery, was submitted and the voters, for the first time mobilized from both parties, rejected statehood for the time being. Kansas still was a territory, and the Democratic party was once again rent by schism. Douglas and numerous Northern Democrats had defied the President and the Southern leadership.

Western development aroused interest in portions of the trans-Mississippi domain other than Kansas. Many were earnestly seeking to improve transcontinental transportation. So far, all efforts to build a railroad had proved futile. North and South could not agree on a route or on a subsidy, nor could private capital be mobilized in any sufficient amount. Travelers therefore had to go by covered wagon or by organized mail-coach service. The first was unsubsidized, private enterprise, but the second operated under various forms of Federal compensation for carrying the mail which contractors now tried to get increased. At first this Federal appropriation for mail service was confined to the steamship companies for mail carried by sea and across the isthmian routes, but California was demanding quicker and cheaper overland service. Private enterprise set up a route from the railhead at St. Joseph, Missouri, via the South Pass and Salt Lake City to Placerville, California. Though it was slow and expensive, and in the winter often blocked for months by snow, pressure increased for government subsidy. Finally Congress yielded, authorizing the Postmaster General to pay $300,000 to $600,000 annually, according to the number of trips made, on condition that the contractor agree to carry the mail through in 24 days, a week quicker than the ocean average. The Postmaster General, Aaron V. Brown of Tennessee, advertised for bids, and awarded the contract to John Butterfield who agreed to follow a southern oxbow route from St. Louis and Memphis down through Texas and New Mexico to Fort Yuma and up to Los Angeles and San Francisco. Brown chose this route, he said, because it was open all the year round and never blocked by snow. This line was opened in 1858 and proved practical, though punishing, to anyone with $200 who would risk the Indian attacks which always threatened.

This transcontinental transportation was affected by the various hazards of western life. The Indian dangers were ever present. Then difficulties developed along the central route because of the peculiar relations of the Mormons with the Gentiles and the Federal government. The Mormons had settled in the Great Salt Lake region believing themselves to be so far from the haunts of their fellow men that they could build their wilderness Zion undisturbed. But the discovery of gold in California had placed them, in effect, on a highway along which thousands passed in various stages of expectation and destitution. The Federal government refused Utah statehood, and it had to be content with territorial status.

The Mormons insisted on going their own way, and in being a law unto themselves, to such an extent that they practically ignored Federal authority. A military expedition of some 2,000 soldiers was sent out in 1857 to remind them of their allegiance. Brigham Young called his people together and preached resistance. He prescribed a "scorched earth" program. They would destroy their handiwork and withdraw to the mountains, harassing the invaders by blocking their supply routes and dooming them to starvation. However, Buchanan was persuaded to authorize a volunteer diplomat, Thomas L. Kane of Pennsylvania, a mutual friend of both Brigham Young and the President, to go out via the isthmus route and seek peace. He succeeded. The

Mormons accepted a Georgian as Federal Governor, and hostilities were avoided. The new Governor did not interfere with the Mormon leadership.

This potential warfare interfered with transcontinental travel and deflected it to other routes. At the same time, supplying the troops increased the freight hauling business from the Missouri railheads to Utah. The discovery of gold in 1858 and 1859 in the Nevada-Colorado area caused a great increase in travel from California to Nevada, and from the East to Colorado. Denver and Pike's Peak became terminal points. Missouri freight hauling contractors began a line which after various mergers took over the central mail-carrying system which competed with Butterfield's southern route.

In the midst of the quarrels and schemes that marked this tense year of 1858 came a great outburst of religious emotion. The financial panic of 1857 had shaken the confidence of many and had acted as a quickener of religious zeal. In their distress people turned to God and enjoyed a season of revival. Not only did ministers in their pulpits call men to repentance for their sins of preoccupation with worldly gain but laymen took the initiative in providing their own means of grace. It was particularly noted that in New York City merchants organized noonday prayer meetings in the business district where they confessed their sins and exhorted each other to renew their covenants with Christ's Church. In Philadelphia and elsewhere appeared Young Men's Christian Associations in which many a youth sought and found God.

This quickening of the Spirit, this Pentecost, made its appearance in many sections of the land and brought multitudes to a renewed consciousness of sin. This concentration on sin, reminiscent of Puritan days, could not fail to arouse scruples against slavery. And those who hated sin had great concern for the unrepentant sinner. This attitude sharpened the sectional antagonism. Northern enthusiasts could condemn Southern slaveholders as sinners and denounced their crimes. On the other hand many

Southerners resented these strictures and in return accused their Northern brethren of the sin of greed; they were slaves of mammon, pharisees, and hypocrites. Such charged emotions and their effect on sectional antagonism were ominous of dangers to come.

Consciousness of and callousness toward sin were further evidenced by demands for the revival of the slave trade. In the Southern commercial convention of 1858 its desirability was vigorously advocated, and there was other evidence of demand. In the latter months of 1858 two examples were featured in the press. A United States naval vessel captured a slaver, the *Echo,* which was brought into Charleston with its woebegone cargo. Despite the fact that there was no doubt about any point in the indictment, the jury brought in a verdict of not guilty. A similar result attended the case of the *Wanderer* whose captain landed a gang of slaves in Georgia. The operators in this instance likewise were found "not guilty." Laws against even such inhuman traffic could not be enforced in the face of a public opinion which either openly favored its revival, or felt so outraged by Northern refusal to render fugitive slaves that such compensatory nullification seemed a remedy.

Southern apprehensions, and perhaps their consciences too, were further roused by the fact that Northern Republicans were actively circulating a book written by a Southern poor white, Hinton R. Helper, called *The Impending Crisis.* By the use of statistics, the book demonstrated, convincingly to many, that the nonslaveholders in the South were victimized by slavery. Helper called upon them to cease supporting slaveholders, and to protect their own interests. Slavery was keeping them povertystricken and degraded.

In the midst of these disquieting signs and disturbing experiences, the nation was increasingly conscious of the approach of 1860, for these various conflicts and emotional upsurges were contributing to an ever mounting tension. The elections of 1858 were watched eagerly as barometers. Would the Republicans capture the House of Representatives and, more particularly, what would happen to Douglas whose term in the Senate was expiring? He was undoubtedly the leading Democratic Presidential candidate, but he must retain his seat in the Senate if he was to have any chance of success, particularly since he had defied President Buchanan and his powerful Southern colleagues. Many believed that Douglas was the only Democrat who could carry the Northern states necessary to beat a Republican in 1860. On the adjournment of Congress in June 1858, Douglas went home to Illinois to fight for his political life.

And what a battle it was to be, for the Springfield lawyer, Abraham Lincoln, was to be his opponent. Lincoln at that time had little reputation outside of Illinois. Save for a single term as a Congressman during the Mexican War, he had scarcely stirred outside his home state. But in Illinois he was known as a shrewd politician, plain and unassuming, a man whom folks liked. "Honest Abe" was a real man of the people. A series of debates which was to attract nationwide publicity was arranged between Lincoln and Douglas. The Little Giant, five feet four, and the "Tall Sucker," six feet four, toured the state in a spectacular series of verbal encounters. In this debate Lincoln not only emphasized the immorality of slavery and its inconsistency with democracy, but he caused Douglas to reiterate most emphatically that the South could have no right to establish slave property in the territories if the people thereof did not wish it. He thereby denied to Southerners what they were demanding, namely, protection of slave property rights in the territories. He likewise pronounced the favorable dictum of the Supreme Court, in the Dred Scott case, as worthless in any territories where the people wished to exclude slavery. These debates were read widely in the South and added more nails to Douglas' Presidential coffin, which had been started at the time of his Lecompton revolt. However, Douglas was re-elected to the Senate, and was more than ever a candidate.

In the Congressional elections, the Democrats were again defeated, but, as four years previously, no one could predict what form of anti-Democratic coalition would control. The Republicans were more effectively organized but the balance of power was left in the hands of a small band of Americans and anti-Lecompton Democrats.

The year 1859 was to produce a horrid climax to this troubled decade. John Brown, notorious because of the Pottawatomie massacre in Kansas, now felt a new sense of divine mission. He would invade the South with an armed force to free the slaves. According to his plan he would establish cities of refuge, supplied with arms, in the Southern mountains, and call the slaves to flee thither for freedom. Were they pursued, they would beat off their persecutors and the refugees would then establish a provisional free state. Brown's expectation was that, in due time, these cities of refuge would attract so many slaves that the Southern states would have to abolish slavery or be overwhelmed by the promoters of this provisional free state. Brown secured the financial and spiritual aid of certain New York and New England philanthropists. His plans, in the making during 1858, were interspersed with efforts to rescue slaves in Kansas and Missouri and transport them to Canada, adventures again marred by killing and stealing.

By the summer of 1859 Brown was through in Kansas, and he had collected several thousand dollars. Now he was ready to inaugurate his plan; he would invade Virginia and there start his mission. He leased a farm across the Potomac River in Maryland and assembled a small force of twenty-one followers equipped with a supply of arms, including some particularly murderous knife-pointed pikes. His first step was to seize the arsenal and rifle factory at Harper's Ferry and there secure a good supply of arms and ammunition. On the night of October 16, Brown struck. He captured his immediate objectives but the Virginia militia quickly rallied and Brown was soon besieged in a fire-engine house. Early on the eighteenth the Marines arrived and, under the command of Robert E. Lee, quickly subdued the invaders. Ten of Brown's small band, including one of his sons, were killed.

Brown was turned over to the Virginia authorities who quickly indicted, tried and convicted him of conspiracy with slaves, treason and murder. Within six weeks of the act he was hanged. The Governor of Virginia sent one of John Brown's pikes to each of the other Southern executives who exhibited them in the state capitals. It became well known that Northern money had financed Brown, and efforts were made unsuccessfully to show that he was in the pay of the Republican party. All this was enough to spread a belief that Northern interests were plotting slave uprisings in the South, and that if the Republicans came into power they would send other John Browns into slave territory to rouse the Negroes to arson, rapine, and murder. In the North, on the other hand, many thought it was barbarous to hang an insane old man. One even likened the execution to the crucifixion on Calvary.

As John Brown was being hanged the new Congress met. Once again it took two months to arrange the coalition that finally organized the House under a Republican speaker. Once again there was a legislative deadlock between the Republican House and the Democratic Senate. The Republicans introduced bills for a protective tariff, for the admission of Kansas as a free state, and for the distribution of free homesteads to those who applied. These were either rejected by the Senate or vetoed by the President. No bill could be passed which would aid the building of a Pacific Railroad. Two advances in transcontinental communication, however, were coming into being. The first of these was the organization of a dramatic "pony express" to dash the letter mails from the Missouri railheads to Sacramento in ten days. This service, started in 1860, represented the height of transcontinental speed attained in this era. Those who dared the perils of coach travel or impatiently counted the slow-moving days waiting for mail, yearned for the safety and speed of steam. But sectional rivalry and Constitutional doubt left them frustrated, except that as the decade closed plans were perfected to build a telegraph line across the continent.

This legislative defeat of much-desired Northern measures was bitterly resented. The power of the South over the Federal government, and its repeated defeat of Northern measures, had created a frustration among Northern voters as dangerous, if less obvious, than was the fear of John Brown raids in the South.

The control of the Federal government by the South during the fifties had been almost complete. While the Presidents were of Northern origin they had been nominated by national conventions dominated by Southern leaders. The Cabinets had generally had four of the seven members from the South. In Congress the most important committees were chaired by Southerners. At one time the President pro tempore of the Senate and the chairmen of the Foreign Relations, Finance, and Judiciary committees were experienced representatives from the South. When the Democrats were in control, the Speakers of the House were Southern. Five of the nine members of the Supreme Court were from that section. These men controlled both legislation and the fortunes of statesmen. The acme of their pretension to dominance was their determination to destroy the ambitions of Stephen A. Douglas who had defied them. The frustration of the North, and the apprehension of the South over losing its power to defend itself against aggression, had created a tension that boded ill for the future of the Republic.

6

The Republican Triumph

IN FEBRUARY 1860, Abraham Lincoln traveled eastward ostensibly to address a church forum in New York City. But he was really coming to step into the political spotlight. The most prominent candidate for the Republican Presidential nomination was New York's Senator William H. Seward. But to many he was too radical; he acknowledged a Higher Law than the Constitution, and predicted an Irrepressible Conflict. Also, there was some doubt whether he could carry Illinois and Indiana, Western states which were essential to Republican success. Certain prominent Easterners opposed to Seward, like the two great editors, Horace Greeley and William Cullen Bryant, wanted to try Lincoln out before an eastern audience.

When the speaker arrived in New York City he learned that the meeting had grown. It would not be in Plymouth Church but in the great auditorium of Cooper Union. So he put the finishing touches on his address, donned his ill-fitting new suit, and faced his audience. He spoke of no Higher Law but advocated carrying out the intent of the Constitution which he proved, by careful reference to the words and votes of its authors, had provided Congress with power to exclude slavery from the territories. He made no incendiary references to irrepressible conflict but appealed to the moral sense of the nation to promote peace and harmony. "Let us have faith that right makes might, and in that

faith, let us, to the end, dare to do our duty as we understand it."
Here was a man of legal soundness and moral stature. The New
York audience went home impressed.

The nation was in fact approaching President-making in 1860
earlier than usual, largely by accident. The Democrats in 1856
had desired to make a concession to the South for defeating
Pierce, its candidate, so they had set the next convention at
Charleston, South Carolina. But to avoid the early summer
tropical heat they were meeting in April, rather than in the
customary June. In consequence the Republicans were planning
to meet in May. With the conventions set so early there was
promise of a long drawn-out campaign.

The year 1860 was the most dangerous and disastrous which
the United States was ever to know. It began in confusion and
ended in disruption. When the American people had scarcely
recovered from panic, and were still deeply moved by religious
revival, the horror of John Brown's raid had placed a frightful
cap on the climax of their emotional instability. It was a national
calamity that in this frightening time there had to be fought a
great electoral contest in which the stakes of power, never before
so huge, were to be placed at hazard. The basic fact in the situation was that the nation was on the eve of a transfer of power un-
like any other ever experienced in the nation.

The Democrats had been operating on the principles of laissez
faire at home and spread-eagle action abroad. Attempting to focus
popular attention on the delinquencies of Britain and France,
and the possibilities of new interests in the Orient and the tropics,
they had avoided any help to manufacturing, transportation and
real estate interests, thus favoring the South at the expense of the
North. If the Democrats were unseated by the Republicans, an
exclusively Northern party, there were bound to be tariffs, subsidies, grants, new territories and states, and a hopeless minority
status for the South.

The Democratic contest at Charleston was to be between Senator Douglas, now for a third time an aggressive contender for the

nomination, and the Southern managers who had long been the principal figures at these gatherings, the same men who had generally exercised decisive influence in Congress. These Southern managers were determined that Douglas should not be nominated. They did not trust him. They felt his Popular Sovereignty was a tricky device to win votes and, knowing that he cared not whether slavery was voted up or down, they had no confidence that he had any real concern over Southern Rights or that he would really exert himself to protect them. They had no candidate of their own; their tactics were to insist that any one nominated must accept a platform guaranteeing Federal protection of slave property in the territories. Adoption of such a platform meant denying the people of the territories the power to exclude slaves. A majority voting for such a platform would defeat Douglas.

Douglas, on his part, was believed by many Northern Democrats to be the only man who could enable them to win back any Northern states or to keep Pennsylvania, New Jersey, Illinois, and Indiana, at least two or three of which the party must hold if it were to stay in power. The Douglas managers were reasonably sure of a majority at the convention but as the Democrats required a two-thirds vote for nomination it seemed certain that the Little Giant must secure a degree of Southern support if he were to obtain his goal. In addition to these two groups of Southern managers and Douglas promoters, there was a third contingent, interested in bringing in a compromise candidate who would secure the united support of the factions and prevent disruption. Certain "practical" New York operators were leaders in this effort.

The task was difficult. The Douglas supporters would not yield. They had indeed a majority of the convention, and they were determined that their Southern opponents should not deprive them of victory. They did not take too seriously Southern threats that, if that section were not promised protection of its rights in the territories and elsewhere, its delegates would leave the convention. In fact some of the Douglas supporters perhaps felt that, if there were seceders, it would be easier for Douglas to get two-thirds of the quorum that remained, and that such secession would rouse sympathetic support in the North for Douglas for daring to stand up and defy the "Slave Power."

The Douglas supporters defeated the Southern demand for "protection of slavery in the territories," and when it became apparent that there would be no backing down on Douglas' nomination, certain states from the Lower South withdrew and set up a rival convention. They, too, were careless of unity. Some undoubtedly felt that if there were two Democratic candidates the election might be thrown into Congress. No party had a majority in the House but the Senate was safely Democratic. This body therefore would choose a Democratic Vice-President, so that, in default of a President duly chosen by March 4, the Vice-President would take over and a Democrat would still be in the White House. Confronted with this impasse the Douglas majority decided to recess the convention for six weeks, and to try to replace the Southern seceders by new and less intransigent Southern delegates, i.e., delegates more friendly to Douglas.

The Republicans also were confronted with deep-seated divisions despite their youth. There were rivalries between Eastern and Western delegations, and among those who had originally been Whigs, Know-Nothings, Free Soilers, and Democrats. The success of the party in 1860 was dependent upon the united action of these factions in support of a candidate who could capture two or perhaps three of the four significant Northern states which Frémont had lost in 1856. Senator William H. Seward of New York had a lead somewhat comparable to Douglas' in the Democratic contest. Despite this lead Seward, like Douglas, had a serious handicap. The Know-Nothings were hostile to him and his association with Thurlow Weed, "boss" of the New York Republicans, led some to believe he was engaged in corrupt politics. Moreover, he was weak in the western states which the Republicans must carry to win.

The Republicans were meeting in Chicago. There the local party had built a great hall, called the Wigwam. The Seward supporters, with plenty of money at their disposal, supplied by hopeful New York capitalists, organized a large crowd to go to Chicago, accompanied by a band and a cheering abundance of champagne. They were expected to impress the denizens of the "Windy City" with their enthusiasm and perhaps infect them with it. They were to make an impressive show to encourage the Senator's delegates and impress those of his rivals. The New York claque designed to take over the gallery.

But the "Tall Suckers" of the Prairie were not caught unawares. They assembled a formidable group of Lincoln supporters led by some of the strongest-lunged hog callers of the West and marshaled by a versatile doctor. They got to the convention hall early and planted themselves firmly in the best seats. The Seward crowd, in the meantime, were marching around Chicago, behind their band, exhilarated by their "noble vintage." When they got to the Wigwam it was full, and their capacity for enthusiastic infection was thus greatly curtailed. The galleries were for Lincoln, no small asset when they were so stentorian in their efforts.

The logical result occurred, the opponents of Seward organized against him and combined their groups into a majority for Abraham Lincoln of Illinois. He had few enemies, was more conservative than Seward, was strong in Illinois and the West. His long support of the protective tariff as a Henry Clay Whig made him acceptable in Pennsylvania. His Cooper Union speech had attracted wide attention. His active managers arrived at strategic understandings with the Cameron men in Pennsylvania and with a faction in Indiana, which probably did not net Lincoln the support they were designed to supply, but nevertheless brought Cameron and Caleb B. Smith Cabinet commitments. Lincoln and Hamlin, a former Democrat from Maine, became the Republican ticket.

Even more clever was the Republican platform-making. The

Declaration of Independence and Free Soil in the territories were included, and so was subsidy to the Pacific Railroad. But in addition there was a tariff plank satisfactory to Pennsylvania protectionists, and a promise of free homesteads which stirred enthusiasm in the West. Thus opponents of slavery, protectionists, and those desiring other subsidies and gifts of land, were wooed. Skillful appeals were addressed to the many who for years had been antagonized and frustrated by the dominant Southern Congressional leadership. It was a craftily devised ticket and platform.

This ticket was to have the advantage of divided opposition. A rather large segment of the Southern Whigs and Americans had joined with a much smaller group of conservatives with the same background in the North, and had formed a new party which had met a few days before the Republicans. They called themselves the Constitutional Union party with but two planks in their platform, support of the Constitution, loyalty to the Union. They nominated Senator John Bell of Tennessee and former Senator Edward Everett of Massachusetts. This was the Kangaroo ticket, so-called because its hind legs were presumed to be stronger than the front. This slate was believed to have much strength in the South where the many Union-loving conservatives might well vote it in preference to Douglas or any Southern radical secessionist. The presumed strength of this ticket alarmed certain of the Southern Democratic leadership and strengthened their determination not to accept Douglas. If they went back south with this "Little Prairie Man" as their leader, there might well be wholesale desertion to their old Whig opponents, and the loss of the control of their State governments won after so many hard contests.

This Constitutional Union move thus improved the chances of the Republicans, not only by creating a third party, but also by driving a deeper wedge into the Democratic ranks. When the Democratic convention reconvened in Baltimore in June it was soon apparent that nothing had been accomplished. The Douglas men, now that Lincoln was nominated by the Republicans, were surer than ever that Douglas was their only hope in the Northern states. The Southern managers, confronted by this formidable revival of the Whigs, were sure that they could not sell Douglas with his trick Popular Sovereignty to their constituents. In vain the trading middle group labored at Baltimore; both sides were adamant. A majority nominated Douglas, and a minority organized a rump convention and nominated John C. Breckinridge of Kentucky, the current Vice-President, and Joseph Lane, born in North Carolina, one-time resident of Indiana and now Senator from Oregon and markedly sympathetic to the South. He might, with four tickets in the field, become President, for if the matter were left to his colleagues in the Senate, he would be the man.

The designation of four candidates, Bell, Breckinridge, Douglas, and Lincoln might indicate to today's observer that the victory was sure to be Lincoln's, and that was it. But results are never so certain before they happen regardless of how logical and inevitable hindsight may see them.

The Republicans were taking no chances. Lincoln would not campaign but there were others who would. The Republican party had some of the characteristics of a youth movement, and it was full of enthusiasm. This enthusiasm was organized. Marching and singing groups, called "Wide Awakes," were marshalled. They were supplied with kerosene torches and oilcloth capes to protect them from the dripping fuel. Then, trained in song as in the "Log Cabin and Cider" days, they were sent marching and singing through the night. "John Brown's Body" together with "Liberty and Freedom" were inspiring when set to music and illuminated by hundreds of flaring lamps. "His soul is marching on!"

Douglas, on his part, was going to emphasize the panacea quality of his great principle. Contrary to custom he would take the stump and warn the nation of its peril. Disunion and secession would destroy it. His platform of "Let the people rule!" would save it. Tirelessly he went up into New England, through his own West and down into the South, calling upon people to preserve the Union and shun treason. Traitors should be hanged

highei than Haman, and he would hang them. Breckinridge
spoke for two hours at a barbecue to prove he was not a dis-
unionist or a secessionist. Bell did nothing.

Some efforts were made to do the only thing that could stop
Lincoln, namely organize fusion electoral tickets of all opposed
to him in the various states, with the electors pledged, if chosen,
to vote in any way which might defeat him. None of these efforts,
which were really tried only in Pennsylvania, New York, and
New Jersey, had any enthusiastic support even among those attempting them. They proved to have no appeal, and eventually
cost Lincoln merely three votes in New Jersey.

All the signs of the campaign pointed to Lincoln's victory.
Vermont and Maine went Republican in September, and Pennsylvania, Ohio and Indiana in October. Apprehension grew in
certain quarters in the South and among Southern officeholders in
Washington. If the Republicans won they would have authority
to change all the Federal officers. Postmasters, customs collectors,
district attorneys, and marshals would be removed and Republican appointees put in their places. These men would not remove
abolition propaganda from the mails, they would be eager to
stamp out the slave trade, and they might wink at future John
Browns or at least at those who might induce slaves to attempt to
escape.

These appointees, probably chosen from nonslaveholders,
would attempt to build up a new power in the South, which to
the slave owners would seem alien and subversive. So that summer people were taking thought of the future. Some bands of
"minute men" were organized who were drilling and planning to
protect their communities against slave insurrections. Others
were thinking of secession, of creating a Southern republic to
protect their "property rights" and their right of self-government.
They would not submit to being terrorized by Republican "John
Browns." They would sooner follow their forefathers who fought
for their rights in 1776.

The election itself in November was a surprise to very few.

Lincoln carried all the Northern states and received all their electoral votes except three in New Jersey which went to Douglas. Breckinridge carried all the slave states except Virginia, Tennessee, Kentucky, and Missouri. Bell carried the first three of these and Douglas the last. What is more, Lincoln had a clear majority of the votes in all the Northern states save New Jersey, California, and Oregon while Breckinridge had a divided majority against him in Delaware, Georgia, Louisiana, and Maryland. Thus the Breckinridge or Southern Democrats carried by majority only seven of the fifteen slave states. Bell and Douglas who represented opposition to secession secured together a majority of the votes in eight of the slave states. In the fourteen slave states that voted by ballot, Breckinridge received 570,000 votes and his opponents 705,000. Throughout the entire nation, Lincoln polled only 40 per cent of the vote while the combined votes of Bell and Douglas, who might be considered "neutral," polled 43 per cent. A plurality of the voters cast their ballots for candidates who were national as opposed to those supporting sectional interests.

The electoral vote was a different story. Here Lincoln had 180, or a clear majority, challenged by nobody. Breckinridge had 72, Bell 39 and Douglas 12. Lincoln had won honestly and constitutionally an election marred by neither fraud nor violence. But he represented a minority of the voters who went to the polls. In the South he received votes in only the four border slave states and in Virginia, and these were negligible except in Missouri. He was distinctly a Northern President. Only 26,000 of his 1,800,-000 votes came from the South, and there a million and a quarter had voted against him. He had won the North by 1,800,000 to 1,500,000.

Despite the fact that the results of the election were a surprise to few, they could not help but be a shock to many. The South had been in power so long that the sense of command had become general and well-established. But now the slave power had been defied and voted out by a great combination of Northern

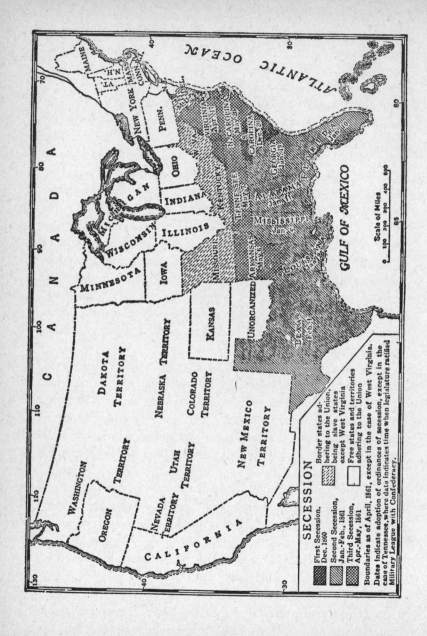

ATLANTIC OCEAN

CANADA

MAINE

N.H'N
VT
MASS.
CONN.

NEW YORK

PENN.

OHIO

MICHIGAN

WISCONSIN

INDIANA

ILLINOIS

MINNESOTA

IOWA

KENTUCKY

TENNESSEE

MISSISSIPPI
Jan 9

ALABAMA
Jan 11

FLORIDA
Jan 10

GEORGIA
Jan 19

CAROLINA
Dec 20

NC AROLINA
May 20

Virginia
Apr 17

MD.

DEL.

N.J.

GULF OF MEXICO

Scale of Miles

0 100 200 300 400 500

Missouri

ARKANSAS
May 6

LOUISIANA

TEXAS
Feb 1

DAKOTA
TERRITORY

NEBRASKA TERRITORY

KANSAS

COLORADO
TERRITORY

Unorganized

NEW MEXICO
TERRITORY

WASHINGTON
TERRITORY

OREGON

NEVADA
TERRITORY

UTAH
TERRITORY

CALIFORNIA

SECESSION

First Secession.
Dec. 1860

Second Secession,
Jan.-Feb., 1861

Third Secession,
Apr.-May, 1861

Border states ad-
hering to the Union,
being slave states
except West Virginia

Free states and territories
adhering to the Union

Boundaries as of April, 1861, except in the case of West Virginia.

Dates indicate adoption of ordinances of secession, except in the
case of Tennessee, where date indicates time when legislature ratified
Military League with Confederacy.

voters which had formed for the express purpose of breaking that power. This had been done while the census of 1860 was being taken, a census which was dooming the South to definite minority status. The day of its power was fast declining.

Mixed emotions involving fear, pride, and honor were roused by the tidings. There was fear lest their cherished way of life be destroyed, fortunes ruined and white supremacy endangered. They had been deeply affronted. They had a cumulative pride in their own capacity for civilization, their superiority, their dignity, their authority. Now the Yankee worshippers of mammon were going to take over and substitute a money-grubbing materialism for this Southern culture. Their sense of honor was aroused. They had sworn not to submit to such degradation, now honor required that they act, that they secede and save their system by creating a new and independent republic.

By an interesting quirk of fate, the state where this urge for independence was the strongest was best placed to start the move. South Carolina which had been the home of nullification and secession ever since the crisis of 1832-1833 was, by virtue of its unique practices, poised for action. South Carolina, of all the states, was the only one in which Presidential electors were still chosen by the legislature. Therefore every four years a special session was prescribed for the day before the general November election at which the electors would be named. In 1860 the legislature met as usual but at the request of the Governor they stayed over to learn the national result. When Lincoln's election was known to be a fact the legislature called upon the voters to choose a convention instructed on the question of secession. The principal Federal officeholders in South Carolina, and her two Senators, resigned almost at once and there seemed no doubt that the Palmetto State would attempt independence. Others soon followed.

In the furor over John Brown's raid the preceding winter, Alabama had prescribed a similar convention if a Republican were elected. The Georgia and Florida legislatures were soon in session and called conventions. The Governors of Mississippi and Louisiana called special legislative sessions to secure the same end. Governor Sam Houston refused to call the Texas legislature but an unofficial convention nevertheless was contrived. However, in the eight more northerly Southern states, Virginia, North Carolina, Tennessee, Arkansas, Delaware, Maryland, Kentucky, and Missouri, there was no significant response. Within the next few weeks the states south of North Carolina and bordering on the Gulf of Mexico provided for conventions in regular, special or irregular sessions of their legislatures. Between December 6 when South Carolina balloted, and January 8 when Texas voted, all provided for conventions which met between December 17 and January 28. These states seceded between December 20 and January 31.

With South Carolina setting off this chain reaction, what force could intervene? Would the Federal Government call a halt? In 1832-1833, when South Carolina had earlier spoken in defiant terms, President Jackson had answered heatedly and threatened action. But now James Buchanan was in the White House, and as Senator Douglas had once pointedly reminded him, Andrew Jackson was dead.

President Buchanan was confronted with two questions, one general, the other very particular. The general question was what policy he would adopt toward secession. The particular one concerned Federal property in the seceding states, civil property such as post offices, custom houses and the like, and military property, forts and arsenals. Forts particularly could be used to quell uprising and secession. Most of these forts were designed for coastal defense, and were slightly garrisoned and meagerly equipped. Some, like Fort Sumter at Charleston, were not even finished. Shortly before the election General Winfield Scott had pointed out that these defenses were vulnerable and, in view of possible secession, needed to be strengthened if the Union were going to use them to protect itself.

Buchanan not only had temperamental defects but he was head

of a defeated party, advised by a divided Cabinet; and his term had only four months to go. Never given to swift or decisive action, he was now prone to temporize. But here were the forts and General Scott's memorandum. He had the Secretary of War send down an officer to discover the military situation at Charleston and he changed commanders. Also, he authorized the new commander, Major Robert Anderson, to take whatever steps he thought wise to protect himself. Other than this he did nothing and spent his time drafting a message on the State of the Union in which he argued that secession was unconstitutional but that coercing a state was equally so. Even this minimum of action stirred up division. His Northern Secretary of State resigned, ostensibly, at least, because it offered so little to the North, while his Southern Secretary of the Treasury resigned because the President was not sufficiently vehement in his reiteration of the rights of the states. Buchanan was to contribute nothing in the way of decisive action.

Almost at the same time Congress was assembling. Would its members take positive action? Upon previous occasions when the Union had been threatened Congressional compromises had averted the danger. The Missouri Compromise of 1820, the Compromise Tariff of 1833 and the Compromise of 1850 had been effective. Would there be a Compromise of 1860? Crittenden proposed one, extending the Missouri line to the coast, thus permitting slavery south of it. The answer was no. Neither Lincoln nor the Republican Congressional leaders were willing to permit any spread of slavery, and this was what the South demanded. Lincoln particularly felt that if slavery were permitted in the Southwest territories there would come demands to secure more of Mexico and Central and South America so that the slave power might gain allies. Failing to secure these demands, the South might again threaten secession. Hence there were to be no concessions to slavery. Many thought that when the South's bluff was called, she would acquiesce. By New Year's Day 1861, hope of compromise was fading.

7

The War Comes

IN THE DYING DAYS of the crisis year of 1860, events were hurrying on. The six southernmost states were seceding. They had begun taking over Federal property including forts, arsenals, and a subtreasury. There was no interruption of this process save in South Carolina and in Florida. At Charleston, the commandant, Major Robert Anderson, had moved his small garrison from easily accessible Fort Moultrie to Sumter on an island in the harbor, while in Florida, Fort Pickens, on an island at Pensacola, together with two forts at Key West and the Dry Tortugas, remained in Federal hands. South Carolina and Florida had demanded the surrender of Sumter and Pickens, but Buchanan refused and even organized expeditions to relieve them. The steamer, *Star of the West,* sent to aid Sumter, was turned back by the Carolinian gunfire. Under a truce arranged at Washington, the Pickens expedition remained offshore.

In the meantime the seceding states had to wrestle with disappointment while they planned for the future. Only seven of the fifteen slave states seemed likely to secede. Less than half had responded and the grand Old Dominion, Virginia, was not among them. Despite this failure, those who had seceded were working to create a new republic. It was decided in South Carolina, and at conferences in Washington, to call a convention of the seceding states at Montgomery, Alabama, on February 4, where the new nation would be set up.

To offset this move Virginia called representatives of all the states to meet at Washington at the same time, to see if some means of restoring the nation could be found. If Congress could not create a Compromise of 1860 perhaps this body could draft a Compromise of 1861. Meanwhile, Buchanan organized a new administration. The places of the Southerners and aged Secretary of State Cass were filled. Buchanan and his reconstituted Cabinet bent their energies to keeping intact what still remained, carefully offering no provocation for further secession. Congress, now that the Senators and Representatives from the Lower South had withdrawn, passed a new tariff with protective features, admitted Kansas as a free state, and organized the territories of Colorado, Nevada and Dakota without mentioning slavery.

The two conventions assembled. That at Montgomery created the Confederate States of America. It drafted a provisional and then a permanent constitution, elected a President and Vice-President, and settled down to act as a Provisional Congress until 1862. It chose Jefferson Davis of Mississippi and Alexander H. Stephens of Georgia to be the executives who were inaugurated February 18, and it passed laws of all kinds, setting up foreign relations, a treasury, an army and navy, a post office and a legal system. The permanent constitution was completed within six weeks. It was designed to protect slavery and to prevent subsidies and a protective tariff. The President was to serve for six years and could not be re-elected. There were no vague clauses which would permit the use of implied powers or other forms of loose construction. The rights of the states were emphasized. This document was submitted to the states and quickly ratified.

The "peace" convention at Washington spent the month of February accomplishing next to nothing. It was not attended by the seceding states nor did all the others send delegates. It met behind closed doors under the chairmanship of ex-President Tyler. The results of its labors were agreed to shortly before Lincoln's inauguration. It differed from the compromise plan defeated in Congress in that, though it extended the Missouri Compromise

line to the coast, it applied only to regions then possessed by the
United States. No new territory could be acquired without the
consent of a majority of the Senators from both the slave and
free states. This was no more acceptable than the other plan.
Congress rejected them both.

The sole effort of the lawmakers to restore the nation was to
send to the states an amendment to the Constitution forbidding
any interference with slavery where it then existed. With that
feeble move the Congress expired, clearing the stage for Lincoln
and the Republicans. The irony of it was that the Congress just
elected was Democratic and, had the Southerners not seceded, the
new Republican President would have been boxed in by a Democratic Congress and a pro-Southern Supreme Court. Buchanan
left office with a sigh of relief. A reinforcing expedition was still
stationed off Fort Pickens and a relief ship was waiting in
case there was need to succor Sumter. As yet, the Confederacy
consisted of only seven of the fifteen slave states.

The issue of peace or war now lay between two new powers,
one in Washington and one in Montgomery. Each was untried
and inexperienced, groping amid strange surroundings. Abraham
Lincoln had been face to face with the problem since November,
Jefferson Davis only during part of February. Each must create
an instrument before he could use it for solving the problem of
division. Lincoln must create an administration and marshal a
new, untried party behind it. Davis must create an administration
which could work with an untried legislative body under a new
constitution, and so build a republic. It is difficult to say who
had the more difficult task. In addition to this backbreaking responsibility, these leaders must come to grips with the possibility
of war.

Lincoln's party had never been in power before save in certain
Northern states. It had had no experience with Cabinet appoint-
ments and Federal departmental patronage. It had never controlled both houses of Congress which it did now because of
Democratic defections. It had almost exclusively enjoyed the

luxury of irresponsible opposition. Now Lincoln had to choose a Cabinet of seven men and join them in supervising the appointment of several thousand "deserving" Republicans who would take over the Federal offices and restaff a government for years operated by an experienced Democratic bureaucracy.

Lincoln's new party had hardly crystallized; and some of its factions had in the not-far-distant past been political antagonists. The President-elect worked on this problem continuously and did not finish it until inauguration day. He chose William H. Seward, his principal rival, for the post of Secretary of State; Seward represented the power of New York and the Free Soil Whigs. To represent the radical Western group he selected, over stiff opposition, Senator-elect Salmon P. Chase of Ohio, former Whig, Independent Democrat and Free Soiler. He honored two patronage commitments made at the convention and appointed Simon Cameron of Pennsylvania, sometime Democrat, Whig and speculator, and Caleb B. Smith of Indiana, former Whig, as Secretary of War and Secretary of the Interior respectively. Cameron was vigorously opposed as a spoilsman and corruptionist. Gideon Welles, a former Democrat, represented that element and New England as Secretary of the Navy; he had been recommended by Vice-President Hamlin. Two men from the border states, one a former Whig and the other a Jacksonian Democrat, made up the balance, when Lincoln appointed Edward Bates of Missouri, Attorney General, and Montgomery Blair of Maryland, Postmaster General. There were three former Whigs, two former Democrats, and two who had been both. Two came from the West, two from the border states and three from the East. Lincoln had tried to get a Southerner without success.

Occupied with this Cabinet-making, Lincoln had to sit by while secession spread and the Confederacy came into being. As leader of his party he was consulted by Congressional leaders on the question of compromise and as Commander in Chief-elect of the military forces General Scott sought to brief him on the military problem which secession was creating.

Lincoln rejected the various compromise plans because they all permitted the extension of slavery. This was contrary to the platform on which the party had been elected and he would have none of it. On the question of surrendering the forts at Charleston and Pensacola, he declared that if the forts were surrendered they would have to be recaptured. On these subjects he was publicly silent and conveyed his views eastward through intermediaries. There is reason to think that he did not take the crisis as seriously as he might because he believed that it was being maneuvered by the Southern radical leadership who feared the loss of power. He was hopeful that there was a submerged mass of Union-loving citizens in the South, men who held few or no slaves who only needed leadership to assert themselves. He, born a poor boy in Kentucky, had been one of them and he hoped they would trust him when he came into power. He therefore was unwilling to yield any vital point.

In this frame of mind Lincoln came to Washington, narrowly escaping assassination it was believed. He was charged with sneaking into Washington in disguise though he had merely arrived on a different train at an unannounced time. In consultation with Seward he finished his inaugural. It was a stirring plea to avoid hostilities. "There needs to be no bloodshed or violence," he assured the South. "The government will not assail you. . . . You can have no conflict, without being yourselves the aggressors." But it is significant that he also said: "The power confided to me will be used to hold, occupy and possess the property and places belonging to the government, and to collect the duties and imposts." However, hardly had these words died on his lips when he was presented with alarming news on March 5.

Jefferson Davis had been at work for barely three weeks. He had been elected February 9 and inaugurated February 18. When he arrived at Montgomery he found Congress at work making laws. It created only six departments, for the Secessionists, with their state rights complex, wanted no Interior Department, a division which signified to them undesirable centralized functions.

Davis had to choose six department heads; they in turn, starting from scratch, had to set up offices and create staffs, for in Montgomery there was literally nothing except some forms and government procedures brought from Washington. There were seven states in the Confederacy; as Davis came from Mississippi he chose his Cabinet from the other six. Robert Toombs of Georgia was to be Secretary of State, Christopher Memminger of South Carolina, Secretary of the Treasury, LeRoy Pope Walker of Alabama, Secretary of War, Stephen R. Mallory of Florida, Secretary of the Navy, Judah P. Benjamin of Louisiana, Attorney General, and John H. Reagan of Texas, Postmaster General. He, like Lincoln, had to create a political power.

When the Administration was assembled it contained none of the original secessionists; neither Yancey nor Rhett had been included. This omission had been by design because Davis and his associates were very conscious of the fact that none of the more conservative Southern states had joined with them. They believed that if they gave prominent place to these "Fire-eaters," great states like Virginia would be even more unlikely to join. But this omission was later to have unfortunate consequences.

One of Davis' tasks, and one that was congenial to him as a military officer and sometime Federal Secretary of War, was the organization of an army. This duty involved responsibility for taking over the forts and Confederate defense. The seceding states had already done much of this but Sumter in South Carolina and Pickens in Florida still flew the Stars and Stripes in sight of Confederate cities; they were Federal enclaves in Confederate territory. Buchanan had respected uneasy truces with Florida and South Carolina. Would the Confederacy tolerate them? South Carolina had sent envoys up to Washington and now Davis was going to attempt to negotiate; his representatives arrived in Washington on the eve of Lincoln's inauguration.

Davis had assumed direction of military operations, particularly at Charleston, on February 22. He had appointed P. G. T. Beauregard brigadier general in the new army of the Confederate States and placed him in command there. Beauregard took up his duties just as the Confederate commissioners were arriving at Washington. He found that the South Carolina militia had seized Moultrie and had been establishing a series of batteries which now threatened Sumter, but to date no overt hostile act had been committed save to fire on the *Star of the West,* when it brought supplies to Sumter, and to send it back North. Would the truce which had been arranged after this by the commander of Sumter and the Governor of South Carolina, and respected by Buchanan, continue now that Lincoln was safely in office?

The day after his inauguration Lincoln received his unpleasant surprise. After the firing on the *Star of the West* nothing further had been done to help Sumter because Anderson had made a truce and had reported he was secure there so long as he was let alone. He had been anxious not to precipitate bloodshed. But the events of the few days prior to March 4 had changed his mind. He had been used to buying fresh food in the Charleston markets but the South Carolina force was threatening to cut him off from that source of supply and he now had to report that he did not have supplies to support him for more than a few more weeks and that the strength of the Confederate force was so great that it would now take 20,000 men to relieve him.

Lincoln found himself confronted not by merely an uneasy status quo which might be prolonged indefinitely, but with an emergency situation. Anderson must be supplied or the fort surrendered. Also, he learned that Fort Pickens had never been relieved and that the expedition sent for that purpose was still on shipboard off the Florida coast. Lincoln himself had held consistently that nothing should be surrendered. He now undertook to investigate the situation at Charleston. He realized that the small relief expedition that Buchanan had held in readiness was not adequate, and he began to secure advice on how help could be sent down. Here he was troubled by divided counsels. Aged General Scott now advised it could not be done though he got encouragement from the Navy. And his new Cabinet was divided.

Secretary of State Seward believed that if no overt act was committed some sort of an adjustment could be negotiated, and he was engaged in indirect communication with the Confederate commissioners. He was coming to the conclusion that it would be politically wise to evacuate Sumter but hold Pickens. He would neither receive the Confederate commissioners nor exchange correspondence with them; but using two Supreme Court justices, Nelson of New York and Campbell of Alabama, as intermediaries, he gave them to understand that if the Confederates made no attack, Sumter would eventually be evacuated.

When Lincoln first put the question formally before the Cabinet on March 15, all but two took the Seward point of view. This did not satisfy Lincoln. He sent a naval officer and confidential friends to Charleston, and dispatched orders for the Pickens relief expedition to land. What the messengers reported to him from Charleston encouraged him to believe that Sumter could be reinforced. At the same time, he was hearing from the country. The spring elections appeared to be going against the Republicans, which might be interpreted as a rebuke. Also, Lincoln was learning that there was no Union sentiment in the South that would rally against the Confederacy. Finally, he was learning that Seward was attempting to direct policy, ignoring the President.

Lincoln and a majority of his Cabinet now realized the futility of a negative policy. Evacuating Sumter would gain nothing and at the same time cause the Administration to lose face in the North and before the world. The final straw seems to have been when obese and partially senile General Scott finally submitted a written memo in his bizarre style recommending that both Pickens and Sumter be evacuated. This was too much. The Cabinet reversed its vote on March 29 and Lincoln started the machinery for sending provisions to Sumter under naval escort and notifying the Governor of South Carolina to that effect. Seward officiously undertook to manage this over the heads of the Secretaries

of War and the Navy. Confusion resulted, particularly as word
came that Pickens was not yet relieved and more help should be
sent there. In organizing the two expeditions the naval strength
needed to make Sumter's relief successful was diverted to Pickens,
and the fleet for Charleston departed without adequate fire power.

In the meantime the Confederate authorities had been hard at
work. General Beauregard had taken over command at Charleston on March 6 and had proceeded to reorganize the armament
of that port, not only to prepare to reduce Sumter, if necessary,
but also to prevent an invasion from the sea. These preparations
proceeded during March and the Confederates encouraged their
commissioners in Washington to pursue their indirect negotiations with Seward and thus gain time. In the meantime Sumter's
supplies were diminishing. The Confederates estimated that
Major Anderson might try to conserve food by discharging the
civilian laborers, so they ordered that no one could leave the fort
until all did. The laborers must stay and eat, yet Anderson was
completely cut off from supplies in Charleston markets. The
Confederates were now effectively mobilized and a ship flying the
United States flag which was innocently attempting to make port
was fired on. Within a week, on April 8, Governor Pickens and
Anderson learned that the relief expedition was on the way.
This news was telegraphed to Montgomery. The expedition
seemed to the Confederates as a violation of a pledge made by
an officer visiting Sumter and also a violation of Secretary Seward's word. The Confederate Secretary of War replied by ordering Beauregard to demand evacuation and, if refused, to "proceed . . . to reduce it."

This order was dispatched on April 10 but only after a lengthy
and acrimonious discussion. For the Confederate, like the Federal,
Administration was divided by political considerations. The Confederate leaders were most discomfited by the fact that fewer
than half of the slave states had joined the Confederacy, and that
some of them, by rather decisive popular majorities, had voted
against secession. Some highly placed Confederates believed that

the lagging slave states would rise to the rescue if hostilities were to break out, and the Federal government sent armed forces into the Confederacy. An opposing group, interestingly enough led by the Confederate Secretary of State, Robert Toombs, believed that the firing of cannon would rouse a united North, destroying all hope of friendship there. The "hard" view prevailed and the order was sent.

On the eleventh the demand for evacuation was made upon Anderson. He refused but stated it was rather a moot question as he had food left for only a few days. Beauregard then telegraphed Montgomery asking for instructions as to bombardment in view of Anderson's impending starvation. Secretary Walker telegraphed back, "Do not desire needlessly to bombard Fort Sumter." If Anderson would say when he would evacuate, and promise not to use his guns unless attacked, attack could be stayed. But if Anderson refused, Beauregard was instructed to "reduce the fort as your judgment decides to be most practicable." In the meantime the relief expedition was assembling outside the harbor bar, but minus the strong warship needed to get the flotilla past the forts; that was on its way to Pickens.

Not knowing the weakness of the Federal force, and uncertain as to when the Federal expedition might enter the harbor, Beauregard made haste. At 1 A.M., April 12, he made his final demand. Anderson replied he must evacuate by noon April 15 but he would make no promises about using his guns. If the expedition entered the harbor he was obviously going to use his fire power to aid its successful consummation. Beauregard's aides did not even bother to row back to Charleston with this reply; then and there, at 3:30 in the morning, they served notice on Anderson that he would be fired on within an hour. At 4:30, a signal gun boomed and the batteries opened fire. The relief expedition had to remain helpless outside the bar.

Anderson returned fire as best he could, but his were no match for the Confederate guns. On April 13 the fort was on fire and the flag shot down. Anderson agreed to evacuate next day, one day earlier than stipulated, and at 4 P.M. Sunday afternoon, April 14, marched out with drums beating and flags flying, saluting the Stars and Stripes with fifty guns.

The flag had been fired on! Fort Sumter had been surrendered! The wires carried these disturbing tidings on Friday, Saturday, and Sunday. President Lincoln spent that Sabbath in preparation. Monday, April 15, he called upon the Governors of the states for their quotas of a total of 75,000 volunteers to put down the rebellion. Four days later he proclaimed the seceding states in a state of blockade, cut off from trade.

American youth rushed to the colors. New regiments were mobilized. Uncle Sam sought to buy ships or to have them built for the new Navy. And, in Montgomery a new, untried, ill-equipped, barely organized government was working feverishly to make itself an effective opponent in armed combat. Within forty days, Virginia, North Carolina, Arkansas, and Tennessee joined the Confederacy. The firing on Sumter and Lincoln's proclamation precipitated war.

At Washington and at Montgomery each government had taken a calculated risk. Lincoln had decided to hold what belonged to the United States. He would not surrender in the hope that this would satisfy the Confederacy and prevent war. And Davis decided not to stay his hand in demanding what he believed was his, also in the hope that hostilities might be averted.

Pride, politics, patience, prudence, pique, petulance, and plotting had all been mixed up in a highly complex emotional mélange. One safe generalization remained: nobody planned it that way.

8

Learning the Art of War

THE WAR, feared but not really expected, had come. Much of the military strategy of the conflict was to be conditioned by three curious accidents. In the days of the founders a political deal had located the capital city straddling the Potomac, partly in Maryland and partly in Virginia. The Virginia half had never been used, but still the capital remained surrounded by slave territory. Therefore, had Maryland seceded, Washington would have been physically within the Confederacy. Then, Lincoln was born in Kentucky. Had Kentucky seceded he would have been, psychologically at least, deprived of his birthright. The third accidental situation was more complicated.

The organizers of the Confederacy chose to meet in Montgomery, Alabama. But as their work advanced and the new confederation became a reality, they became increasingly dissatisfied with the seat of their new government. Obviously Montgomery was small and poorly equipped to house a burgeoning bureaucracy. More subtle was the influence of its cultural location. The founders had been used to operating from Washington. They paid a sort of unacknowledged cultural tribute to the social centers of the Old South, such as those in Virginia and South Carolina, at Richmond and Charleston. Furthermore, the uncertainty of Virginia's secession had made the Confederates eager to solidify her stand by according her a superior position.

Inconveniently and uncomfortably crowded in provincial Montgomery as they were, deprived of political and cultural contacts they valued, the architects of the new government decided to move their capital to Richmond almost as soon as Virginia joined the new adventure. Much of the military history of the conflict depended upon the location of these peculiarly situated capitals and the political implications of their sites.

Thus, the Federal government could not let Maryland secede. Lincoln felt he must keep his native state. And the Confederacy hoped that the Union would accept peaceful coexistence, or be compelled to do so by the capture of Washington. On the other hand Richmond was considered to be within easy striking distance of Washington, and there were many who believed that a quick campaign would capture the Confederate capital and end the war. As it happened, neither Maryland nor Kentucky seceded. Washington and Richmond remained glaring at each other for four long years and the efforts of hundreds of thousands of soldiers were spent in trying to capture these border-situated seats of government.

The waste of effort and manpower in this prolonged stalemate cannot be calculated. Nor can any estimate be made of how many lives would have been spared had the Union been content to protect Washington while penetrating the Confederacy at various points along the coast and splitting its hinterland, as it finally did. Pride and politics governed the terrific four-year campaign over the narrow area between Richmond and Washington. Had the Confederacy retained its capital at Montgomery, where it would have been relatively safe and from which it could have waged war from a central interior location, there is no way of telling what the consequences might have been; the strategy at least would have been different.

Two armies and navies had to be created by a people who were very unwarlike. An Army had been improvised in 1846-1848 for the campaigns in Mexico, but even in that conflict the Navy had scarcely been used. There had been some Army experience and a number of the officers in that conflict were still available. In fact, its principal officer, General Scott, was now commander of the Union Army though most of the other Mexican War veteran officers had been lieutenants or captains with little practice in the handling of large bodies of troops. With slight exaggeration, the Army could be best described as one whose officers were limited in experience to handling fifty dragoons in Indian country.

The organization of the armies was complicated by the fact that the President of the Confederacy was a graduate of West Point, had been a gallant officer in the Mexican War, and more recently Secretary of War in the Federal government. Also, many of the officers of the United States Army were men of Southern birth or sympathy. A significant number of them, most notably Robert E. Lee, elected to follow their states, and were available to staff the new commands.

The United States government was less fortunate. It had been left with the skeleton of a superannuated military bureaucracy, tangled in red tape, lackadaisically managing 17,000 men, scattered in Indian posts. Its commanding officer, Scott, "the giant of three wars," was almost incapacitated and he had now lost so many of his younger associates. The War Department had been presided over during the Buchanan Administration by a secretary of very doubtful capacity, John B. Floyd. Lincoln filled his place with a very politically and contract-minded Pennsylvania politician, Simon Cameron.

The Army, which at the beginning of hostilities was found to number only 13,000 effectives, was increased to 300,000 within a few months. First, 75,000 volunteers were called, then 42,000 more. Lincoln then enlarged the Regular Army by fiat, ordering the recruitment of eleven new regiments or 22,000 men. The calls made upon the states for volunteers were met during 1861 with great enthusiasm. More were organized and sent on by the Governors than Lincoln had asked for. There was much initial confusion, some of which continued. All during the conflict the Regular Army structure was maintained while regiments of volunteers were accepted. The President appointed the commanding generals of the various armies and the officers of the Regular Army. But in many of the volunteer regiments the men themselves elected their company officers, and these in turn elected the regimental officers. The state Governors appointed many of the generals of their contingents, and certain influential men raised regiments and brigades of which they themselves became commanders. A simple system was never worked out because the Army did not want to find itself at the end of the war with a great surplus of officers who would have to be provided for when the men were demobilized. During the four years there were 2,778,304 separate enlistments in the Union forces, probably representing service by about 1,500,000 men. At the end of the war there were 800,000 under arms.*

In mobilizing the Union forces, Lincoln not only had the expert advice of General Scott and the trained talents of Generals Irwin McDowell and George B. McClellan, but he thought it politic to appoint such ambitious rivals as John C. Frémont, Nathaniel P. Banks, Benjamin F. Butler, and others. Their points of view were essentially political and seldom did they show any great degree of military talent.

The first steps in creating a new Federal Army were sketched out on Sunday, the day Sumter surrendered. On Monday the press bore countless printings of Lincoln's requisitions on the Governors of the thirty-four states for quotas of militia. Immediately, regiments of state troops began to move on to Washington where the aged commander, Scott, was preparing to train them into a fighting force. Those from the North were to encounter the obstacle of fragmentary railroad service: there was no through track from the North to Washington. These troops had to detrain and march across Baltimore to another station. A hostile pro-Southern element in that city beset a Massachusetts regiment, and in the melee soldiers and citizens were killed. For a while Wash-

*The Confederacy enlisted about a million men, but at the end Lee had only 400,000 to surrender.

ington was cut off until a transport service was organized by way of Annapolis. Before long troops were encamped in Washington by the thousand.

Four days after the proclamation calling for 75,000 volunteers was issued, President Lincoln issued another on April 19, declaring the ports of the Confederate States to be in a state of blockade. The Navy was now called upon to close the harbors on a coastline 3,550 miles long, and the new Confederacy was challenged to keep them open. The United States Navy had not been used much since the War of 1812; it was largely old-fashioned and scattered among a variety of stations in Europe, Asia and the Pacific. It had ninety ships but only forty-two were in commission, and of these only twenty-nine were steam vessels. Its manpower consisted of 1,457 officers and 7,600 men, and of the officers some 322 shortly resigned. The Confederacy, on its part, had to build a navy from nothing. Both Secretary Gideon Welles, in Lincoln's Cabinet, and Secretary Stephen R. Mallory, in Davis', began a search for ships. Welles had the advantage because the shipyards and the available commercial fleets were Northern. He began purchasing, adapting and building an armada which contained everything from ocean packets to ferryboats, from sailing vessels to fishing smacks. The only advantage which the Confederates had was the seizure of the navy yard at Norfolk, Virginia, after the Union force had partially destroyed it.

As the War and Navy departments were feverishly mobilizing, the State Department was grasping the fact that battles must also be fought in the chancelleries of Europe. Secretary Seward undertook to persuade the European powers that the conflict was a rebellion, a private concern of the United States of which the European powers should not take cognizance. Above all, Europe must refuse to recognize the Confederate States of America. The Confederate State Department on its part felt that its chance of victory would be aided infinitely by successful diplomacy. If the foreign powers would recognize the South as a nation, then it would be so much easier to borrow money, to buy arms and equipment, and to establish trade abroad.

The Confederacy had faith in an ancient instrument which they had inherited with so many of their other ideas and items of political paraphernalia from the American Revolution. Harking back to 1776 they sought to exert economic coercion. They would prevent any export of cotton and thus stop the supply upon which they believed the cotton textile industry of England depended. Some 80 to 85 per cent of her raw cotton came to England from the United States. A fourth of Britain's population lived on earnings in the cotton textile industry, for 50 per cent of her export trade was in cotton cloth and 10 per cent of her total wealth was invested in cloth manufacture. The Confederacy believed that if these cotton factories had to shut down, their idle operatives would exert enough pressure upon their government to ensure the recognition of the new venture. They did not seem to realize that the large cotton crops of the two preceding years had piled up such a surplus that the factories would not soon be in need of new imports. Nor did they understand the British workers' hostility to slavery.

Lacking a navy, but expecting recognition, the Confederacy hoped that its most effective sea weapons would be privateers. Jefferson Davis announced on April 17, 1861 that he was ready to supply such vessels with letters of marque and reprisal. Secretary Seward thereupon undertook to put the Confederacy at diplomatic disadvantage. The peace conference ending the Crimean War, held in Paris in 1856, had proposed to the world that privateering be abolished. The United States had not agreed to this. Seward now instructed the new diplomats leaving for Europe, particularly Charles F. Adams and William L. Dayton assigned to London and Paris, to inform these governments that the United States would accept the Declaration of Paris. Washington hoped that this action would emphasize the fact that the Confederates were as much out of line in the methods of warfare as in the matter of slavery.

The Europeans, particularly the English, did respect the United States blockade. They themselves liked to use loose blockades. They consequently forbade the use of their ports in disposing of prize cases which made privateering a highly unprofitable speculation. Other than this, the action of the European powers, particularly England's, was pleasing to neither side. England did not wait for Adams' arrival but on May 13 recognized the belligerency of the Confederacy. This meant that though Britain did not recognize the new government or agree to exchange diplomats, she did deny the United States' contention that this was merely a local uprising of rebels who could be punished for treason. The armed forces were large enough to invoke the laws of war. Privateers could not be treated as pirates, and hanged; captured soldiers were to be treated as prisoners of war, not as traitors to be shot. Britain's decision, despite its concession of belligerency, fell short of recognition and was bitterly disappointing to the Confederacy.

While these diplomatic maneuvers were in process, plans for military campaigns were brought nearer perfection. But as military campaigns were put in motion it became painfully obvious that the ancient and obese commander of the Union forces was hardly less than a liability. President Lincoln respected and deferred to General Scott's knowledge, but everyone knew that Scott could not take any field command. He was so affected by the dropsy that he could hardly be hoisted into a carriage, much less mount a horse. His mind, however, was clear, and he applied himself at once. He devoted himself to increasing the Regular Army for he had little confidence in the military utility of the three-months men who were pouring into Washington, often even without arms or uniforms. But here was Virginia across the Potomac, now a part of the Confederacy, and a strange flag could be seen flying in Alexandria.

The political and journalistic mouthpieces of the nation were demanding that the new army move "On to Richmond," and end not only the menace to Washington but the war itself. This urge Scott resisted; his untrained mobs were not ready. But the pressure was too strong. The army must advance. This meant that a field commander had to be assigned, and General Irwin McDowell was given the unenviable task of invading Virginia at the head of a blue-clad rabble. The only redeeming feature was the fact that he would meet a gray-clad rabble. Battle was joined at Bull Run July 21 and after an amazing day of grotesque military moves, the Confederates were reinforced by a second army. The Union high command had mistakenly believed this body was being carefully kept in the Shenandoah by General Robert Patterson, an ancient Pennsylvania veteran of the War of 1812. Disaster followed.

The Union troops, and the politicians who had come out to watch the victory, were carried back to Washington in panic while the exhausted Confederates relaxed and rejoiced in the fact that the battle was won. Some even thought the war over and demanded to go home. It was an eye-opener all around. Particularly in Washington was it obvious that raw troops could not end the war in ninety days.

While this first campaign for Richmond was being ineptly developed, there was grave concern about the border states. It is true that fears about Maryland had been somewhat quieted. The legislature had refused to call a convention; Baltimore had a Federal garrison enforcing martial law, and the spring elections showed Union sentiment predominating in the state. Also, there were hopes of salvaging part of Virginia despite the fact that the state had seceded. The western counties beyond the mountains refused to accept this decision. The Governor sent the state commander, Robert E. Lee, to quell their spirit, but the Federal commander in Ohio crossed the river and worsted him. By July 14, General George B. McClellan had driven the Virginia forces out. The West Virginians were therefore free to establish themselves as the loyal state of Virginia. They held a convention which elected a "loyal" Governor of Virginia, Francis H. Peirpoint, who continued in office all through the war, supervising the moves which transformed most of the "loyal" state into the state of West

Virginia which was admitted in 1863. In the meantime McClellan had gained in reputation from the defeat of Lee.

Operations were similarly significant in the other border states. Like Virginia, Arkansas and North Carolina had joined the Confederacy after the call for volunteers and so had Tennessee, although there was decided dissent in the eastern counties. In this region, under the leadership of Senator Andrew Johnson, Union feeling was strong. Though this pocket of resistance to the Confederacy failed to materialize as a Union state, as had West Virginia, it greatly aided the Federal cause.

The other three border states, Delaware, Kentucky, and Missouri, though divided, never joined the Confederacy. So long as Maryland stayed in the Union, Delaware had to do likewise. But in both the other states there were difficulties of no slight order. Kentucky was Lincoln's birthplace and he was determined not to be spiritually outlawed by secession. With the Governor pro-Southern and the legislature badly divided, the state government declared itself neutral. However, congressional and state elections in June and August showed Union sentiment predominant. Lincoln acted very cleverly. He made General Robert Anderson of Kentucky, the hero of Sumter, director of recruiting for Kentucky, but established him across the Ohio in Cincinnati. Then he sent a young naval officer into the state itself, with arms but no instructions, to supply the loyal militia. Finally, the Confederates precipitated action by sending troops into the state in September as a "defensive" measure. The Kentucky legislature almost immediately decided for the Union, flew the Stars and Stripes over the Capitol, and Grant and Sherman were established at Paducah and Louisville. Blood would soon stain the Blue Grass, but Kentucky would never be Confederate.

Missouri was a highly strategic area, particularly at St. Louis where there was the Federal subtreasury and arsenal. Here as in Kentucky the Governor was pro-Southern but the commander at the arsenal, Captain Nathaniel Lyon, was a Union ball of fire although, according to some authority, a rash and misguided one.

With the help of the Governor of Illinois, who sent in troops under authorization of the War Department, he captured the Missouri militia which the Governor was mobilizing, thus saving St. Louis. The Southern element then set up a military command under General Sterling Price. He and Lyon fought a miniature civil war which in August cost Lyon his life. But by that time the Union supporters had gathered in convention and deposed Governor Jackson. Missouri was safe for the Union, even if divided.

In both Kentucky and Missouri many enlisted in the Confederate Army and Representatives and Senators from these states sat in the Confederate Congress. But their constituencies were shadowy and unreal. The Confederacy never realized its expected potential among the slave states. Eleven proved its maximum strength with two of these, Virginia and Tennessee, badly split.

The defeat at what was the first Bull Run had been momentarily paralyzing. Lincoln almost immediately realized that a military reorganization was required. General George B. McClellan had been winning victories in West Virginia, and the day after the disaster he was summoned to Washington to relieve McDowell and to assume the administrative work that General Scott was unable to carry on. McClellan took over vigorously, but it soon became clear that he could not work with the old general and that he was contemptuous of Lincoln. But the President soon became convinced that Scott was no longer needed and, despite McClellan's ego, he appointed him on November 1 to become the new commander.

McClellan in his new post continued to devote himself to his great passion, organizing a grand army. He was thinking not of thousands but of hundreds of thousands, and as the force grew, its needs expanded. The same situation prevailed in the Confederacy. But behind the mobilization of fighting men there was another, even more intricate, process to be organized, that of providing for their supply. The wants of an army proved most complex. The 200,000 men of both armies had to be fed,

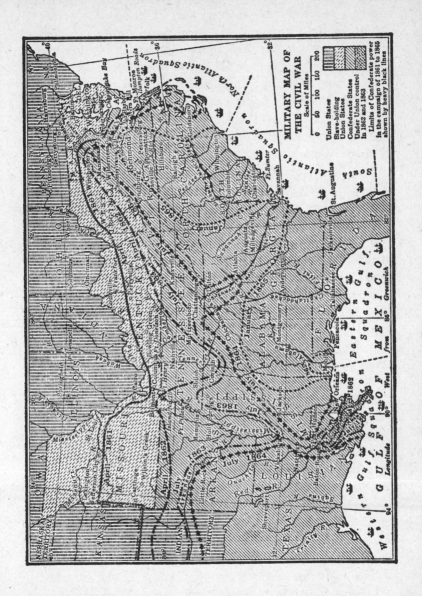

MILITARY MAP OF
THE CIVIL WAR
Scale of Miles
0   50   100   150   200

Union States
Union States
Slave-holding
Confederate States
Under Union control
in 1862 and 1863
Limits of Confederate power
in the campaign of 1861 to 1865
shown by heavy black lines

clothed, sheltered, fortified, armed and otherwise equipped,
transported and given medical care. Also they would waste and
destroy much which would call for replacement. All these needs
made extra demands upon the capacity of both of the belliger-
ents to produce while at the same time men, first by the hundreds of thousands, and then to the number of more than a million, were taken out of economic usefulness. And the payment
for these services called for financial expedients vitally affecting
the American economy.

The ancient bureaucracy which was the United States Army
had never dealt with a force larger than 20,000 save in the brief
Mexican War. Its red-taped routine had to be adjusted to supply
more guns and uniforms than the nation's foundries and factories could immediately produce. The Confederacy, on its part,
had practically nothing except what could be found in Federal
arsenals and state armories within its bounds. Both sides had to
turn to Europe. The Confederates got there first and cornered
most of the market. Unfortunately for them their credit was
limited, and the Federal agents who arrived more tardily, but
supplied with money, bought up many of the Confederate contracts when their negotiators found themselves without funds.

While this competition for foreign supplies was at its height,
the domestic economies of both sections were responding. The
farmers adjusted most quickly. Wheat and corn were needed
for breadstuffs in vast quantities, hogs, sheep and cattle for meat.
Vegetables and fruits must be raised and preserved, canned and
bottled. Coffee was imported. This meant that flour milling,
meat packing and canning as industries were called upon to
process food in great quantities in the North. These operations
in the South were more in the nature of home industries and the
soldier diet there was much simpler, largely restricted to corn and
pork. Their coffee imports were soon cut off and chickory sub-
stitutes had to be tolerated.

The need for great wheat supplies in the North came at the
same time that thousands of farmers and their sons were volun-

teering, or being drafted, into the Army. The labor shortage would have been much more serious than it was had not new farm machinery, notably the McCormick reaper, been available to make possible the garnering of huge crops with a reduced farm labor force. The South continued its agricultural system with slave labor. Though it transferred some of its efforts to raising food, it persisted in raising cotton crops in the vain hope of exporting them for cash.

Clothing and shoes for the armed host gave another spurt to Northern industry. The need to supply uniforms and shoes by the hundreds of thousands came at a time when industrial advance was ready. Mass production on machines was now possible. Ready-made clothes and shoes could now be turned out in quantity, and improved methods were hereafter to rule merchandising. Hart, Schaffner and Marx got their start in the new ready-made clothing industry. The South tried to depend on importation but eventually had to rely largely on "homespun butternuts." Too often men went barefoot.

Arms and munitions spurred the metals industries. Cannon and small arms must be acquired in quantity. United States arsenals worked overtime and shipments were bought abroad, often snatched from the Confederate agents who did not have the favored cash position of the Northern agents. The construction of new naval vessels, particularly of the *Monitor* and the ironclad type, brought a union of shipbuilding and metal industrial activity. Powder, percussion caps, cannon balls, grape shot, shells must be manufactured in great quantity. The casting of many cannon called for caissons and ammunition wagons. The transportation of food and other supplies and the need for ambulances caused a great expansion of wagon building, and here the name of Studebaker became famous.

Housing the troops and fortifying them called for tents and tools, stoves and hut lumber. Establishing hospitals called for surgical instruments, medicines, anesthetics and liquor. Here Northern industry was able to supply most of what was needed, but often the South had to make do with expedients. In one way or another the South could contrive most things, but frequently in insufficient quantity. Serious shortages hampered the Confederacy and their lack of medicine, particularly anesthetics, made the surgery of the time frightful, particularly in amputations.

The great armies and their equipment were to call for gigantic transportation projects on land and water. This responsibility fell largely on the railroads. These were not too well fixed for long-distance carrying. Most of these roads were short lines; little attention had been paid to connecting their tracks for through travel. In fact through travel often had been discouraged so people would have to stop over and spend money locally for meals and lodging. Sometimes lines leading to the same point would be of different gauges so there could be no shift of rolling stock. Now these deficiencies had to be rectified and much new track laid to connect roads. Locomotives and cars were built. The construction of rails, wheels, and locomotives—all of this stimulated the iron industry. In the South the need for railroad operation was likewise great but success in dealing with the problem was hampered by lack of facilities. The Confederacy devoted all of the capacity of its iron foundries to manufacturing arms and ammunition. The overworked railroads wore out rails and rolling stock, yet little was done to repair or to replace. Not one bar of railroad iron was rolled in the Confederacy during the war.

These great supply projects which were inaugurated in this dreary year of 1861 had to be paid for. In the years that followed, more and more money had to be raised. The expenses mounted into billions and the mobilization of these dollars was to prove as intricate a process as that of mobilizing the men and the supplies. The Federal government which had been operating on a budget of $70,000,000 a year was soon called upon to spend $2,000,-000 a day. The political leaders were hesitant about heavy taxes; at first it was hoped that the needed money could be obtained by the sale of bonds, by borrowing. The state banks would lend gold and silver coin and issue paper money which was presumed to be redeemable in coin. However, the heavy expenses of the war and its risks soon made gold too scarce and neither the state banks nor the treasuries could pay their obligations in coin. So specie payment was abandoned in the North. There had never really been any such thing in the South.

When the Northern Congress came together in December 1861 for its first regular war session, it resorted to financial stratagems to raise the gigantic sums of money required. As the supply of gold and silver coin was utterly inadequate, Congress soon authorized the issuance of paper money, called greenbacks, to be legal tender for all debts public and private except customs duties. These bills were to amount to over $400,000,000 before the war ended. At the same time loans continued to be authorized and a variety of notes and bonds was issued, some payable in gold, some in coin, some in "dollars," eventually amounting to over $2,000,000,000, and bearing five different rates of interest and nineteen different dates of maturity. Three-fourths of the money needed during the four years was to be borrowed. The Confederacy was even more involved in issuing paper. As it had little coin to start with, it immediately issued paper money and floated loans. It was an inflationary operation from the start, and continued to get more and more unreal with respect to maintaining any standards of value.

While these great processes of supply were being initiated, the weary months of mobilization, defeat, disappointment, dominated by McClellan's dreary caution, dragged on to the end of 1861. But the catastrophic year was not to die without one last crisis which might have precipitated a foreign war. The diplomatic agents which the Confederacy had sent abroad to seek recognition had failed. They had proved to be men who could not impress European politicians. Davis determined on a new diplomatic effort late in the year. He sent two of the South's foremost politicians, men who had been United States Senators intimately connected with foreign relations under Pierce and

Buchanan, James M. Mason of Virginia and John Slidell of
Louisiana. Both of these men had extensive foreign connections.
These gentlemen slipped through the blockade and transhipped
to a British mail steamer, the *Trent,* en route to Europe. At this
point a United States warship, the *San Jacinto,* Charles Wilkes,
U.S.N., commander, stopped the *Trent* and took the diplomats
back to the United States in December 1861. This high-handed
act, not justifiable under international law, almost brought on a
European war. The British government protested vigorously.
American opinion, which had been fired by admiration for
Wilkes' bold act, was in a mood to answer back defiantly. But
Lincoln, like Queen Victoria and Prince Albert, appreciated the
danger and reasonable counsel prevailed. The United States was
in the wrong. Lincoln admitted it and sent Mason and Slidell on
their way to Europe. It was a dreary ending to a disastrous year,
for there was still no action by McClellan; rather he was laid
low by typhoid while his army continued the constant grind of
drill.

9

The Strain of Defeat

THE MEETING of the Union Congress in December 1861
soon brought into unpleasant prominence the fact that there was
a political conflict going on behind the military lines. The contest
for the stakes of power had become more complex than a military
clash between the United States and a league of seceding states.
Two civil contests were being fought, one among the political
activists in the Union government, and another of similar character within the new Confederacy. These civil conflicts were oc-
casioned by the need to create two new political and war-making
powers. Lincoln must create one of these mechanisms and Davis
the other.

Since Lincoln had been nominated he had been laboring to
make a unified party out of the coalition of northern Whigs,
Free Soilers, Know-Nothings, and anti-Nebraska Democrats so
recently fused into the Republican party. The instability of this
coalition was exaggerated by rivalries between its eastern and
western wings. In making up his Cabinet and distributing his
patronage, Lincoln had sought to give fair representation to these
various elements. This he had been compelled to do in the midst
of rumors of war and of war itself.

As Congress assembled during this first war winter it was apparent that dissatisfied elements in the party were going to
challenge his leadership. Certain Congressional factions, led by

Senators, wished to create a cabal of Senatorial committee chairmen to control the lawmaking process as a similar Southern group had done during the Democratic Administrations of the fifties.

The dawn of 1862 was made no brighter by mounting evidence that Lincoln must fight this political war behind the military lines tediously forming under McClellan. The hardbitten group of radical zealots within the Republican party was determined on the destruction of the political power of the South, based as it was on slavery. But Lincoln believed that the purpose of the war was to save the Union, the great experiment in democracy, and if that end could be achieved he was willing to permit slavery to continue to exist within its boundaries. When the defeat at Bull Run proved that the war would not be won in ninety days and that the Union government would need every resource, especially the cooperation of the border states, Lincoln and his moderate associates, Republican and War Democrat, secured the passage of a Congressional resolution declaring the objective of the conflict was to preserve the Union. This roused the Radicals who were henceforth more troublesome opponents than the Democrats.

The uncertain fortunes of the first year of the war, particularly McClellan's reluctance to fight, led Lincoln's enemies to raise the slavery issue by way of forcing its piecemeal abolition by the Army. They were joined in this effort by Cameron, the Secretary of War, and General Frémont. The determination of the Radicals, and the irresponsible conduct of Cameron and Frémont, led the President to conclude that he must organize coalition support. He therefore worked with the moderate Republicans and a group of Democrats who were willing to support the war. Cameron was appointed Minister to Russia. Edwin M. Stanton, a Democrat who had been in Buchanan's Cabinet, replaced him as Secretary of War. But Lincoln was never to have an easy relationship with the Radicals and many a contest was to be fought between them. The stakes of power were often in the balance.

Jefferson Davis, like Lincoln, had to fight a political conflict behind the lines. Within the Confederacy little attention was paid to the old party designations, Democratic, Whig, or American, and no official parties ever developed. But if there were no parties, there were factions, Upper South, Lower South, Radical Secessionists, the more conservative Cooperationists, Old South, New South, all fighting for power. As the war advanced a new cleavage developed. President Davis had to strain every resource to establish a government and mobilize a war machine. To make this difficult task possible Davis sought to centralize power. The Southern states, however, had always been very conscious of state rights and had often resisted the centralizing tendencies of the old government. The same impulses in the new government were no more pleasing and even the necessities of war-making did not reconcile the new Confederacy to such concentration.

Davis was bitterly opposed by powerful Governors in Georgia and North Carolina. Moreover, there were Union enclaves in Virginia and in Tennessee, and to a lesser extent in Alabama and North Carolina. West Virginia actually seceded from the Confederacy and the mountain regions of North Carolina, Tennessee, and Alabama were alien ground. Davis succeeded, in most instances, in persuading his Congress to follow his lead. But the opposition in the States, and the steady penetration of the Confederacy by Union military and naval power, ultimately reduced Davis' political authority almost to nothing, a fact he never seemed to comprehend because his beleaguered Congress continued to enact legislation, in large part according to his bidding.

President Davis was particularly unfortunate in that he had none of Lincoln's capacity to attract popular support and to confound his enemies. He was basically a kindly man at heart but he was in poor health much of the time, and he had a talent for making enemies whom he proceeded to hate rather than conciliate. His temperament found relief in preoccupation with the petty details of war-making, and he never could quite rise to the over-all demands of a complex situation. His relations with some of the generals were most unfortunate, particularly with Generals Joseph E. Johnston and P. G. T. Beauregard; two of his favorites, General Braxton Bragg and Commissary General Lucius B. Northrop, were resented and distrusted. His principal Cabinet adviser, Judah P. Benjamin, was very unpopular, and he had virulent enemies in Congress and among the press. The editors of the Charleston *Mercury* and the Richmond *Examiner* were particularly bitter in their attacks.

Despite his inability to conciliate his foes, Davis fared reasonably well with Congress. The only major policy which they refused to support was his desire to suspend the privilege of the writ of habeas corpus in order to prevent state judges from limiting Confederate power and freeing drafted men from army service. Even this, however, was granted for some limited periods. Davis was elected unanimously in the only Presidential election which the Confederacy held, that in the fall of 1861. This unanimity, however, was specious. President Davis had to suffer constant attacks as a "dictator."

While Lincoln and Davis were organizing their political lines to ensure their necessary war powers the former was wearily engaged in trying to get his military machine in motion. McClellan's tedious perfectionism was depriving him of any chance at early or decisive success. Victories were won, but by other instruments. Success first crowned the efforts of the Navy. Not only was the blockade slowly becoming effective but the fleets were undertaking to capture the Southern ports themselves. The attack had begun upon the North Carolina shore in the Hatteras area with the objective of controlling the Albemarle and Pamlico sounds. The first assault had been victorious and its objective was accomplished on August 29, 1861. In November another penetration was made with the capture of Port Royal, South Carolina, where the Federals secured a second base. During the winter, the dominance of the Hatteras coast was improved by the capture of Confederate fortifications on Roanoke Island on

February 8, 1862, and the occupation of New Bern and other places by forces under the command of General Ambrose E. Burnside.

While this campaign of coastal penetration was advancing, a startling naval event occurred that was to mark a new era in American naval history. Experiments in using iron naval vessels had begun in 1839 in England, and shortly thereafter in France. As neither of these governments thought them satisfactory, the United States, when it enlarged its Navy after the Mexican War, continued to use wood. Thus in 1861, the principal ships—the *Brooklyn,* the *Powhatan,* the *Merrimac,* the *Minnesota,* the *Congress,* the *Cumberland,* and the *Hartford*—were all so constructed. But England and France had been converted to iron during the Crimean War, and had introduced armor plate, turrets, and rifled guns. The Confederacy immediately took cognizance of this innovation. When Commodore Faulding was destroying what he could before abandoning the Norfolk navy yard in 1861, he had sunk one of the best ships in the Navy, the steam war vessel, the *Merrimac.* However, the Confederates had succeeded in salvaging the ship and, following the new fashion, made her into an ironclad. The Confederacy covered the *Merrimac* with armor plate made from iron rails, attached an iron ram to her prow, and armed her with ten guns. In March 1862, she was ready.

The Union Navy had a fleet stationed at Hampton Roads. On March 8, the *Merrimac,* renamed the *Virginia,* steamed out to smash and sink the ships. The ironclad rammed the thirty-gun *Cumberland* which soon sank, her captain refusing to surrender. The *Virginia* now turned on the *Congress* which was trying to run for it, delivering a broadside. The slaughter was hideous, and when her captain was killed a lieutenant sought to surrender. Union shore batteries continued to fire on the *Virginia,* so she drew off and hurled red-hot cannon shot at the *Congress* until she was afire in many places. The triumphant ironclad now expected to finish the fleet but the tide was going out and she could not come within effective range. Tomorrow boded ill for the *Minnesota* and her two companions. But tomorrow was to be a different kind of a day.

All was not lost. In the preceding October the first real naval victory for the Union had been won, not on the sea, but in the offices of the Navy Department. There it had been decided to contract with the Swedish engineer, John Ericsson, to build a *Monitor*-type warship. This was an iron hull with a revolving turret equipped with two rifled guns. She looked like a cheese-box on a raft. She had been finished during the winter and had recently steamed south. And it was just in time. Washington was panic-stricken. News of the fate of the *Cumberland* and the *Congress* caused officialdom to believe that the Capital was doomed. What could stop the renamed *Merrimac* from coming up the Potomac? The answer was the *Monitor*. It arrived the morning of March 9, and as the *Merrimac* steamed out the *Monitor* began a day-long engagement with her. At night the *Merrimac* beat a retreat and never returned. The day of the ironclad in United States naval history had begun.

The Navy proceeded to accumulate more laurels. In April, advance was made in Georgia; on April 11, Fort Pulaski which controlled the approaches to Savannah surrendered. By this move all Atlantic ports were pretty well closed except Wilmington, North Carolina, and Charleston. The climax of naval success came between April 23 and May 1 when Admiral Farragut captured New Orleans by his spectacularly brilliant and daring run past Forts Jackson and St. Philip. Shortly after, Admiral Porter took Pensacola and thus gave the Union forces most of the Gulf Coast.

Action on both land and water brought victory in the west. General John C. Frémont had been sent out to take command even before Captain Lyon was killed. He set himself up in style in St. Louis, surrounded by a glittering staff. Fleets of river steamers, ironclad in the new fashion, were assembled on the western rivers, the Mississippi, the Tennessee and the Cumberland, with Flag Officer Andrew H. Foote a prominent commander. The failure of Kentucky to rise, and the knowledge that a large section of Eastern Tennessee was not Confederate-minded, early induced the Confederacy to turn its attention westward. President Davis now undertook to direct a western campaign, but here distance necessitated remote control. Davis was never able to achieve this, nor did he maintain any real interest in these distant operations. He placed the matter in the hands of his third general and great friend, Albert Sidney Johnston, just arrived from the Far West.

General Frémont, on his part, seemed more interested in head-quarters activities than in field operations which he delegated to General U. S. Grant, a rather nondescript Mexican War veteran who had returned to the Army from a life of persistent failure. He blocked Johnston's efforts to establish control of Kentucky and, in February 1862, penetrated into Tennessee where he cap-tured Forts Henry and Donelson with Foote's naval help. John-ston then organized a counteroffensive to wipe out Grant, and nearly succeeded at Shiloh where he caught Grant off base on April 6. Johnston lost his life in this battle. Grant saved himself, and the campaign against him was a Confederate failure. The Western conquest of the South had begun.

At this point, April 1862, McClellan finally undertook to move. Illness and perfectionism, together with a curious reluctance to put his army in danger, had kept him in camp all winter. Almost in desperation Lincoln had issued a peremptory order to him to move, on Washington's birthday. This only precipitated a long argument. Lincoln and certain of his military advisers wanted the campaign to proceed over the land via Bull Run. McClellan had other ideas. He wanted the troops transported to Fortress Monroe, and then to proceed up the peninsula between the James and York rivers with river supply lines. McClellan carried his point after much debate, and his army was shipped south. On April 2, he arrived at Fortress Monroe. There he delayed some more, trying to secure troops which had been withheld from him. The Confederate General "Stonewall" Jackson had been so active in the Shenandoah Valley that Lincoln feared an attack on Washington and kept an army from McClellan to defend the capital. The Union commander also wasted a month besieging Yorktown which the Confederates finally evacuated without a blow. Only then did the General finally get braced for fighting. On May 27, he attacked General Joseph E. Johnston's forces and fought a complicated campaign which brought his men within sound of Richmond's church bells but not to victory. By July 1, the Peninsula campaign, so elaborate and so costly, had to be conceded a failure.

Lincoln was forced to conclude that salvation had to come from the West. Because of his almost unrelieved failure to get results, Frémont was displaced there by General Henry W. Halleck, a professional soldier turned lawyer. This savant, spoken of as "Old Brains," now faced Beauregard, General A. S. Johnston's successor, and he proceeded to clear the Mississippi. He sent General John Pope successfully against Island No. 10, and then in most classical fashion proceeded to invest Corinth. By the time his scientific siege arrangements were completed, Beauregard slipped away. The climax of the campaign came when the Navy reduced Memphis.

Kentucky was now safe for the time being. The Confederates had little left in Tennessee and the Federal Army was established in northern Mississippi. Also, the dramatis personae changed. Davis got rid of Beauregard whom he didn't like, and appointed his favorite, Braxton Bragg. Lincoln brought Halleck and Pope to Washington to teach the Eastern generals the art of victory. Grant was left in command in the West while Don Carlos Buell was supposed to finish the conquest of Tennessee by securing Chattanooga. This was the situation in the West by the summer of 1862.

In the East, operations continued to be concentrated in the region between Washington and Richmond. "Fighting" John Pope was in fine fettle. He ridiculed planning, strategy, bases of supplies and the like. He proclaimed heroically, and somewhat ambiguously, that henceforth "headquarters would be in the saddle." He tried to go to Richmond via Bull Run and that was just as far as he got. Lee and Stonewall Jackson badly defeated him in the Second Battle of Bull Run, August 29-30, 1862.

While the Army of the Potomac was demoralized by the loss of their beloved McClellan and by this second defeat, a new peril threatened. There had been a change in the Confederate high command. General Joseph E. Johnston had been wounded in the Peninsula campaign and had been replaced by Lee who took the initiative after defeating Pope. He and Jackson planned to invade Maryland, reclaim that state and march on to Washington. His army was soon in motion, and Lincoln had barely time to recall McClellan to stop him. The two armies clashed at Antietam on September 17. After an exhausting battle Lee withdrew.

Lincoln used this victory to enable him to win a contest on the political front. The Radicals were constantly pressing him to move toward the abolition of slavery. Congress, on its part, had freed the slaves in the District of Columbia and in the Territories, and Lincoln himself had worked out a plan for compensated emancipation. Yet the pressure for direct action continued. At the same time criticism of the President's assumption of power, suspension of the privilege of the writ of habeas corpus, arbitrary arrest, increasing expenditures, and the conduct of the armed forces, continued to mount.

The President also felt pressures from abroad urging him toward emancipation. The Confederacy had been continuing its fight for recognition across the Atlantic. Lincoln found he must fight a propaganda battle in Europe, taking advantage of a conflict of ideologies on that continent. Most of the governments there were monarchies resting upon hereditary, aristocratic principles. There were, however, liberal elements in most of these nations, some of which had fomented the recent revolutions of 1848. Also, particularly in Britain and France, there were working-class and republican movements. As a slave economy, ostensibly ruled by slave owners, the Confederacy was looked upon favorably by certain European aristocrats. This same situation aroused liberal hostility. The United States government sought to take advantage of this division.

That the Confederacy would ultimately fail to obtain recognition was certainly not apparent in these first months of 1862. The Confederacy had strong support among monarchs and upper-class statesmen who were apprehensive of the advance of the United States and who were relieved to see it split, and demonstrating the unworkability of democracy. The Confederacy had little appeal to liberals but it could emphasize its virtues to the conservatives. To which purpose they too sent out propaganda agents, public relations men, notably Henry Hotze who set up a Confederate propaganda paper, *The Index.*

Lincoln carefully selected clever agents to work on public opinion in England. Thurlow Weed, prominent journalist, was one; Robert J. Walker, financier and ex-governor of Kansas, another; Henry Ward Beecher, famous clergyman, and brother of Harriet Beecher Stowe of *Uncle Tom's Cabin* fame, a third. Beecher was particularly successful in addresses to workingmen, stirring up their hatred of slavery and persuading them to support the freedom-loving North even if their employment was precarious.

Despite its later success, the North was at an initial disadvantage in this propaganda contest. The slavery question was embarrassing. European liberals, and particularly the wage workers in England and France, were opposed to the Confederacy because it made slavery the cornerstone of its political economy. However, the Union government could not capitalize on the antislavery opinion because it had to retain the loyalty of the border slave states. Consequently, for nearly a year and a half, the objectives of the war were declared to be the preservation of the Union, that great experiment in self-government and equalitarian democracy. It was further stated that slavery would not be disturbed if the Union could be maintained while it still existed. Coexistence of freedom and slavery was still held to be possible.

After some months, it became clear not only that the governments of Great Britain and France were inclined to be sympathetic with the Confederacy, but that liberal elements would remain cool to the Union government so long as slavery was tolerated. Lincoln decided to make capital in several directions. By a pronouncement for emancipation he would conciliate world liberal opinion, remove the Radicals' grievance, weaken the Confederacy's labor force and its military potential, and at the same time strengthen his own war powers and his political position. In July 1862, after McClellan had failed, the border states had rebuffed him on compensated emancipation and since opposition to the war was mounting, Lincoln decided to issue a proclamation abolishing slavery, but only within the bounds of the Confederacy. When Secretary Seward urged that it be postponed until a victory was won so that it would not look like an act of political desperation, Lincoln saw the sense of this and waited. After the Union victory at Antietam, Lincoln published his preliminary Emancipation Proclamation on September 22, 1862, and followed it with the final document on January 1, 1863.

Lincoln's initial Emancipation Proclamation appeared only a few weeks before the midterm Congressional elections. Another round in the fight for power had to be slugged out. Despite the fact of war in this disastrous 1862 the biennial Congressional election was held without hesitation, though there was a vigorous and relentless opposition to Lincoln and the Republicans. A bitter campaign was put on in many states by the "peace" Democrats. The Republicans suffered disasters, notably the loss of the New York governorship and various offices to the Democrats in Pennsylvania, Ohio, Indiana, Illinois, and New Jersey, but they maintained their Congressional control though by narrow margin.

The sighs of relief at the scant victory at the November elections had scarcely been emitted when a new blow struck. After his success at Antietam, McClellan relapsed into his old habits of inaction, and Lee escaped across the Potomac. Nothing Lincoln could do would get him to move. At one point McClellan pleaded that his horses were exhausted and their tongues sore. This dispatch brought from Lincoln the tart and exasperated inquiry, "Will you pardon me for asking what the horses of your army have done since the battle of Antietam that fatigues anything?" It was evidently no use, there must be a new commander.

Lincoln rather inadvisedly turned to the bewhiskered Burnside who loudly, almost tearfully, proclaimed himself incapable of such a responsibility, and then proceeded to demonstrate the correctness of his self-appraisal. His great strategy was to massacre his own men at Fredericksburg by the simple device of ordering them to storm a position impossible to capture by assault. Not until dusk on that disastrous day could his associates persuade him to stop. This December 12 cast new gloom over Union hopes.

The Eastern defeat, the failure of Union forces to make any further progress in the West, and the return of Congress to Washington in December reopened the political warfare. The Radicals were bitter because of the narrow escape from defeat in the elections as well as because of the defeat in battle. They had forged a weapon which they were growing adept at using. They had succeeded in securing a committee to investigate the "Conduct of the War." These committeemen devoted themselves to discovering why victories were not being won, and did much to harass the generals who failed. They were developing a thesis that Lincoln appointed too many Democrats as generals, and that he neglected sterling Republicans like Frémont and Banks. McClellan, a Democrat, was anathema to them.

In the minds and emotions of his Radical enemies, Lincoln was becoming more and more blameworthy, inefficient, and disloyal to the Republican party. What was worse, he was on occasion frustrating and outmaneuvering them. He had defeated them first by securing his definition of the war, and then by prescribing emancipation under his own fiat, thus strengthening his own power. They sought to retaliate by forcing him to reorganize his Cabinet, notably by getting rid of Seward whom they held to be his evil genius. In this they were encouraged by Chase who always thought of himself as the big man in the Administration, and who had hopes of succeeding Lincoln. The Radicals made it so hot for Seward that he resigned in December 1862. But Lincoln would not accept this. He had come to value Seward, and he was aware of Chase's ambitions. By a clever move he got together the leading Radical Senators and his Cabinet, save Seward, to discuss the dissatisfaction. He cleverly maneuvered the discussion so that Chase, in the company of his fellow members of the Cabinet, had to contradict what he had been telling the Senators about disunity in the Cabinet.

This so embarrassed Chase, caught in his own deviousness, that next day he felt he must go to Lincoln and, at least, offer to resign. Lincoln seized the resignation from Chase's very reluctant fingers. He now had what he wanted, resignations from both Seward and Chase. He thereupon announced that he would accept neither, that he wanted his Administration to be well-balanced, containing representatives of all shades of opinion. Once again he had won.

Thus, in this militarily disastrous year of 1862, even if the Union forces had not been able to win much on the field of arms, their great commander had shown himself capable of holding his political forces intact, and demonstrating his mastery of making democracy work. Most significant was the fact that he had made it the year of emancipation. As Lincoln reported to Congress, "In giving freedom to the slave, we assure freedom to the free. . . . We shall nobly save or meanly lose the last best hope of earth. . . . The way is plain, peaceful, generous, just—a way which if followed, the world will forever applaud, and God must forever bless."

10

The Tide Turns

DESPITE THE FACT that 1863 opened with the publication of the final Emancipation Proclamation, the Union skies were gloomy. Burnside's defeat meant that once again Lincoln had to seek a commander. Richmond was still to be won. Union power was not yet great enough.

For his fourth general, the President wearily chose a politician's favorite. Jovial Joseph Hooker was hand-picked by Secretary Chase, a handsome man who appeared well to the Radicals, and who certainly was no Democrat. His campaign that spring seemed to start off well; in fact, he got Lee pretty much in a box near Chancellorsville. But in the battle joined on May 2-4, he became all snarled up and his judgment was not improved by a blow on the head from a spent cannon ball. He could still issue orders, but they made even less sense than usual. It was a victory, however, that the Confederates could ill afford for it cost them the great Stonewall Jackson. The commander was slain when in the dark he rode unannounced into a company of his own men who shot him, mistaking him for an enemy.

Chancellorsville emboldened Lee to try another northern thrust, this time into Pennsylvania. Here was plenty of food, and rich towns might be ransomed. Harrisburg and Philadelphia might be seized—perhaps Washington pounced on from the rear. There were many Southern sympathizers in the North who might take this chance to rise and strike their foes on the streets of the cities.

Lee once again marched across the Potomac. Hooker, though psychologically incapacitated, was still supported politically in his command. He could do nothing to stop Lee except to wail for more men. When these were refused by Lincoln and Stanton in the almost vain hope that he might resign, he gratified them. Instantly, they put General George Gordon Meade in command. He drew his forces together at Gettysburg. There Lee hoped to beat him and gain his objective of exacting a peace by a victory on Union soil. Three days of desperate fighting taught Lee his first real lesson in defeat. For the North, the Fourth of July was made glorious by this victory.

In the West, Grant's fortunes were at first somewhat discouraging. He himself undertook to fight off some minor Confederate commanders while he hoped to keep Bragg out of Chattanooga through Buell. However, Bragg got to this city first, and then undertook to strike out for Kentucky. Grant left Buell to deal with this situation while he turned his attention to freeing the Mississippi by capturing Vicksburg with the assistance of William Tecumseh Sherman. Buell prevented Bragg from staying long in Kentucky but failed to capture him. While these two commanders settled down for a winter of watching each other in Tennessee, commands were again changed. Buell was set aside, not for General George H. Thomas as Stanton wanted, but for a divinely handsome Adonis, William S. Rosecrans. Davis, on his part, was forced to turn direction over to Joseph E. Johnston, now recovered from his Peninsula wounds. Johnston immediately turned his attention to capturing Grant and Sherman, and gave Bragg the task of bringing in Rosecrans. Neither succeeded.

Then Grant's luck changed. After various failures, he finally reduced Vicksburg and the "Father of Waters once more flowed unvexed to the Sea." This was the Western message of July 4, 1863. Surely this Fourth had been glorious; Gettysburg and Vicksburg on one great day of triumph in East and West, won by Meade and Grant. Lee was defeated, the Mississippi free, and the Confederacy split in two. But, unfortunately, there was no matching victory on the political home front. Opposition to the fighting had taken the form of organizing campaigns to elect men committed to "peace." Such efforts were carried on not only in regular, open party contest but more dangerously, it was believed, by secret organizations. Prior to the war there had been a band known as the Knights of the Golden Circle created in the romantic atmosphere of the South to promote the extension of United States influence in the Golden Circle of the Caribbean islands. This order was especially designed to secure the annexation of Cuba, the isthmus region, and more of Mexico. It had been particularly strong in Texas and Louisiana. Its numbers on the eve of the war were thought to be in the neighborhood of 60,000. After the commencement of the conflict there were reports that this organization was spreading its influence in the Middle West, particularly in certain counties in southern Ohio, Indiana and Illinois where there were many whose family origins were Southern. There were also some other organizations known as the Sons of Liberty.

Political warfare behind the lines continued unflagging. The Democrats continued their battle for existence by seeking possession of state power. Their victories in 1862 had given them the governorship in New York, and they controlled the legislatures in Illinois and Indiana. In those states the Republican War Governors, Richard Yates and Oliver P. Morton, found themselves hard-pressed. The Democrats were using defense of civil rights, opposition to centralization and demands for peace as their principal weapons. Some of their number formed secret societies. Their attacks upon Lincoln and their criticism of the war could, and probably did, discourage some from enlisting, and did give the Confederates reason to believe that the South had friends in the North who might join in intrigues to help them. The Republicans made the most of these situations and cries of treason were raised. These Democrats and others like them were eventually called "Copperheads," snakes that would strike to kill. A number were indicted for treasonable activity, but in many instances local juries were hard to convince and acquittals resulted. The prosecuting officials believed that this result often occurred because "Copperheads" were on the juries.

On occasion Lincoln and Stanton abandoned civil process, and put the suspects in forts and Federal prisons from which they could not be "sprung." This practice, together with the use of military courts-martial, and the suppression of one or two newspapers presented the opponents with an issue. They charged violation of sacred liberties and civil rights. In the spring of 1863 one of the Copperhead leaders, Clement G. Vallandigham of Ohio, was tried by court-martial and convicted. Lincoln then cleverly banished him to the Confederacy. He soon tired of it there, and returned to the United States via a blockade runner, the West Indies, and Canada. The peace Democrats of Ohio then nominated him for Governor.

Another danger arose from the passage of the Draft Act designed to make sure that the ranks of the Army were kept filled. As this legislation contained a provision that anyone paying $300 or obtaining a substitute might be exempt from service, it became unpopular as favoring the rich. Hostility to it developed to such an extent in certain poverty-stricken districts in New York City that when the draft was put into effect, riots broke out sporadically for three days in mid-July 1863, causing a loss of life variously estimated from fifty to more than 1,000, and destruction of over $1,000,000 worth of property as estimated for the payment of damages. Negroes, alleged to be the cause of it all, were the object of insane fury; some of them were hanged to lampposts, and even more brutally murdered. The Democratic Governor of New York issued proclamations and authorized the arming of the police; at length, Federal troops had to be brought in.

To make the situation more hazardous, new dangers loomed in Europe this summer of 1863. Again diplomatic weapons had to be forged. One of the Confederacy's great problems continued to be the maintenance of an adequate Navy. Secretary Mallory continued to devote himself to keeping commerce destroyers busy on the high seas, and building ironclads to keep his ports open and to damage the Union Navy. He was able during the war to get some eighteen cruisers into commission, most notably the *Sumter,* the *Florida,* the *Alabama,* and the *Shenandoah.* He likewise achieved several ironclad rams, the most famous of which were the *Merrimac* and the *Albemarle.*

The Confederacy's principal European naval agent was Captain James D. Bulloch who succeeded in making shipbuilding contracts in England. Such deals with a belligerent in a conflict in which England was neutral were camouflaged. The ships would leave English dockyards on peaceful ventures; at some distant point, perhaps a barren island, a new crew, armament and the Confederate flag would be taken aboard, a new name emblazoned on the bow and a Confederate warship would be in commission. The American diplomats knew what was going on and vainly sought to stop this violation of neutrality. Two raiders, particularly the *Florida* and the *Alabama,* thus secured in England, got away and began depredations on American commerce which were to reduce the American merchant fleet drastically, and to cost the Union millions of dollars. Emboldened by this success Bulloch undertook to have some new-type ironclad war vessels, known as rams, built by the Lairds, British shipbuilders. The Union Navy had no vessels capable of defense against such formidable warships; as they neared completion in 1863, the future seemed ominous.

The Confederacy's policy of economic coercion had failed. The embargo on the export of cotton had not produced a cotton shortage in the European textile industry large enough to be effective. New supplies were procured from India and Egypt. Even more important, slavery had been abolished. Vicksburg and Gettysburg had just been won; the Confederates' hope of military victory seemed much less likely of realization than previously. The Union Navy had been growing in size and fire power. The Union Congress had passed a law authorizing privateers, and Seward did not have to point out to the Foreign Office some of the consequences if American privateers were turned loose on Britain's far-flung merchant fleet. The American minister in London, Charles Francis Adams, in a final demand that the Laird rams be stopped, eloquently concluded with the words, "It would be superfluous in me to point out to your lordship that this is war."

As a matter of fact the British government had already determined on a course of action. Adams was reassured September 8, 1863. The rams were detained and later bought by England. This change of policy did not, however, stop the depredations of the *Florida,* the *Alabama* and their sisters, and later those of the *Shenandoah*. The depletion of the United States merchant marine by privateers, eventually numbering eighteen, reduced the number of ships under American registry from 66.5 per cent to 27.7 per cent of those engaged in the nation's carrying trade, inflicting losses for which the United States was eventually awarded damages of $15,500,000 against Great Britain by the Geneva Tribunal.

The United States had likewise to deal with France on the same subject, though less dramatically. In her quest for aid the Confederacy received great sympathy from the government of Napoleon III. France, like England, was always concerned by the expansionist tendencies of the United States and the breakup of the Union could not help but seem to make this growth less likely to continue. Napoleon winked at a project for building war vessels in French shipyards undertaken by a M. Armand under contracts involving two ironclads and four swift steamers. However, the American consul in Paris secured proof that these were under construction for the Confederacy. At about the same time that the British were putting a stop to the Laird rams deal, Napoleon found he had scruples. The vessels were sold to foreign governments.

France, however, was helpful to the Confederacy in financial matters. While seeking munitions and ships, the Confederate agents were also seeking credit. They had neglected to sell cotton abroad to establish a cash balance, or even to store a supply in Europe as a basis for a loan. But as the war advanced certain

French financial operators dreamed up, or were persuaded into, a speculation. The Paris banking house of Erlanger and Company undertook to float a loan secured by cotton held by the Confederacy, and priced very favorably to the investor. This 7-per-cent loan of 75,000,000 francs was floated partly in London in 1863. The Erlangers were sold the loan at 77, and were able to market the bonds at 90. For a time they sold well. But as defeat and speculation took their toll, prices began to fall. To stave off a collapse on the market the Confederates kept the price up by buying back more than half of the securities sold. Thus, for bonds of 7½ million face value, the government realized only about $2,600,000. The cotton value of this loan was some $45,000,000. In the end the final holders lost everything; but Erlanger had sold out long before that. This company enjoyed its profits and continued to do business for the Confederacy. Treasury officials were proceeding with plans for a loan of $75,000,000, and the establishment of a Franco-Confederate bank in Paris, as late as January 1865.

The Union Treasury made no such efforts to secure European financing. In fact its agent, banker Jay Cooke, who managed the marketing of the United States bonds, did not favor letting foreign bankers in on the discounts and commissions. He did sell one lot of $10,000,000 to German investors, but it was done in New York and for their account. Eventually a number of United States bonds were bought in Europe. American dollars were very cheap and these bonds could make highly profitable investments—if the Union won. By the end some $250,000,000 worth were held in Germany and Holland, and some $70,000,000 elsewhere. Many Europeans bought American paper cheap and watched the advance of the dollar to their very great profit.

In the course of this exasperating diplomatic fencing, the Union cause gained a strange ally, autocratic Russia. During the last months of 1863, two units of the Imperial Navy appeared in the harbors of New York and San Francisco. They bore messages of good will, and their crews came ashore to fraternize. The officers appeared much in society and were lionized as they brought the encouragement of the Czar who in 1861 had freed the serfs. All this was very heartening. It was not until many years later that more of the story was revealed. Russia was having difficulty subduing a revolt in Poland and she feared that the British and French might attempt military intervention. In that event her navy might be blocked up in port by the superior British fleets and the Russian winter. So her warships were sent to the security of American harbors from which, in case of war, they might go forth and prey on enemy shipping as Confederate war vessels were doing. The friendly gesture was merely one of self-interest. But the value of the gesture in boosting morale was in no way lessened thereby.

These advantages could not blind the Union State Department to a serious defeat. Lincoln and his government had been helpless to prevent a flagrant violation of the Monroe Doctrine by their European rivals for interest and influence in America. Spain and France took advantage of the desperate preoccupation of the Union to feather their own nests on the Western Hemisphere. The Spanish government had never become reconciled to the loss of most of its American colonies. The insecure adventurer, Napoleon III, Emperor of the French, was forever looking for ways to add to his power and his security, and cherished thoughts of recouping and advancing his fortune in America. Weak government and revolutions in Latin America gave these European governments certain opportunities which they could seize safely only when the United States was too preoccupied to enforce the Monroe Doctrine.

In the late 1850's Mexico had been plagued by revolution. Property had been destroyed and debts defaulted. Much of this loss bore heavily on foreign investors. Even before the American conflict, England, France, and Spain had been planning intervention to secure financial redress. After the outbreak of the conflict, the United States was too busy to spare any strength to protect its interests in these southern regions. The European powers therefore could do as they would. In the fall and winter of 1861-62, after Mexico had suspended all payment on the foreign debt, the three nations signed a convention arranging for military intervention. Landing in the troubled Mexican republic, Spain captured Vera Cruz in December. But her real interest was elsewhere. She had already occupied Santo Domingo and now wanted her troops in Mexico where they might be useful in the recapture of Peru. England, for her part, never did get involved in Mexican military action. The real responsibility was left to Napoleon.

His forces penetrated to Mexico City in 1863 and these, with a small foreign legion, maintained themselves along the road from Vera Cruz to Mexico City. Napoleon at the same time completed plans to put over a scheme. He encouraged the Conservatives in Mexico to issue an invitation to Maximilian, one of the Austrian Archdukes, to become Emperor, and promised an army and loans to keep him in power. This was arranged and the new Emperor placed on the throne. The United States was helpless while a European monarch was established and a European army stationed at the Union's very doors. As soon as the war was over, Napoleon realized what the victorious Union army might do. He withdrew his troops and left Maximilian to his fate, a Mexican firing squad.

During this season of hectic diplomacy there was a favorable turn of fortune in Union domestic politics. The victories at Gettysburg and Vicksburg were to aid Lincoln and his party in the local elections of 1863. These political leaders had been busy devising machinery to ensure better organization. They had developed Lincoln's idea of a coalition party dedicated to winning the war. In Illinois, the Lincoln Republicans invited loyal Democrats to join in forming a National Union Party. For some months, James M. Edmunds, Lincoln's Commissioner of the Land Office, had been directing the organization of Union Leagues designed to unite the influence of all who wished the war pushed to successful conclusion. This idea was strongly promoted in Lincoln's home state. A huge mass meeting was arranged for

September 3, and Lincoln was invited to address the throng. He did not go but he sent a significant letter. The results were eminently satisfactory. In the October elections war supporters won handily in Pennsylvania and Ohio; in the latter, Vallandigham was roundly trounced. In November the Union ticket triumphed in all Northern states save New Jersey. On the political battlefields, as at Gettysburg and Vicksburg, the tide was turning.

With the advent of winter good news again came from the war theater. In the East, after Lee had retreated from Gettysburg, it had been once again, and for months to come, "All Quiet Along the Potomac Tonight." But in the West there was a renewal of fighting. Though the Mississippi was free, the Confederates were still in Tennessee and had never given up hopes of striking back into Kentucky though they had been blasted at Murfreesboro, December 30-31, 1862. Rosecrans and Bragg had been watching each other southeast of Nashville for the first six months of 1863, while Grant was fighting Pemberton and Joe Johnston for Vicksburg. Then, just before the climax on the River, Rosecrans decided he was ready to get Bragg out of the state and to occupy Chattanooga. He did drive the Confederate down into Alabama, but only to have him slip back into well-protected Chattanooga.

After a rest period, Rosecrans made another effort. He beguiled Bragg out of Chattanooga and by pushing up through the Chickamauga Valley he hoped finally to dispose of his antagonist. But it was not to happen just that way. At Chickamauga, Rosecrans suffered a terrific defeat and his army was saved only by the great tenacity of General Thomas who had a capacity for saving other generals, and was thereafter known as the "Rock of Chickamauga." Rosecrans himself fled into Chattanooga where Bragg neatly bottled him up. Rosecrans was removed in short order, and Thomas was assigned the dreary task of commanding a starving army. Food could not be gotten into Chattanooga.

Stanton felt that Grant was the answer to this problem, and summoning Grant to Louisville placed him in command of a force gathered to relieve Thomas. Grant succeeded spectacularly and Thomas' army began to eat again. But there was to be more. Grant, Sherman and Sheridan, and, yes, Hooker, who had recovered, set out to destroy Bragg and did it at Lookout Mountain and Missionary Ridge at Christmastide 1863. The Confederates were now back in Georgia, Bragg was taken home to Richmond where Davis could enjoy the society of his favorite, and Joe Johnston was once more in command, warily seeking to prepare for he knew not what. Events of the year 1863 had indeed turned the tide.

Lincoln had perfected his war machine in its military phase. He was about to approach a test of his political power in the election of 1864. In the Confederacy, Davis was in ever-increasing difficulties. His eastern war operation, superbly led by Lee, was holding the line, but his western efforts continued to be discouraging. Politically he had suffered defeat in the Congressional elections in 1863, though interestingly enough he was to continue to get much of what he wanted from Congress. The states were his political Waterloos, as the Union forces penetrated ever farther into the Confederacy.

11

Victory

IN THE YEAR 1864 the Union high command at long last achieved a grand strategy. It was at this point that Lincoln launched what he hoped would be the last offensive. A new and coordinated high command was contrived for the Union armed forces. Congress revived the rank of lieutenant general, hitherto held only by Washington and Scott, and Lincoln conferred it upon Grant who was called to Washington to plan a new campaign. He was to be general-in-chief; Halleck was to be merely a staff coordinator. The new commander was to proceed against Richmond while Sherman was to command the western armies and attack Atlanta.

The opening days of May 1864 saw the first new effort. Grant started through the Wilderness not far from Chancellorsville. He was beaten, but there the usual pattern was abandoned. Grant did not retreat. He kept on. Spottsylvania was followed by Cold Harbor; both were costly defeats but in each battle Lee lost so many men that he found himself not only with decimated ranks but without the freedom of action essential to maneuvering. Grant might be called "Butcher Grant," but his ranks were kept replenished while Lee had no such resources. What could there be ahead for the Confederate commander? In the meantime Grant had won no victories, and was denied his objective.

The Union Navy was more successful in continuing its work on the rivers and in sealing up the seaports. The river boats had participated valiantly in the reduction of Vicksburg. Efforts were made to close Charleston in 1863 and Mobile in 1864. Despite the efforts of two generals and two admirals, Charleston had withstood heavy pounding. Fort Sumter had been largely reduced to rubble, but the port had not yielded. In August 1864 Farragut repeated his New Orleans exploit at Mobile, and after an even harder fight met with similar success. It was during this same 1864 that the Confederates made their one successful counterattack aided by the ram *Albemarle*. They succeeded in recapturing Plymouth in the North Carolina Sound region, which in turn stimulated a dashing Union naval officer to anticipate commando tactics. Lieutenant William Cushing, in the dark of an October night, exploded a torpedo which sent the ram to the bottom.

The most exasperating task of the Federal Navy was that of eliminating the commerce-destroying cruisers. All in all, these ships had captured at least 258 prizes and had continued their depredations almost unmolested despite all that the pursuing Union Navy could do. One of these rovers, however, came to a spectacular end in this fourth year of the war.

The *Alabama* had been sailing almost at will for two years, but finally the USS *Kearsarge* caught up with her while she was anchored at the French port of Cherbourg. The Union commander challenged her to do battle, and in the resulting contest, June 19, 1864, she was sent to the bottom. Her captain, Raphael Semmes, became one of the Confederacy's naval heroes. The *Florida* was captured in a Brazilian port the next October.

Yet even in this late year, another raider started on her career. The *Shenandoah* performed her exploits in the Pacific, and from February to June 1865 nearly wiped out the American whaling fleet. Despite this last spasm, by midsummer 1864 it was quite clear that the war on the seas was almost won. A blockading fleet of 300 ships had seriously curtailed the Confederacy's foreign trade. The Federal Navy, grown from 90 to 671 ships, and now including many ironclads, was hardly second to any in the world.

As in former years, political warfare continued and, in fact, was

even more bitter than ever. President Lincoln stirred his enemies
again when he assumed the power to set the pattern of political
reconstruction, to direct the return of the seceding states to their
former allegiance. He had been at work on reconstruction for
nearly two years, but it was not until the close of 1863 that he
undertook to make public pronouncement of a general policy
in his annual message to Congress in December. In reconstruction,
as in war-making, he planned to be the leader.

When he had dedicated the national cemetery at Gettysburg on
November 19, he had described with superb feeling the American
people. He described them dedicated to the unfinished job, to the
task remaining before them, the task of ensuring the great objective of the conflict—the nation's new birth of freedom. To
achieve this great end the President rejected any policy of punishment or retribution. He wished to restore the old Union as
quickly as possible. It was now time to make a master plan. The
Union armies had advanced to such a point that Jefferson Davis
appeared to be President of only four states, Virginia, North
and South Carolina, and Georgia. And the Governors of North
Carolina and Georgia held such exalted views of state rights that
it was doubtful if Davis could exercise much authority there.

Lincoln had been working at reconstruction from the very
first invasion of the Confederacy. When Grant had penetrated
Tennessee, when Farragut had run past the forts at New Orleans,
and Union forces had seized power on the North Carolina coast,
Lincoln had begun action. He appointed provisional governors
for Tennessee, Louisiana, North Carolina, Texas and Arkansas.
In the spring of 1862, Senator Andrew Johnson became the executive of Tennessee and General Shepley, of Louisiana. These were
most effective in their endeavors and by December 1862 new
steps toward reconstruction had been taken. Lincoln authorized
General Shepley to hold elections for Congress in two districts,
and two antisecessionists were duly chosen and admitted to
Congress.

By December 1863 Lincoln had worked out the general policy

under which the states that were being detached from the Confederacy might be readmitted to the Union. He announced the proposal in a proclamation. He offered amnesty to any who would take an oath to support the Constitution of the United States and the emancipation of the slaves, and declared that when 10 per cent of the voters of 1860 in any state had taken such an oath, that state could begin the process of reconstruction. Louisiana proceeded under these provisions, Michael Hahn was duly elected Governor and, in March 1864, inaugurated. Arkansas soon followed. The next step would depend upon whether Congress would admit the Senators and Representatives. The previous Congress had accepted Congressmen elected by Louisiana before Lincoln's amnesty, but would this Congress be so minded?

The reconstruction required because of the war was by no means entirely political. Economic reorientation was likewise involved. In this reordering, the national Congress took the lead. The lawmakers had early decided that the terrific cost of the war must be met by borrowing and by the issue of paper money as legal tender, a method of financing which proved highly inflationary. The purchasing power of money fluctuated continually, standards of value almost disappeared, and anything with economic implications had become highly speculative.

The varying fortunes on the battlefield were reflected in the gold values of the various bills and bonds. Gold was traded on the exchanges, and its value had become an index of popular faith in victory. At one low point in 1864, a paper dollar would buy only 36 cents worth of gold. There was much speculation, as well as feverish business activity. Fortunes were made on all sides, and vast sums of liquid capital created, but the condition of those living on fixed incomes, and those working for wages, was often desperate.

In the South these policies were carried to even greater extremes, for the war in the Confederacy was financed almost entirely by inflation. There was relatively little gold there and hopes of establishing cotton credit in Europe had been thwarted by

government policy and by the blockade. The government therefore resorted to loans and paper money, together with various
forms of taxes, even to taxes in kind, toward the end. So great was
the inflation that prices skyrocketed and eventually the paper
money became practically worthless. Here, too, people living on
incomes and wageworkers were in a deplorable situation.

But all was by no means economic woe within the Confederacy.
To make up in part for their industrial deficiencies, the Confederacy carried on some foreign trade all during the war. A new
type of commerce burgeoned, blockade running. Various types of
European goods, military and noncontraband, were dispatched
to Bermuda and the West Indian islands, particularly to Nassau
in the Bahamas. At these various island ports, swift, low-lying
blockade runners would take on cargoes and attempt to spirit
them past the Union sentinels at the Southern harbors. Many of
these voyages were successful and the profits great. They were also
continuous for though the coast was gradually captured by the
Union forces, several ports, notably Wilmington, North Carolina,
and Charleston, South Carolina, were in Confederate hands almost until the end. Because of the runaway inflation, and because
of this highly speculative and uncertain trade, the Confederacy
had its profiteers who accumulated fortunes in greenbacks, especially as there was much cotton marketing northward and pay for
this was in Federal money. The final defeat would find the South
still with a certain amount of capital. Had the Confederacy not
been so doctrinaire about laissez faire, the government might have
controlled blockade running and compelled these adventurers to
bring in things needed by the Army in greater quantity with less
attention to high-priced luxuries of no military value.

The reconstructed economy was shaped by new Federal legislation other than that which provided for loans and legal-tender
paper money. Changes were made in the tax and banking
structure. The tariff duties which had been the main source of
peacetime revenue were increased until by 1864 they averaged
47 per cent of the value of the goods and were highly protective,

designed in part to compensate for ever-higher internal taxes which would otherwise have priced American manufacturers out of the markets. A direct tax was levied on the states according to population. An income tax was established and an almost infinite number of internal revenue taxes were levied, not only on the usual liquor and tobacco; an elaborate series of stamp duties was required for all sorts of business and legal transactions.

Significant changes in the banking structure of the Union were achieved in the last year of the conflict. The prolonged war and its uncertain fortunes, the gradual fall in the value of the green-back, and the increasing difficulty of selling new bond issues led Congress to experiment with a new banking system set up by laws passed in 1863 and 1864. Businessmen were invited to buy bonds and use them as capital for new banks. If the new bankers would deposit these bonds with the U.S. Treasury as security, the Federal government would supply the bankers with paper money in the form of national-bank notes up to 90 per cent of the market value of the securities deposited. The new banks then could use these bank notes for banking operations, earning interest on the notes which they loaned while collecting interest on the bonds deposited in the treasury. This system was slow in getting started but it established a government-private banking relationship which was to be in operation for more than half a century. Thus, national finance was reconstructed.

Even more significant in the economic reconstruction of the nation was a change in basic policy brought about by the withdrawal of the Southern members from Congress. This bloc had prevented enactment of significant subsidy legislation much desired by Northern interests. The withdrawal of these representatives left a clear field for those desiring government aid. Not only were protective tariffs for industry, and government connection with banking, achieved, but long-sought subsidies were finally obtained.

Business was to be stimulated by distribution of the public lands. Under one act, each state was to receive an amount of such land, depending on its population, which was to be used to promote higher education in agriculture and the mechanical arts. By another, the famous Homestead Law, any applicant could receive a quarter section of land free after five years of residence thereon and the payment of a nominal fee. These laws would not only speed up western development but they would invite foreign immigration from Europe where land was scarce. This immigration would aid in recruiting the Federal armies, an objective further encouraged by the enactment of a Contract Labor law. This statute permitted agents to contract abroad to import labor in companies. These immigrants not only brought labor to farm and factory, but also released Northern youth to enter the army.

Still another great subsidy was designed to provide, at long last, for the much-desired transcontinental railroad. A land grant had been voted to a company for this purpose in the early months of the war, but this Pacific Railroad Act had failed in its purpose of starting transcontinental rail construction so Congress in 1864 tried again. This time two acts were passed, one to provide more attractive inducements for building the Union Pacific Railroad as originally projected, and the other to give similar help to a Northern Pacific Railroad. The first of these would follow a central route from Nebraska to California, while the second would run from Minnesota to Puget Sound.

Taken as a whole this economic legislation constituted a giant reconstruction project. On the eve of these enactments the United States had been a laissez-faire, individual-enterprise state. It was now transformed into a nation with grand ideas of Federal subsidy, encouragement and protection to corporate enterprise. These grants and subsidies, added to the giant war expenditures, were to stimulate the national economy to take great strides in the mobilization and accumulation of wealth.

Congress, however, was not content with economic reconstruction alone. The Radicals in its leadership wished to be the guiding force in the political reordering. If they were to succeed in this, they must be able to gain victory over Lincoln. As it was 1864, and a Presidential election was due, they would try to defeat Lincoln's hopes of re-election. The Radicals were determined that the Democrats must not return to power assisted by Southern representatives. Therefore they sought a candidate who would deal harshly with all Democrats.

Their first job was to gain control of the national nominating convention. For this purpose they hoped to capitalize on Chase's ambitions. Early in the year they published bitter attacks on Lincoln's policies and performance, denouncing him as an utter failure as a war leader and praising Chase as the only statesman who could save the nation. However, General Frank P. Blair, Jr., arose in Congress and delivered such a withering attack on Chase and the authors of the propaganda that Chase ran for cover and disclaimed any connection with the move. The Lincoln leadership, through the New York machine and the Union Leagues, extended the method tried out in certain of the states and reorganized the Republican party as the National Union party. To give this coalition real substance, it was decided to choose a War Democrat as Lincoln's running mate; Hamlin had been too close to the Radicals. The War Governor of Tennessee, the Democratic Senator who had refused to secede, Andrew Johnson, was picked as the best possible symbol of Union.

There were certain elements, however, in the Radical group who were going to try to organize against Lincoln despite Chase's defection. They set up a special convention May 31, just before that of the National Union party was scheduled to meet, and nominated General John C. Frémont for the Presidency. This move did not deter the Administration forces one whit. Lincoln and Johnson were endorsed as scheduled.

The political summer of 1864 thus inaugurated was a particularly depressing season. The war was again producing disappointment, and even despair. Grant's great effort seemed to have been stalled. A spectacular plan to capture Petersburg, one of the outer defenses of Richmond, by exploding a mine within its walls miscarried with fearful loss of life on June 30. The Union Commander could then think of no better plan than to settle down to besiege the bastion. Thousands of men had been slaughtered, and yet Grant seemed no more able to capture Richmond than his predecessors had been.

Nor was Sherman's progress in the West glowing. The campaign in that region had been directed along the railroad line from Chattanooga to Atlanta where the most important transportation and industrial center of the Western Confederacy was established. General Joe Johnston, by employing a masterly example of Fabian tactics, of fighting and retreating, had slowed down Sherman's advance materially.

Most alarming was a new invasion of the North. Once again the Confederates, this time under General Jubal A. Early, rode into Federal territory. They came up the Shenandoah, crossed the Potomac and on July 11 were actually on the outskirts of Washington. The timely arrival of a corps from the Army of the Potomac and a division from the West saved Washington and sent Early galloping, but it had been a close shave. Lincoln himself had been under fire.

During these dark days the Radicals had continued to undermine Lincoln's power and prestige. Within the walls of the Capitol, under the lead of Senator Benjamin F. Wade and Representative Henry Winter Davis, they had produced a reconstruction policy of their own. The Wade-Davis measure was duly passed by Congress, July 30, just as the session adjourned. This act provided that a state might begin reconstruction only when 50 per cent or more of the voters pledged loyalty, and Confederate military or civilian officers were debarred from participating in the process. Furthermore, slavery must be prohibited and the Confederate debt repudiated. Lincoln would not sign this bill. Rather, he issued a proclamation declaring that he would neither set aside his own work, nor acknowledge the power of Congress over slavery in the states. To this Wade and Davis replied with a bitter "manifesto" declaring Lincoln's proclamation the "most studied outrage on the legislative authority of the people." But theirs was an impotent gesture. Lincoln had won again.

In these dreary months, despite military disappointment and dread, no one even thought of postponing the election. Lincoln would submit himself to the people just as though it were a normal period of peace. But there were those in the new National Union party who despaired of victory, and therefore were determined to seek a substitute candidate. Inner circle meetings were held and powerful influences mobilized to persuade the President that he must step down so that someone with a chance of winning might be substituted. Yet Lincoln himself was convinced that he must carry on. In the meantime the tempo changed.

The Democrats finally met on August 29, and nominated General George B. McClellan on a platform declaring the war to be a failure. Some rather complicated negotiations produced Lincoln's acceptance of the resignation of Montgomery Blair, his Postmaster General whom the Radicals found particularly obnoxious and Frémont withdrew from the race. McClellan, in turn, repudiated the platform which declared that the war was a failure. Lincoln, though still half-convinced that he would be defeated, determined to push the war more vigorously than before, for he believed that if McClellan were elected all hope of victory would be over. But there was help coming from the West.

The situation in front of Sherman had changed. Jefferson Davis, who never liked Joe Johnston, was irked by his failure to smash Sherman's invasion, and sent Bragg to investigate and report. On the basis of Bragg's findings and his own distrust, the Confederate President removed Johnston and substituted the valorous, impetuous Hood. By this time Sherman was almost in sight of Atlanta. Hood rushed in with his headlong courage but he achieved no more than casualties though he did delay matters a little. Sherman's long-hoped-for triumph did not come until September 2. His telegram to Washington, "Atlanta is ours and fairly won," arrived in time to banish the pre-election gloom. Nothing more was said about Lincoln's retirement.

The October elections were the first contests which could indicate what the November results might be. Pennsylvania and Ohio, two of the three states holding these key referenda, had provided for voting by the soldiers in the field; Indiana had not. Lincoln therefore wrote to Sherman asking him to give furloughs to as many Indiana boys as possible so they could go home to vote. They went and voted right. The October elections were Union victories.

Just before the final balloting came another military triumph. When Early had consummated a second raid that summer, and on July 30 had burned Chambersburg, Pennsylvania, Lincoln would stand no more. Grant was summoned to Washington and told that he must stop these Valley raids. Grant immediately decided to send Sheridan with a great force to destroy not only Early but the Valley. Hardly more than a week after the welcome news from Atlanta, Sheridan started. Within five weeks Early's army and the Valley were devastated. Thereafter a crow flying through the Shenandoah would have to carry his rations. The climax of the campaign came on the day of Sheridan's famous ride from Winchester to turn the disaster of Cedar Creek into a decisive victory.

Election day, November 8, 1864, was dreary and rainy in the national capital. After the nation's polls had closed, President Lincoln went over to the telegraph office in the War Department to await the wires. They soon came and before long tidings of a smashing victory were pouring in. Lincoln carried every state but three, Delaware, Kentucky, and New Jersey. A popular majority of 400,000 showed the people's faith in Father Abraham. His power, political as well as military, had been perfected.

Sherman's capture of Atlanta, and the growing certainty that Lincoln would continue to lead the Union cause, were preludes to a final military thrust. Its nature was to some extent decided by the Confederates. General John B. Hood had fallen back into Alabama to plan new blows. After several unsuccessful efforts to sever Sherman's railroad connections, he decided to go up into

Tennessee and there cut off Sherman's supplies at the source. At this point Sherman completed his strategy. He would divide his force. Thomas would be sent back to Nashville to deal with Hood, while Sherman would do an unheard-of thing. He would march through Georgia to the sea, without supply lines, living off the country. November 12, he and Thomas parted and the famous march began. By Christmas each commander had achieved his objective. Thomas had destroyed Hood. Sherman was in Savannah, and ready to march northward.

While the Union military and political campaigns of 1864 had been moving to a successful climax, the Confederates were in the midst of the last phase of their tragic internal conflict. They were not called upon to appraise Davis' leadership in an election but, in a sense, Congress sat in judgment. In this last lawmaking session, his foes rallied for a final attack. His principal foe, Vice-President Alexander H. Stephens, who had remained away from Richmond during much of the war, was back. The President's other enemies were even more bitter. As a last desperate measure, General Robert E. Lee was made military dictator. Duncan F. Kenner was sent abroad to assure Europe that in return for recognition the Confederacy would agree to the gradual abolition of slavery. But these measures were far too late and no advantage accrued. Defeat continued to be the lot of the Army.

With the start of the new year of 1865, and despite the winter weather, Sherman marched north into the Carolinas, and Lee made a desperate effort to stop him. Joe Johnston for the last time was placed in command of an army and sent southward to prevent Sherman's advance. Unless he could succeed, the jaws of the nutcracker would finally meet and crush the Confederacy. To the north, Grant was waiting.

As these last military plans were being implemented, Lincoln was preparing to enter his second term. Great as was his grasp and wide his perception, it is doubtful whether he could realize the great changes that had come to the nation which he was spending himself to save. As a war measure he had ordered the destruction of human slavery, an institution so at variance with the spirit of the Declaration of Independence. It was to be abolished finally with the ratification of the Thirteenth Amendment. This was a tremendous change, a social revolution.

It was also unlikely that Lincoln grasped another basic fact of greatest significance. So many people had had the tenor of their lives changed by military experience. Hundreds of thousands had been away from home, had suffered hardship, had been in danger, had felt the thrill and the terror of combat, had been trained and disciplined. All of these were experiences which normally would not have come to them. Some of them had been wounded, had suffered loss of limb, had been victims of disease, had experienced what today would be called shell shock or battle fatigue. They emerged from the experience with impaired health, nervous instability, or with that altered outlook on life which comes from strange and dangerous experiences.

Many of those who had not been in the armed forces themselves had had their lives disturbed and altered. The thousands who went to camp and combat left homes, family and neighbors. It was a romantic age when emotions were easily roused, tears came easily, anxiety was prevalent because life was so uncertain. Parting brought emotion. There was the anxiety, the waiting for news. After each battle there was the anxious scanning of the death lists in the papers. Frequently the news was bad. Somewhere in an unmarked grave on a distant battlefield lay the hope of a family. Occasionally the body could be brought home to the family plot, and the funeral services held in the home town. Sometimes nothing was ever heard, and the waiting and hoping stretched out into a never-ending eternity.

In other words, the war experience had been so vivid to so many that it was to remain with countless individuals so long as they lived and to affect them in many ways, often unrecognized. A legend of the war was to become a part of the nation's definition of itself. And in this legend Lincoln would be the hero. But of this he could have no inkling as he was writing some of the words which were to ensure his place in the great epic.

The President, as he prepared to take his second oath of office, could never suspect these subtleties and complexities, nor could he realize how the war was going to create the legend. But he knew that Americans had engaged in a great contest to preserve the nation's ideals, and that in the minds of many in the North it had been a fight to put down rebellion, to save the Union and to destroy slavery. As Lincoln phrased it in his second inaugural, "Both parties deprecated war; but one of them would *make* war rather than let the nation survive, and the other would *accept* war rather than let it perish. And the war came."

In the South it had been a struggle to preserve a cherished way of life dedicated to the welfare of Southern men and women and their dependents. They had resented attacks upon their virtue and their patriotism, and fought rather than submit to the tyranny of what they believed to be a greedy materialistic majority who would deprive them of their rights, despoil them of their property, disrupt their society, and destroy their power to protect themselves. It was a noble effort even though it was a lost cause. Southern tradition could worship the leadership of Robert E. Lee, and enshrine the sacrifices of the warriors in as imposing an emotional structure as their Northern kinsmen. In all this there was a strange folk unity of emotion for it was a brothers' war.

This Lincoln understood. "Both read the same Bible, and pray to the same God; and each invokes His aid against the other." It seemed strange to Lincoln "that any men should dare to ask a just God's assistance in wringing their bread from the sweat of other men's faces," but he was prepared not to judge. "The prayers of both could not be answered; that of neither has been answered fully. The Almighty has His own purposes. 'Woe unto the world because of offenses! for it must needs be that offenses come; but woe to that man by whom the offense cometh.' " He fondly hoped and he fervently prayed that the "mighty scourge of war" might speedily pass away. But if God willed it to continue until all the wealth piled up by the slaves should be spent, and until every drop of blood drawn with the lash should be paid by another drawn with the sword, he was prepared to affirm that "the judgments of the Lord" were "true and righteous altogether."

Thinking in this vein, on March 4, 1865, he gave the world one of his classic utterances expressing his ultimate purpose: "With malice toward none; with charity for all; with firmness in the right, as God gives us to see the right, let us strive on to finish the work we are in; to bind up the nation's wounds . . . to do all which may achieve and cherish a just, and a lasting peace, among ourselves, and with all nations."

Even as he was saying these words, the lines were closing in on the Confederacy. Again Sherman had accomplished the impossible. By February 7 he had crossed the impenetrable South Carolina swamps and was outside Columbia, the capital. Johnston tried to rally his army at Raleigh, North Carolina, where he was joined by the Charleston garrison, by Bragg and the remnants of Hood's army. He made one last effort to beat Sherman at Bentonville, North Carolina, on March 18 and failed. North Carolina was Sherman's and it would only be days before he would be in Virginia. All Grant need do would be to wait.

To Lee and Davis there seemed to be only one slim hope: if Lee could break out of Grant's grip, abandon Richmond and entrain south to join Johnston. On March 26, General Gordon, Lee's Hood, tried it, but his guides were killed; he lost his way in the dark and the attack failed. Grant now determined to end it; Sheridan was with him and they started. Lee saw what was up, and marshalled every available man to try to smash this final blow. But he failed. Sheridan won at Five Forks on April 1 and Petersburg, the bastion which had held Grant from Richmond so long, fell.

Sunday morning, April 2, Lee notified Davis that he could no longer protect Richmond. It was nearly over. Lee sought to retreat to the mountains. But Grant caught up with him and Lee saw he was trapped. He sent to Grant asking for a meeting, and on April 9 at Appomattox Court House he surrendered. Seven-

teen days later Johnston yielded to Sherman at Durham Station
in North Carolina. The sound of cannon at last was stilled. The
attempt of Davis and his associates to create the Confederate
power had ended in gallant failure.

When on Sunday, April 2, a messenger brought word to President Davis, in his pew in St. Paul's, that Richmond must be
evacuated, he yielded to the necessity of the moment. Mrs. Davis
and the children had already gone on into North Carolina, and
that night, the President and his Cabinet proceeded by train to
Danville, Virginia. It was a long and tedious night ride, punctu-
ated by many stops. The long hours were somewhat enlivened
by Secretary Trenholm's generous store of peach brandy. As
the hours passed Davis may have summed up the gallant but
unfortunate career of the Confederacy. He could never forget
the initial disappointment at the failure of all the slave states to
join, or the lack of success in obtaining recognition from European governments or help from Northern Democrats. The
damned Yankee counterjumpers had fought, and fought as well
as their Southern brethren. Now Lee was in retreat and Sherman
pursuing Johnston. But Davis was not yet ready to face reality.
When he arrived at Danville, he issued yet another proclamation: "I will never consent to abandon to the enemy one foot of
the soil of any of the States of the Confederacy . . . let us . . .
meet the foe with fresh defiance, with unconquered and un-
conquerable hearts."

But it was no use. Monday, April 10, the news of Lee's surrender reached Danville. That night Davis and his Cabinet
resumed their flight still buoyed up by a vague hope of making
a stand somewhere. They were really undertaking a flight into
oblivion, for the Confederacy was dead.

On Palm Sunday, the day of Lee's surrender, President Lincoln
was finishing a visit to Grant's headquarters in Virginia which
had begun March 23 and had included an impromptu inspection
of Richmond the day after its evacuation. On the day of Appomattox, the President reached the White House at dusk and
eventually went to bed ignorant of Lee's capitulation.

During this momentous fortnight, Lincoln had found good reason to believe that the task was almost over. And it had been a mighty one. A million men had been mobilized and accoutered. The great armies had achieved victory. The Union had been saved. The slaves had been freed. The processes of democracy had been carried on almost uninterruptedly despite the fighting. Two Congresses had been elected and Lincoln himself had submitted his second bid for power to the voters for their verdict. The world had seen that democracy was workable even in the midst of civil war.

Lincoln's judgment regarding the true purpose and end of the war had been demonstrated to be sound. He was already turning to the task of binding up the nation's wounds. During his stop at Richmond he had given counsel to recent Confederate dignitaries and had expressed the hope that cooperation in restoring civil government might be universal. He had created the power. Would it be strong enough to accomplish his purpose?

Early Monday morning, April 10, Washington awoke to hear the glad tidings of Lee's surrender and to enjoy to the full a joyful Holy Week. The President himself, after a public speech and a Cabinet council on the process of the reconstruction which he was eager to start expeditiously and to finish as speedily as possible, turned his thoughts to an evening of relaxation. Friday evening he and Mrs. Lincoln would go to Ford's Theatre to see *Our American Cousin*. The day itself dragged, but finally it was time to enter the carriage though even then callers followed him to its very step.

At last the door was slammed shut and they drove off. Not many minutes later they were in the President's box. They had enjoyed the familiar strains of "Hail to the Chief," and at last Mr. Lincoln could settle back in the comfortable rocking chair to watch the unfolding of the play which had already begun. Outside the door of the box the President's guard left his post so that he might see the play. A little after ten a silent figure entered the box unobserved and fired just one shot.

12

Reconstruction

It was a night of terror. Less than a week ago had come news of Lee's surrender, and then what a contagion of rejoicing. So many were looking forward to the most joyous Easter the nation had ever known, the Easter of the nation's resurrection. On Good Friday night came tragedy. During that awful night, the President was murdered and another assassin barely missed killing Secretary Seward. A third, assigned to shoot Vice-President Johnson, lost his courage. General Grant escaped because he had left Washington. Almost as soon as the fatal shot was fired, Secretary Stanton was summoned and began taking testimony. By morning a conspiracy had been unearthed to wipe out the government, and a curiously inept manhunt was on. Rumor raced around Washington that night, and during those dark hours it seemed to many in high place that death might strike anywhere. It was commonly believed that this was a last blow of the Confederacy to drag down the Union too.

That night fixed in the minds of many in responsible position the final evidence of the traitors' guilt. As people realized their loss in the murder of their beloved President there was a cry for vengeance. Andrew Johnson, who had lived a turbulent life in Eastern Tennessee and who had battled the Confederates there in a struggle to redeem the state, was inaugurated in such an atmosphere. Stunned by the turn of fate that brought him to the

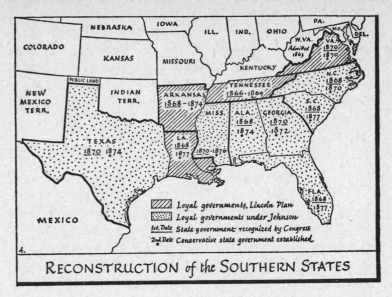

Loyal governments, Lincoln Plan
Loyal governments under Johnson
1st. Date State government recognized by Congress
2nd Date Conservative state government established

RECONSTRUCTION of the SOUTHERN STATES

White House, and aware that he had been marked for assassination, it was not surprising that he led the demand for the punishment of traitors, particularly as Stanton was soon convinced that the Confederate government had planned the assassination. He proclaimed a reward for the capture of Jefferson Davis.

It was indeed a curious concatenation of events and accidents which ushered in the process usually spoken of as the reconstruction of the South, but which was in reality the reconstruction of the nation. The surrender of Lee, the assassination of Lincoln, and the accession of Andrew Johnson, all occurred in April 1865 when Congress was not in session. The laying down of arms found the erstwhile Confederate States without recognized government. At the same time there was the gravest kind of social situation to be dealt with. There were more than three million ex-slaves who had no civil status, let alone any political rights or privileges.

But this Southern situation was only one of several which the end of the war precipitated. There was a great demobilization of armies numbering more than a million men. These soldiers had to be reabsorbed into civilian society and into the economy. Great government spending would now stop, orders would cease and industry and agriculture would have to adjust to a decreased demand. Furthermore the national currency supply was greatly inflated, money was cheap, gold scarce, and values of all sorts were distorted and in chaos.

More immediate was the fact that the coming of peace, with its hysterical rejoicing, and the horror of the assassination, particularly the terror that had swept over Washington on that night of murder, had made a substantial contribution to an emotional instability, uncertainty, and incapacity. These were to prolong and exaggerate the wartime psychosis which so complicated the processes of government. Those who had political responsibility, and the voters who would pass upon their work, were in various stages of emotion. Yet they must deal with complex phases of a redistribution of power which would be in process for years.

Before the conflict started in 1861 political power had been vested largely in the hands of a group of Southern Congressional and state leaders. Now that this power was broken who would inherit it? How would they exercise it?

When Johnson undertook to solve the problems of reconstruction, the work had already progressed. Lincoln had recognized a "Governor" of Virginia all during the war though, after West Virginia had been admitted as a state, this executive held sway over only Alexandria and Norfolk and their environs. Provisional Governors had maintained some Union authority in Louisiana, Tennessee, and Arkansas though not elsewhere. At various times, Congress had admitted loyal members from Virginia and Louisiana. The legislative arm had also passed a reconstruction bill in the recent summer, but Lincoln had vetoed it. There was no statute when Johnson assumed the Presidency, and Congress was not in session. The new President soon determined to follow Lincoln's idea that the responsibility was his. The basic question was the disposition of the victorious Union armies, and he was commander in chief of the armed forces.

Johnson's plan was formulated within six weeks. He would recognize the governments already established in Virginia, Arkansas, Louisiana, and Tennessee and appoint provisional Governors in the other seven states. These Governors would offer an oath to all those who wished to resume their allegiance. If 50 per cent or more of the citizens of any state swore to support the Constitution of the United States, these men would be given the responsibility of choosing a Constitutional Convention in a special election to be called by the provisional Governors. These conventions were to repeal the ordinances of secession, repudiate the war debt, and recognize the abolition of slavery. When these tasks had been accomplished, elections could be held in the several states for state officials, Representatives and legislatures, which in their turn would choose United States Senators. When these steps had been taken to Johnson's satisfaction, he would recognize the result and withdraw his provisional Governors.

In issuing the proclamations setting up this program, the President expressly excepted from participation any who had once taken an oath of allegiance to the United States and had then become citizens of the Confederacy, any who had held civil or military office in the Confederacy, or any who possessed property worth $20,000 or more. Such people would have to apply individually to him for pardon. In setting up this program, the President followed Lincoln's plan in the main, except for adding the property disqualification. Johnson wished to free the new South from planter domination, and to place it in the hands of the plain people such as he represented.

The President's plan was put into operation during the summer of 1865. The several states proceeded on schedule and followed instructions. They repealed their ordinances of secession, accepted the abolition of slavery, and repudiated the Confederate war debt. The President himself invited applications for pardon, and granted 13,500 out of 15,000 submitted, until in 1867 he issued a

proclamation providing amnesty for all but 300 of the most prominent Confederates. In the meantime the state Constitutional
conventions in most instances undertook to revise their fundamental documents.

In the main, these changes were in the direction of providing
greater self-government. More officeholders in the various
branches hitherto appointed would now be elected. Property
qualifications for voting and holding office were generally
abandoned. In at least two instances, legislative reapportionment
transferred power from the tidewater to the back-country
regions. But in not one of the states was any provision made for
the Negro as a voter or officeholder.

When the constitutional conventions had adjourned, elections
were called and legislators, state officers and Congressmen were
chosen by those white males who were willing to swear allegiance
to the United States and vote. Johnson, in the meantime, was
appointing Federal officials from among those who could take
an ironclad oath that they had never willingly given aid or
comfort to the Confederacy, a task sometimes difficult, often impossible. The legislatures in due course chose United States
Senators.

The former Confederate states thereupon undertook to lead as
normal a political existence as was possible with the United States
Army distributed at strategic intervals and constantly interfering.
However, they had to labor under difficulty because the privilege
of the writ of habeas corpus was still suspended, and officially a
state of war still existed. The military were really supreme in
many areas, and remained so until August 1866 when the President finally declared the rebellion at an end.

These revised state governments entered upon their duties facing one of the most complicated cultural situations ever produced
in human history. In the midst of war, the civil status of some
3,000,000 people had been changed without any prior study or
plan. In the population of the former Confederacy numbering
9,000,000 there were more than 30 per cent that had recently

been untutored Negro slaves, none of whom had ever had any responsibility or any social or civil independence. They had lived their lives sheltered from any need to direct themselves, secure under the control of masters. Then came military invasion by those whom they believed to be "liberators" who spread among them a mystic sense of "freedom" present or at hand. Eventually there followed the first Emancipation Proclamation which mainly announced that there would be a second, and when the second came it set free only those slaves who were not within reach of Federal power to secure for them this boon.

The result was confusion which grew as the Union armies had advanced. Wherever troops appeared slaves gathered to welcome the liberators and to enjoy their new liberty. But the difficulty was that they then had to be fed, housed and given medical care, for arrangements were so chaotic that they were prey to sicknesses which might reach epidemic proportions. The problem of meeting this situation had been left almost wholly to the various generals, and as they had no knowledge or training in such social engineering the efforts were generally blundering and often bizarre. Finally, in the last days of the conflict, Congress belatedly sought to deal with the perplexing and growing problem. On March 3, 1865, President Lincoln signed a bill creating a Bureau of Freedmen, Refugees, and Abandoned Lands. As its title indicated, this Freedmen's Bureau was designed to see to it that the ex-slaves were established in their freedom so that they would have a real chance to care for themselves and learn social and economic independence.

President Lincoln called upon General O. O. Howard to establish this Bureau and develop its functions. He organized the late Confederacy into ten districts, to each of which he assigned assistant commissioners whom he had chosen from the Army because they had had experience there in dealing with the Negroes. These men undertook to provide relief, to secure employment and, in general, to guide in the difficult process of social readjustment to freedom.

Most of the Negroes were content to remain where they were, but some means must be provided to enable them to earn a living as free men. Certain politicians advocated breaking up the large estates, and taking over a number which would have to be abandoned because of unpaid taxes, so that farms might be given to the slaves. On the other hand, many ex-slaves were wandering around in search of "freedom." These were reluctant to settle down to work; many were deluded by the rumor that Uncle Sam was going to give each one "forty acres and a mule." This unsettlement meant that some were constantly on the move, crowding into a few cities which had no means of housing them, suffering hardships and spreading disease. In dealing with this confusion, the former slave states revived the old "black codes," used to keep the slaves in order on the plantations, to which were added provisions taken from West Indian laws and Northern vagrancy regulations. Negroes were required to show passes if they were on the roads, and they were forbidden weapons or liquor.

Thus it can be seen that one of the many tasks of the Freedmen's Bureau was to get the Negro back to work. To that end its agents sought to promote the idea of labor contracts with the former masters for wages or shares in the crops, and then to enforce them. They sought also to insure health by creating hospitals. Finally, not the least of their responsibilities was to establish schools and to get teachers, many from the North. The Federal government appropriated millions for food and medicines, and in six years spent more than five millions on schools, primary and secondary, and upon colleges and universities.

The Bureau also assumed judicial and political functions. The most significant of these came to be the organization of an extension of the Union League. These Southern branches were now known as Loyal Leagues, and successful efforts were made to enlist Negro membership to work toward Negro suffrage. These Leagues were organized as secret lodges; some were military units and given arms. The Freedmen's Bureau commissioners thus early became political organizers devoted to the creation of a Republican party in the South. The Bureau became a source of patronage, and many of its later agents were to be spotted with corruption.

These results of Johnson's plan brought on a violent quarrel between the President and the Congress. He had failed to call upon Congress, and had proceeded to develop his plan without it. This independence opened old wounds. The more radical leaders had suffered much frustration under Lincoln. Men like Stevens, Wade, and Sumner were not going to yield to Johnson the influence they had been forced to accord to Lincoln. At first they thought that Johnson would work with them along radical lines of punishment, but when he neither called them in nor heeded them when they advised, they began to loose the vials of their wrath upon him.

Their great objective was to prevent the return of the Southern bloc to the control of Congress which it had held before the war. The Democratic party must not regain its sway. Consequently, a Republican party must be built up in the South to control those states. The best way to insure this, they thought, was to establish the Negroes as voters who would cast their ballots under the leadership of obscure Southern white politicians who were now coming to the front and those Northerners who were migrating south to aid in or profit from reconstruction.

But Johnson's program was not working out that way. The ex-Confederates were resisting the acceptance of the Negroes as civil equals and voters, and their actions were producing political consequences alarming to the Radicals. The Democrats seemed to be returning to power. In some instances ex-Confederate generals were elected to state office or sent to Washington. Georgia, in fact, elected Alexander H. Stephens, recently Vice-President of the Confederacy, to represent her in the United States Senate. This outcome of Johnson's "arbitrary and unconstitutional" policy seemed likely to spell the return of ante-bellum Democratic control and the doom of the Republican power.

The Radicals rose up in wrath when Congress convened in December 1865. They prevented the swearing in of the new Senators and Representatives, and caused their credentials to be referred to a joint committee of fifteen of both houses charged with studying the workings of the President's plan. When Congress convened, the Radicals were in a minority and, if President Johnson could have secured the support of the moderate Republicans, he probably could have kept his foes at bay. A test vote seemed to indicate he might succeed.

Congress passed a Freedmen's Bureau Bill in February 1866, extending the life of the agency indefinitely, and giving it judicial powers to decide whether Negroes were being deprived of their rights as citizens and then to punish any who might be found to be offenders, even calling upon the Army if necessary. Johnson held this to be a violation of the Constitution, subjecting the whites to the arbitrary action of bureaucrats without the protection of a jury trial. He vetoed the bill and was sustained.* When Congress then concluded approval of a Civil Rights Bill designed to establish the new rights of the Negro under the protection of the Federal courts, Johnson also vetoed the bill. This time he was not sustained.

Johnson had contributed to his own defeat by behavior that was increasingly maladroit, and by foolish public utterances. They had worked on the Tennessee stump, but were beneath the dignity of his high office. Many of the original Republicans could not forget that he had been a prewar Southern Democrat. So that the Radicals could carry their point, the Senators and Representatives from the seceding states were not admitted. At the behest of the Committee of Fifteen an amendment to the Constitution was drafted and sent to the states. Certainly no Southern state would be recognized which had not ratified the Fourteenth Amendment.

This proposed amendment was designed to give the Negro

---

* Later in the session Congress passed a second Freedmen's Bureau Act, extending its life for only two years. Johnson's veto this time was overridden.

citizenship. It defined United States citizenship in terms which freed it from state determination as heretofore prescribed. "All persons born or naturalized in the United States . . . are citizens." States were forbidden to "abridge the privileges or immunities of citizens of the United States," to "deprive any person of life, liberty or property without due process of law," or to "deny to any person . . . the equal protection of the laws." Thus Negro rights were in the hands of the Federal courts if any wished to seek redress there.

The amendment further guaranteed the Union war debt, and repudiated Confederate obligations. It disqualified most of the Confederate leaders, civil and military, from holding office until Congress might remove the disability. It indirectly sought to secure for the Negro the privilege of voting by authorizing Congress to reduce the representation of any state in the national House of Representatives in proportion to the number of its male population not permitted to vote. This proposition was so unpalatable to the Southern states that it was forthwith rejected by all of them save Tennessee. Therefore Tennessee was the only Southern state whose Senators and Representatives were admitted to Congress in 1866.

Much disturbed by the rejection of his work, and by a growing series of overridden vetoes, President Johnson undertook to rally support. He sought to secure the election of a Congress which would cooperate. To that end he organized a national convention at Philadelphia in the summer of 1866 to call upon voters to give him backing and to restore the rights of the states under the Constitution. He himself went on a speechmaking "Swing Around the Circle." On this unfortunate journey, he permitted hecklers to make him angry. Once again he forgot the dignity of his office. His pleas fell upon deaf ears, and the Congress chosen gave every evidence of being of like mind with the Radicals.

When Congress reassembled in December 1866, the Radical leadership felt it had won a mandate. Murderous riots, like those in Memphis and New Orleans, and the rejection of the Fourteenth Amendment by the Southern legislatures, indicated to them that the Negro needed protection. Men like Thaddeus Stevens, Benjamin F. Wade, and Charles Sumner were determined to revive the Republican party and to build a strong new organization which could be promoted in the South. To do this the Negro must be made a voter, something for which the Johnson governments had no use. New governments must be provided in the Southern states, except for Tennessee.

For this purpose, the Military Reconstruction Act of March 1867 was placed on the statute books, together with several supplements. Under the terms of these acts, the ten unaccepted Southern states were now organized into five military districts. Each of these was placed under the command of a United States general with troops at his disposal. These generals were to arrange for new elections in the ten states. They were to see that the Negroes were registered as voters and protected in their right to vote by the presence of soldiers at the places of registration and at the polls.

Congress likewise sought to prevent the Supreme Court from interfering with this policy which possibly could be construed as a military invasion of civil rights in time of peace. They passed laws taking certain types of cases from its jurisdiction, and they stopped any possibility of appointment of judges to the Supreme Court by Johnson if vacancies arose. Finally they sought to make the Executive over after their own image. They would impeach Johnson and make Benjamin F. Wade, President pro tem of the Senate and one of their own, President. Congress was to be supreme, controlled by the Republicans. The Military Reconstruction Policy was put into operation during 1867 under Congressional supervision. Congress provided for a continuous session, calling the body elected in 1866 to assemble immediately after March 4, 1867, omitting the customary break from March to December in each odd year.

During the summer of 1867, the generals undertook to register the voters, who were to be all the Negro males over twenty-one, and those whites who had not been disfranchised for participation in the rebellion and who had taken an oath of allegiance in a manner satisfying to the registrars. When their task was finished, 703,000 Negroes had been registered while only 627,000 whites were so enrolled. Some 150,000 whites were excluded. In Alabama, Florida, Louisiana, Mississippi, and South Carolina the Negroes were in the majority. In the elections which followed thousands of whites who were entitled to vote refused to do so.

The conventions that were chosen assembled under the management of a combination of "scalawags," practical Southerners who accepted the facts of the war, Northern migrants or "carpetbaggers," and Negro leaders—a combination which had things nearly all their own way. Their first task was to write universal manhood suffrage into the new documents, thus enfranchising the Negro. They likewise prescribed universal free education, and quite generally abolished imprisonment for debt. Representation in Congress and the legislatures was to be based on a count of all the population. Governors were generally given more power. There was little effort, however, to penalize ex-Confederates. In Mississippi and Virginia efforts were made to exclude them from office-holding, but these sections of the constitutions were at length submitted to the voters separately and defeated. In the end restrictions of any sort upon ex-Confederates were found only in the constitutions of Alabama, Arkansas, and Louisiana.

These new governments, composed so frequently of people, most particularly the Negroes, who had had no experience of any kind, were poorly equipped to carry on the duties of government. They undertook their tasks in a fumbling, ignorant manner. Their mistakes were staggering, their extravagance amazing, and their corruption humiliating. They increased salaries, they secured appropriations for perquisites and travel mileage which, had they not been so criminal, would have been grotesque. The amounts spent on printing and sundries, such as furnishings, supplies and liquors, were unbelievable. In one of the most unfortunate states, South Carolina, legislators bought clothes for their ladies, and even coffins, at state expense. They reimbursed their "Speaker" for an unfortunate day at the race track to the amount of $1,000 as a reward for his efficient service as a presiding officer. In Louisiana the legislature purchased a hotel recently sold for $84,000 for three times that amount, to be used as a Capitol building.

The greatest harvest of rascality was reaped in the realm of railroads. Carpetbaggers came South immediately after the war to reconstruct and develop the railroads which had suffered grievously by the destruction of war. They also saw possibilities of consolidating and extending these transportation arteries. And Southern leaders new and old were not loath to join in. The new legislatures readily acquiesced in making appropriations, granting franchises, voting subsidies, loaning money, guaranteeing bonds and even selling roads already constructed by the states, sometimes at ruinous discounts. Bribery and corruption figured prominently. North Carolina authorized a bond issue of $27,-850,000 to aid railroads which involved $200,000 in bribes and of which very little ever got into railroads. The North Carolina promoter who had managed this deal, operating later in Florida raised some $2,800,000 by selling bonds, but the railroads got only $309,000 of this sum. Where the balance went was best known to the carpetbagger. In Louisiana a state-owned railroad upon which two millions had been spent was sold quietly for $50,000 despite the fact that much higher bids were available. And so it went.

While one shudders at this saturnalia of extravagance and corruption, certain significant facts must not be forgotten. The Southern states before the war had been dominated generally by landed elite and their business and professional associates. These interests sought to keep down real estate taxes and, by and large, were unsympathetic to public spending. The farms were usually rather self-contained, self-supporting units, where even education was considered a private matter. The great number of Negroes were slaves, and their masters felt responsible for their welfare as well as their control. Ante-bellum state governments kept their functions at a minimum, and budgets and taxes were small. The idea of social services for the public welfare was not entertained.

The emancipation of the Negro and the problem of making him a responsible citizen brought a new need for public service which would cost money. There was a public school system to be created. The Negroes must now be subject to law, not the discipline of their masters. Therefore courts, police, and jail facilities had to be enlarged. Hospitals, poorhouses, and insane asylums were needed. Roads and bridges destroyed or damaged by the war must be reconstructed. Also, the tendency of some of the Negroes to flock to cities, and the growth of railroads, industries, and commerce expanded urban communities. Slums grew, and with them disease. Yellow fever and other epidemics aroused fear. New boards of health made recommendations for drainage and sanitation. Waterworks and sewers, street paving and lighting, better police and fire protection were called for. So too were street railways. All these cost money and the Reconstruction legislatures, made up as they often were of people without much if any property, were not loath to pile up land taxes to meet these costs, or to grant franchises to enterprising promoters of these public improvements. When the period was over the eleven Confederate states had piled up a huge debt. The cost was great, but the idea of state responsibility for education and welfare was thereby introduced into the South. This was no small part of the process of reconstruction.

During these years of license and irresponsibility public expenditure rose in the several states anywhere from 200 to 1,500 per cent. Taxes increased anywhere from 400 to 1,600 per cent. Property values, adversely affected by the devastation of war as well as by reconstruction, declined as much as 75 per cent. In 1870 tax valuation in the former Confederate states was but half what it was in 1860 while taxes were four times as great. When Reconstruction was over these states had piled up a combined debt estimated at $140,000,000.

In the midst of this extravaganza, the Southern states proceeded to adopt their new constitutions, to elect Representatives and Senators, and to ratify the Fourteenth Amendment. Finally, in the spring of 1868, North and South Carolina, Georgia, Florida, Alabama, Louisiana and Arkansas were ready and Congress, finally satisfied that the Negroes were voting, and the states Republican, undertook to admit them. Only three were not ready; Mississippi had rejected her new constitution by popular vote, because it proscribed the Confederates, and Virginia and Texas were still working at theirs.

While these bizarre travesties were being enacted in the states the tragedy came to a climax in Washington—Johnson's foes had been working for two years and more to find some grounds for his impeachment. But, despite a sort of hysterical and highly unwise habit of public speech, he lived a blameless, if not too perceptive life. Finally, however, the Radicals seized on a rather desperate expedient which they thought they could use. President Johnson found it more and more difficult to get along with his Secretary of War, Edwin M. Stanton, who was, to say the least, peculiar. Certainly he was not bound by any real sense of loyalty to the three Presidents whom he had served. He was sympathetic with the Radicals, yet he would not resign and, on occasion, carried Johnson's plans to them. A Tenure of Office Act had recently been passed which required the consent of the Senate before a Cabinet officer could be removed. The Senate would not consent to Stanton's dismissal so the President seemed to be stymied. However, there was some legal opinion that this act did not apply to Cabinet officers appointed before its enactment, and Johnson hoped to get the matter before the courts for decision.

To that end he removed Stanton early in 1868 despite the Senate's refusal to consent. The Radicals in Congress seized upon this as their opportunity. They impeached Johnson for violating the Tenure of Office Act and ordered him to be tried before the

Senate, counting on the Republicans, who had more than a two-thirds majority, to convict him and make Benjamin F. Wade President of the United States. But so arbitrary a plan to make the Presidency subservient to Congress failed. Seven Republicans failed to vote Johnson guilty, and Benjamin F. Wade never became President.

While this Radical dream of power was assuming such nightmare proportions, the new Republican organization building up in the South was made politically effective by the admission of the seven "Republican" states. In this year the Republicans resumed the custom of holding a national convention, abandoning the Union party of 1864 and 1866. The convening state leaders and their Congressional associates were unanimous in their choice of the war hero, General Grant. He had no political knowledge or interest; in fact he seemed to have voted in but one Presidential election when he cast his ballot for a Democrat. But he was a hero who, it was thought, could be easily advised. Wade was passed over for the Vice-Presidency in favor of the much younger Schuyler Colfax of Indiana. Andrew Johnson was given no consideration for renomination, and he turned to the Democrats.

The Democrats were not in a happy position. They were considered by many to be involved in war guilt. Some of them had sympathized with the rebels. On their part they sought to promote their fortunes by advocating quick reconstruction and the restoration of the Constitution and state rights. They were still the party which had opposed subsidies and protective tariffs, and had vigorously striven to keep government and business apart. The war had brought the government into a great business operation, and taxes, loans, subsidies, and purchases had involved close contact between government and many phases of economic enterprise. Now that war was over could not the spending, the borrowing and the taxing be suspended and laissez faire, the separation of business and government, be restored?

The Republicans did everything they could to keep the idea current that the Democrats were Copperheads and rebels, and to mobilize the veterans in the Republican ranks. State rights and the restoration of the Union and the Constitution did not seem very appealing issues, particularly if they meant the return of the Confederate politicians to Washington. The Democrats had to grasp at straws. But, in fact, they were to grasp much more clearly some of the realities of the situation. There was a new politics emerging from a redistribution of power which was being directed not so much by the incidents of Southern reconstruction as by more complex changes in the life of the nation. A new group of men of enterprise and imagination were planning great things for the restored Republic. To this end they were seeking to make the government an instrument of their purpose.

13

The Power of Money

THE RECONSTRUCTION of Southern society was but one phase of postwar adjustment. The truth of the matter was that a change was taking place in the power structure directing national development. The power of the states claimed by antebellum advocates of state rights had perforce to yield to the strength of nationalism. Federal power was at length supreme, the nation was redefined in those terms, and a great political problem was likewise solved. The United States was a nation, not a confederation of independent states. The resolution of this uncertainty removed from politics a question which had demanded the nation's best statesmanship. Politicians could sit back now and relax. The test had been met and the work done.

But those with organizing genius who loved power, and knew how to exercise it, were not to be without occupation. New vistas were opening up. These new opportunities, while seemingly nonpolitical, had significant political implications, implications which were to alter the nature of democracy. The realization of these opportunities was bound to dictate a redistribution of power for though the war had caused a great increase in money, the new supply had not been widely distributed. Its very concentration produced a new power in the land.

The population was growing fast. The war had stimulated the process of producing and distributing great quantities of food, clothing, military equipment, and other war material of all sorts. New commodities and processes were brought into the business world, and certain of them made large profits possible. Great wealth was becoming almost a certainty to the enterprising. The Civil War had produced much activity in all forms of business and placed a premium on mass production. Meat packing, flour milling, shoe and clothing manufacture and steel production had all been accelerated by new methods. Oil had been discovered, refined and marketed. Railroads had been unified and extended. Much had been learned of operation on a grand scale.

Most spectacular was the expansion of the railroad business. Between the end of the war and 1872 the mileage had doubled, increasing from 35,000 to 70,000 miles. The Union Pacific Railroad was completed. Jay Cooke was pushing the Northern Pacific. Railroad promoters, east and west, were working on a project for a road to the Pacific along a southern route. At the same time the consolidation of small roads which had been going on since the fifties was being engineered by such operators as Cornelius Vanderbilt, J. Edgar Thomson, Thomas A. Scott, Grenville M. Dodge, Collis P. Huntington, Leland Stanford, and their associates.

During the war, railroad operators had learned the advantages and the necessities of consolidations and through-lines. The postwar period saw the results. It was to be the age of railroad empires. A number of business statesmen, tycoons and rascals participated in this great surge of organization; their methods were various and sometimes devious. When their work was done, there was a vast network of rails covering the nation. Giant corporations and millionaires with masses of capital had achieved great power over business in particular, and over the lives and destinies of their fellow men in general. A new power was rising in the land.

The most spectacular of these figures, and some of them were indeed bizarre, was "Commodore" Cornelius Vanderbilt. This ruthless warrior had started out in water transportation, operating

ferries, coastal steamers, and ocean liners. During the Civil War
he had turned to railroads, and had begun to plan an empire on
land with the same spirit of statesmanship and brigandage that
had motivated him in mobilizing his fleets at sea. The Commodore's objective was a rail system from New York City to Chicago, paralleling the Hudson River and the Erie Canal in New
York State and then striking out from Buffalo in several directions to Chicago.

Not only did he want this system, but so far as New York State
was concerned he wanted a monopoly. For although he was
statesman enough to recognize system, he was even more the
speculator seeking money and power. He had begun in the midst
of the Civil War by securing a railroad running from New York
City up the Hudson Valley. When he had secured access to Al-
bany he turned his attention to the Albany-Buffalo stretch. During the preceding double decade, other railroad enterprisers had
completed a system known as the New York Central. The Commodore's abilities included not only planning combines but
making doubtful railroad ventures pay, so there was no great
resistance when Vanderbilt attempted to buy control of this
property. By 1867 he had achieved this goal and had a system
running from New York City to Lake Erie. But he did not have
a monopoly. He would acquire the Erie Railroad.

This road from Piermont on the Hudson to Dunkirk on Lake
Erie had been a long time in building. But in the fifties its track
had been completed, and it had acquired a director and treasurer
in the person of Daniel Drew, another railroad name to conjure
with. He, like the Commodore, was an elderly speculator without
much conscience. But whereas Vanderbilt was constructive in his
gambling and improved his properties, Drew was merely a money
grabber who cared nothing for the future of the oranges he was
sucking dry.

Both Vanderbilt and Drew were adept at manipulating the
prices of their railroad stock for their own advantage; both had
sold short and then had lowered prices so they could buy cheap

and sell dear, covering their short contracts always at a profit.
Drew was treasurer of the Erie and apparently saw no distinction
between the money in the treasury and whatever he chose to call
his own. On one occasion after the war, he led people to believe
that he had sold Erie stock on future delivery contracts that he
could not honor; that he was broke. Then, at the last minute,
he took $3,000,000 of convertible Erie bonds which he held as
security for a loan he had made the railroad, converted them into
stock, dumped that stock on the market, and so lowered Erie
shares in value that he could easily buy enough at low prices to
honor his future delivery contracts and write a comfortable profit.

But now Vanderbilt wanted a monopoly, and that meant control of the Erie. So he went into the market blithely, as was his
wont, in March 1868. Knowing Drew, he was taking extra pre-
cautions. Drew as treasurer of Erie had access to millions of
convertible bonds which had been authorized by a secret meeting
of the board of directors. If these bonds were converted into stock
and sold, Vanderbilt would have to pay outrageously for his
control. He thought he had prevented some such trick by securing
an injunction from a "friendly" judge whom he found convenient. But Drew, skillfully working through a dummy and
arranging for 50,000 shares to be "snatched" from a messenger
as he was carrying them between offices, got these shares on the
market.

Vanderbilt kept buying until he learned what had happened.
Then he went before his judge to get a process issued against
Drew and the Erie directors for contempt of court. But before it
could be served the Erie officials fled across the Hudson with
$6,000,000 of the Commodore's money. Here they set up head-
quarters in the Erie station at Jersey City where they surrounded
themselves by armed guards. This was their "Castle Erie." Their
final coup was to get the New Jersey legislature to make the Erie
a Jersey corporation. The Commodore's money seemed safely beyond his reach.

As Vanderbilt contemplated the 100,000 shares which had cost him $7,000,000 without giving him control of Erie, he did not stay idle. Finding his judge helpless in New Jersey, Vanderbilt turned to Albany. Here the Erie was trying to get a bill legalizing all that the Erie directors had done. Vanderbilt undertook to get this bill killed. Both sides soon found this legislative battle altogether too expensive, and rather than permanently enrich the members of the New York legislature and certain lobbyists, Vanderbilt and Drew got together and the Commodore got back $5,000,000. He gave up the idea of control. Jay Gould became president of Erie in October 1868, and took charge of a railroad that had been milked of $9,000,000. The Erie did not recover from this pillage until the twentieth century.

The Commodore went on to acquire the Lake Shore and Michigan Southern, the Michigan Central and the Canada Southern Railroad which brought him to Chicago by several paths with many branches reaching south to the Ohio, west to the Mississippi and north to Canada. The Erie limped along, but it still ran and was extended until it reached New York City and Chicago. Gould, Drew and a blatant rascal, Jim Fisk, continued their piratical forays.

Two other systems were organized but without the instrumentality of such exotic figures as Vanderbilt, Drew, and Gould. The Pennsylvania Railroad, under the leadership of J. Edgar Thomson and Thomas A. Scott, at the beginning of the Civil War consisted of a recently consolidated line from Philadelphia to Pittsburgh. In 1869 the management succeeded in securing the Pittsburgh, Fort Wayne and Chicago. It got to the Atlantic Coast by acquiring the lines crossing New Jersey which brought passengers and freight to Jersey City. Further expansion in Ohio brought it to Cincinnati and to St. Louis. These three systems—Vanderbilt, Erie and Pennsylvania—found themselves in competition with a fourth which John W. Garrett was organizing from Baltimore. This operation was based on the Baltimore and Ohio which had succeeded in getting access to Chicago, Cincinnati and St. Louis, and was fighting the Pennsylvania for an approach to New York City.

These lines were operating east of the Mississippi but even more difficult projects were being constructed west of the great river to bring the Pacific states into the transportation orbit. The building of the Union Pacific Railroad had gotten off to a slow start. When at length the enterprise got under way, the vice-president of the company undertook to organize a construction company of which he was to be president which would enter into a contract with the directors of the Union Pacific to build the road. The railroad would let this contract to this inner ring of the directors who would then monopolize a profit. Under this arrangement the construction company, or Crédit Mobilier as it was called, began work near Omaha in July 1865.

The Central Pacific Railroad which was to come east to meet the construction of the Union Pacific likewise organized a construction company from within, and was built largely by labor imported from China. As each railroad's share of the public land donated by Congress depended in size upon the number of miles built, a race in construction developed which ended at Promontory Point, Utah, on May 10, 1869. Here, in a colorful ceremony, trains from each direction bearing officials from the Union Pacific and Central Pacific Railroads steamed to a meeting point. The final spikes of gold and silver were then driven into the ties and through-transportation from Omaha to San Francisco was now possible. Connecting railroads united the ports of the Atlantic and Pacific seaboards.

Simultaneously, projects were on the boards to penetrate the northwest. Congress had authorized a Northern Pacific Railroad. Financier Jay Cooke was optimistically working to finance and construct it, even though there was little in the way of either freight or passenger traffic in immediate prospect. Lesser roads like the Kansas Pacific, the Missouri Pacific, the Chicago, Burlington and Quincy, the Rock Island and the Chicago and Northwestern, together with connecting roads from the East were

making Chicago, Kansas City, and Omaha great railroad centers
and providing freight lines to carry the products of the grain and
meat producers.

These great construction projects brought with them intense
competition for freight and passengers. During the seventies there
were rate wars which reduced fares and freight rates on competing lines, and tempted them to charge all the traffic would bear
when there were monopolies. These situations, together with the
scandalous financial manipulations of men like Drew, meant that
in the eyes of many the railroads were piratical and thieving. On
the other hand, the fact that certain of them, particularly the
Pacific roads, had great subsidies of public land meant that in
order to realize their resources they must promote sale of their
lands and encourage settlement thereon. They therefore became
great pioneer developers, establishing agencies to sell real estate,
foster migration and create communities. They were to lead in
the last frontier operations.

Railroad expansion was much influenced by revolutionary developments in the iron and steel industry. In the 1850's, William
Kelly in Kentucky and Henry Bessemer in England invented a
technique for making steel cheaply by an air-blast process. These
inventors secured patents in the United States, and near the end
of the war the commercial manufacture of steel by these processes
was begun at Detroit and at Troy. Shortly, the use of the two
patents was combined under one management. The greatest
works were established in Pennsylvania, the Cambria plant at
Johnstown, the Bethlehem Works, and Andrew Carnegie's enterprise at Pittsburgh, the J. Edgar Thomson Steel Co. By 1875 the
output had reached three hundred and seventy five thousand tons,
and four years later it was to be more than twice that. Most of
this steel was in the form of rails snapped up by the great railroad builders, for the cheap and plentiful production of steel made
the construction of railroads much more durable and efficient.
Iron rails had been unable to bear anywhere near so much strain
and wear as could those of steel. In like manner the coming of

steel was to revolutionize machinery manufacture and building construction of all kinds, bridges, factories, ships, locomotives and other railroad rolling stock. A new age had begun.

As striking as the developments in railroads and steel were to be those in a new commodity—oil. Oil had been commercially discovered in Western Pennsylvania in 1859. During the Civil War its possibilities as a fuel, an illuminant, and a lubricant had made it a highly profitable commodity. A refining industry had developed in the Pittsburgh-Cleveland area. The most active promoters were John D. Rockefeller and his associates, Flagler and Harkness in Cleveland. They found the industry a chaos of small refiners engaged in cutthroat competition. These men undertook to bring order and profits out of the new industry by organization. In 1870 they formed the first Standard Oil Company in Cleveland. By 1872 they had secured the property of twenty of the twenty-five competitors, and did 20 per cent of the nation's refining. They sought to increase their control, wealth and power by securing rebates from competing railroads which carried their tank cars, and by constructing pipe lines through which the oil could be pumped long distances, thus freeing the oil men from dependence on railroads. By the end of Reconstruction the Standard Oil operators were well on their way, but the fabulous days of the Standard Oil trust had not yet dawned. However, their power was already mighty.

Industrial mechanization, efficiency and concentration of management were making the pattern increasingly evident. Stemming likewise from Civil War needs, large-scale operations in meat packing, food canning, flour milling, machine-made shoes and ready-made clothing were all continuing to grow in size and strength. Manufacturing of all sorts was forging ahead. Measuring by the increase of factories alone, the statistician senses the growth when he learns that in 1859 there were 140,000 factories, in 1869 252,000.

Side by side with the growth of industrialization there was the expansion of retailing, wholesaling, export and import business,

and banking. The financing of the Civil War, with its outpour-
ing of bonds and greenbacks, the discovery of greater quantities
of precious metals, and the more stable banking provided by the
National Banks which were created at the war's close—all of
these made their contributions to business enterprise. What is
more, many new savings banks and trust companies mobilized
capital for business use.

Much of this economic activity was concentrated east of the
Mississippi, but great advances were being made beyond that
great stream. The Homestead Law, the Land Grant College Act,
and the Pacific Railroad land subsidies were all waiting when the
million soldiers were demobilized. Such largesse was equally in-
viting to immigrants from across the seas. In 1871, 6,000 homesteads were taken up; in 1872, 10,000, and in 1875, 22,000. Between
1873 and 1878, 2,988 purchasers bought 1,723,580 acres of Northern
Pacific lands. In this area, mining, cattle and farming industries
were booming. Just prior to the Civil War, gold had been discovered in Nevada, Colorado, and in the Frazier River region in
the Northwest. In the 1870's great deposits of silver were found
in Nevada, and gold and silver in the territories of Idaho and
Montana. Prospectors made their way thither, and stampedes
and boom towns sprang up overnight. Speculation in gold and
silver mines added to the feverish nature of business, and produced mining kings to take their places with the empire builders
in railroads, steel, and oil.

Cattle raising on a large scale, begun in Texas during the war,
spread over the plains after the conflict. The Texans began driving their cattle up to the railheads, particularly to those in Kansas,
and between 1869-1879, 4,000,000 head were driven into these
stockyards. Out on the great plains, ranches were organized and
the cowboy became a figure in American enterprise, taking his
place with the miner and prospector. But the plains were not to
be left to the cattle and the cowboys. The homesteaders were
pressing steadily on with their prairie plows and their windmills
for irrigation. With their barbed wire fences they were to cut off

the free range of the cattlemen and to prepare huge acreages for the commercial crops of wheat and corn. New states, Nebraska and Colorado, were already in the Union, and nine territories were looking forward to eventual admission.

All this feverish activity had stimulated enterprise and mobilized great wealth. This was in the hands of a growing number of men of brains and power. Their relation to government was to change the nature of the nation's leadership. The politician was to be eclipsed. In a sense the Civil War and Reconstruction had finished the problem of political definition, or so it seemed. Nationalism had triumphed over localism. The great task now was the development of resources, the organization of industry and services to supply an enormous population and the mobilization, control and direction of capital. A new figure was emerging to direct this task. He was to be a man of money, not politics. He was to overshadow and, to a certain degree, control, the politician and make him a secondary figure. Certain of his activities were frightening.

Shortly after the war that group of men who had been training in railroad financing became active in the New York money market. They were unscrupulous operators who were seeking new fields of exploitation. Certain of them were ready to try a great coup. After taking over the management of the Erie railroad, Gould and associates ousted Drew. Together with a peculiarly obnoxious operator, James Fisk, Jr., Gould began planning new raids on bank credit, foreign exchange and on stock prices in general. Their most spectacular rascality was in the realm of gold.

The United States had not been on the gold standard since December 1861. Consequently gold was a commodity bought and sold at various prices depending on whether the greenbacks seemed likely to be redeemable. Their fate had seemed uncertain during much of the war, and their purchasing power small. The nation's importers had to have gold to pay foreign creditors and certain taxes. The result was a steady market for gold. Now

Gould and Fisk would "corner" the supply of gold and make the many who must have it "pay through the nose." But this would involve politics, for the United States Treasury had a supply of gold and a "corner" could only be arranged if the government would keep its supply out of the market. But here these enterprisers were not without expedients.

One of President Grant's many relatives was a brother-in-law, A. R. Corbin, who had some acquaintance with Gould and Fisk. They undertook to give him a share of their proceeds. He was to bring Grant and Gould and Fisk together in order that Gould might explain to the President why government gold should be kept locked in the Treasury. The reason was the welfare of the farmers. Thereafter Grant was entertained by Gould and Fisk, appeared in an opera box with Gould, and was a guest on Fisk's Fall River Line. The public could assume that the President saw no evil in these men.

On these occasions, Gould carefully explained to Grant his plan to aid the farmer. It was this: The price of wheat was set in Liverpool in English gold values. The proceeds of wheat sales came to the farmer in the form of the greenbacks he got in exchange for the gold which the wheat brought. Thus, if gold was scarce and dear, the farmer would get a larger number of greenback dollars than if gold was cheap and greenbacks therefore fewer. If gold was made scarce and dear the farmer would profit. Gould represented to Grant that his plan to aid the farmer depended upon the Secretary of the Treasury keeping the government's gold off the market.

Grant said nothing to show any disagreement and so, some weeks later, in September 1869, Gould and Fisk started to buy gold. Grant was at a mountain resort in southwestern Pennsylvania at the time. Before long word of what was going on got to him, and he authorized the selling of government gold. The Gould-Fisk plan collapsed. However, the public had been treated to a spectacle which seemed for a time to involve the connivance of the President, the Treasury and two ruthless speculators in an operation to enrich a few and ruin numerous others.

These spectacular rascalities, featured as they frequently were by the manipulation of fabulous sums of inflated dollars, underlined a situation dangerous to democratic government. This was a period of inflation. The salary scale in government had never been generous in the best of times, and salaries which might have been barely adequate before the war were now painfully small. The civil service from the President down, through the Cabinet and the departmental bureau chiefs and clerks, the judges, the Senators and members of the House—all were confronted with the shrinking purchasing power of the dollar and no public sympathy large enough to permit increases in salary. Cabinet, Judiciary, Congressmen, all had to keep up appearances and live in competition with the extravagance and display of inflation-born *nouveaux-riches*. It was a time when the obvious chicaneries of the Drews and Fisks showed how low private morality had fallen. It was a period of desperation and temptation, encouraging all manner of doubtful schemes.

Among these were some of the transactions of the Crédit Mobilier, the construction company which had been organized by some of the officers of the Union Pacific to build the road for their own profit. One of its principal promoters, Oakes Ames of Massachusetts, had entered Congress in 1867. He and some others in the administration of the railroad had decided that it might be to the advantage of the road if it had more friends in Congress. They placed in Ames' hands a block of stock. He undertook to sell this to certain of his influential associates in the House, offering a convenient plan of purchase. The buyers need pay no cash. They could take title at a price well below the market, and their generous dividends would be withheld until the price was paid. In the meantime the stock would be held for them, and delivered when the payments were completed. To Congressmen suffering from small salaries in this inflationary period, this proposition to hedge seemed a godsend.

Speaker Blaine presented a spectacular example of similarly undesirable practice. He had become, in effect, a bond agent for the Fort Smith and Arkansas Railroad, and had persuaded his friends to buy certain of its securities which soon proved altogether too insecure. Corruption in some of the newly reconstructed Southern states was glaring. One particularly terrible example can be cited to illustrate the degradation of local government, namely the crimes and larceny of the Tweed Ring in New York City. Here a band of pilferers stole right and left from the treasury of that metropolis; no device was overlooked to rob the taxpayer and to enrich the members of the ring who made Tammany a by-word of corruption and New York's municipal government a stench in the nostrils of the nation.

The fact of the matter was that a large degree of power was in process of transfer from the government to the leaders of the growing business world. A shift was under way, a shift from Washington to what was popularly but rather loosely termed Wall Street. In this era it became apparent that certain significant policies of government were being shaped to suit the wishes of the rising money power.

Its prejudices and preferences were reflected particularly in financial and tax legislation. At the conclusion of fiscal year 1864-1865, there was a chaotic and unorganized debt of $2,682,-593,026.53, of which $432,687,966 was afloat in legal-tender greenbacks, the value of which fluctuated from day to day. This was an inflation which made prices and values uncertain. Some banking interests wanted stability of money and prices. To them this meant the greenbacks should be retired and the debt consolidated into series of bonds payable in gold, that is, a return to the gold standard by means of deflation. By the Act of April 12, 1866, deflation was begun, and the Secretary of the Treasury was authorized to withdraw from circulation greenbacks at the rate of $4,000,000 a month. However gold continued to fluctuate. It took anywhere from $1.24 to $1.67 in paper to buy a dollar's weight in gold. The pressure of those who wished to redeem the bonds in paper increased to such an extent that an Act of Congress, February 4, 1868, stopped the retirement of the greenbacks on the eve of the Presidential election. But the wishes of that part of the business world which desired gold payment of the bonds were incorporated in the Republican platform of that year when a pronouncement was made for redemption in gold.

In the matter of taxes, there were the tariff, the income tax and other internal taxes to be dealt with, including a myriad of stamp levies. There was a particularly high tariff averaging 47 per cent of the value of imports. Many felt that this unnecessarily restricted foreign trade and kept prices of commodities too high. But the protected industries were strong enough to defeat a general tariff revision downward in 1867. Two acts reducing duties on wool and copper in 1867 and 1868 were all that passed. Further tax reordering must wait until after the election.

While the political leadership of the nation was struggling with the problem of restoring the South to normal functioning in the Union, wartime inflation, social expansion, and economic development had invited new leadership. Men of great enterprise and ingenuity were appearing in business rather than in politics. They were acquiring great wealth which could be transmuted into power. They were overshadowing the political leaders and using their power in a fashion destined to reconstruct the operation of democracy.

14

Revolt

THE CONFLICT OF ARMS concluded in 1865 had, indeed, in Lincoln's inspired phrase, given the nation "a new birth of freedom," but it had placed many in a situation where they thought their independence and their liberties were threatened. The slave, to be sure, was free, but the war had loosed forces which some feared would, in effect, enslave others. The great inflation had upset all standards of values. Prices had skyrocketed, fixed incomes and wages had lost much of their purchasing power. The great fortunes amassed by the few had put much economic and even political power in their hands, and the use which they made of it to their own advantage could and did destroy the independence and security of many of their fellow men, particularly among the ranks of labor and of those who tilled the soil.

The difficulties of wage workers and farmers were to produce discontent, and defensive organization. This had occurred in the ranks of labor even before the end of the fighting. The great increase in industry during the war, despite the fact that much of it was mechanized, had brought a great demand for an increase in the ranks of labor. This had been met, despite heavy enlistments and the supporting draft which had made the Army a serious competitor for manpower. One important instrument in keeping pace with the demand was mechanization; another was the Contract Labor Law enacted by Congress in 1864. This legislation had enabled employers to contract abroad for companies of workers who were brought over to keep the work benches full and the machines at capacity. The labor force which numbered 1,300,000 in 1860 had increased to more than 2,000,000 by 1870.

These workers were, as ever, concerned over wages and hours, and their interest in wages was heightened by inflation. At first blush, inflation had seemed to improve their lot because wages had increased 60 per cent, but cumulative experience dashed that illusion as labor began to grasp the fact that living costs had increased 90 per cent. Higher wages were demanded, and increased pressure was applied for an eight-hour day and the repeal of the Contract Labor Law.

In order to make this pressure more effective, labor organized and a new era began. There had not been a great deal of such organization in the 1850's. The war years had stimulated interest. The railroad engineers had organized the Brotherhood of the Footboard in 1862, starting with those working on the Michigan Central. Then the unionization movement spread to the iron molders. William H. Sylvis, son of a Philadelphia wagon maker, marshalled them. Shortly thereafter, Jonathan Fincher started his *Trades' Review* as a labor periodical. Sylvis promoted the Industrial Assembly of North America which was held in Louisville in 1864. Two years later he assembled a Labor Congress at Baltimore which created the National Labor Union, embracing more than half a million workers organized by crafts. This body projected annual congresses and reached a membership of 640,-000. Pressure for an eight-hour day bore fruit almost at once. In 1867 New York, Illinois and Missouri passed eight-hour laws, and in the year following Congress enacted legislation instituting an eight-hour day for those laboring on public works, and repealing the Contract Labor Law. Bad legal draftsmanship, however, made these Federal laws of little use.

In these same years, the shoemakers formed the Order of the Knights of St. Crispin at Milwaukee. Likewise, a romantic Phila-

delphia garment cutter, influenced even more than the shoemakers had been by Masonic ritual and his reading in medieval
history, created an even more elaborate secret society. In 1860,
Uriah H. Stephens and ten other tailors in Philadelphia organized the Noble Order of Knights of Labor. Their idea took form
slowly. This Assembly No. 1 of tailors was shortly augmented by
Assembly No. 2 of ship carpenters, and later by another composed of carpet weavers. Within six years there were some four
score of these Assemblies in the Philadelphia area, and by the end
of the Reconstruction era the Knights were perfecting a national
body in the form of a General Assembly composed of state representatives. The order maintained its secrecy and its ritual. All
who worked for wages, whether skilled or not, were welcome in
its ranks. General programs for the improvement of the lot of
mankind were shaped by the idealistic thinking of its members.
Its leaders were dedicated men, not always too practical.

The farmer's difficulties also drove him to protest and to organization. His fortunes, at first, had been greatly improved by
the war and the attendant inflation. The demand for food for
the armies had been immense. Many a farmer had increased his
acreage in order to take advantage of the high prices. But to do
this he often had to borrow inflated dollars to pay for the land
at inflated prices. So long as the price of his crops remained high
he could pay his interest, and reduce the principal of his debt.
Contrary to labor's experience the farmer seemed to profit from
the first phase of inflation.

At the end of the conflict the agricultural situation began to
change. The demand for food fell off with the demobilization of
the armies. The government stopped its vast quantity purchases.
This in itself induced a fall in prices, but there were influences
evidently at work to accelerate the decline in prices even faster.
Now that the need for such great quantities of money had ceased,
the obvious policy seemed to be to stop issuing legal-tender notes
and to retire them. Certain bankers and "sound money" men demanded a return to the gold dollar as standard, a return to specie

payment which had been abandoned in 1861. Legislation to start
this process had been passed by Congress in the first postwar
session in 1866. The implications of such deflation were disturbing to some businessmen whose prices were falling.

The basic fact was becoming apparent after 1870 that the
farms were producing an unsalable surplus at the same time that
advocates of deflation were demanding a decrease in the supply
of money. Such contraction would work particular hardship on
those burdened by farm mortgages. They had borrowed dollars
when dollars were cheap, now they must pay back dollars when
dollars were scarcer and dearer. If a farmer had borrowed $6,000
when wheat was selling at $2 a bushel, he could pay off his
mortgage with 3,000 bushels. But in the seventies, had he not
paid off his debt, he must still pay back $6,000; but if the price
of wheat had fallen to 50 cents a bushel he would have to raise
12,000 bushels to meet his indebtedness. In other words, measured
by the work he must do to free himself from debt, his obligation
had increased 400 per cent. How could he work that much harder
when he was already doing all that he could?

The farmer in the corn and wheat states of the Middle West
saw himself beset by enemies. When he raised his crop it was
sold at harvest time, the point of lowest price. It was hauled
away by railroads which often held monopolies and could charge
high freight rates. Middlemen stored the grain in huge elevators until the spring when prices were high; then the middlemen sold and gained the profit. Contributing to the farmer's
financial woes was the local banker who held his mortgage,
charged him high interest, and foreclosed and made him a
tenant if he couldn't pay. Local storekeepers charged him high
prices for his supplies. Finally, it was a new age of farm machinery. This machinery was made expensive by the protective
tariff, and the farmer had to buy it on credit with high carrying
charges. His machinery notes were often discounted at the local
bank by the manufacturers, and he was placed even more in the

power of the local banker. As the farmer looked at his prospects, his sense of grievance grew.

The plight of the farmer, like the handicaps of labor, stimulated an impulse to a romantic style of enterprise. As early as 1866 the Commissioner of Agriculture was permitted by President Johnson to send a clerk down South to find out the extent of the agricultural disaster which the war and the disruption of the farm labor force had brought upon the broken Confederacy. Oliver Hudson Kelley, born in Massachusetts and migrant to Minnesota, had the assignment. In gathering material for his report and in drawing up his conclusions, he was most impressed by the defeatist quality of the farmer's attitude. He was isolated, apathetic, backward looking. Seemingly, he was incapable of anything but a passive acceptance of misfortune. Kelley concluded that what the farmer needed was some form of communication and fraternization. If enough farmers got together occasionally they would naturally talk about their troubles, and this discussion might suggest action. Kelley, like Stephens, was impressed by the pattern of the Masonic order and he began to think of a secret ritualistic organization in which farmers could have the stimulus of swapping gripes.

Soon Kelley changed jobs. He moved over into the Post Office Department. He proceeded with a handful of other clerks to carry out his idea. He, and an associate in the Agricultural Bureau, William Saunders, organized on December 4, 1867 the National Grange of the Patrons of Husbandry, with Saunders as Master, and Kelley, Secretary. Each Grange meeting was to be conducted according to ritual but it was also to offer an educational program, often in the form of a lecture or a discussion of some farm problem. The farmers' wives were included, and there was usually something substantial to eat. Thus was the Grange, as it was often called, created in a Washington office

Kelley soon resigned his Post Office job, and set out to organize the order on a national basis, living on the initiation fees. At first, growth was painfully slow for the farmers had not yet felt the pinch; after three years of effort there were establishments in only nine states. There was most activity in Minnesota, Iowa, Wisconsin, Indiana and Illinois, although there were units in Vermont and New Jersey, in Mississippi, and South Carolina. All these state organizations were joined in a National Grange which met annually. There were units in thirty-two states; only in Connecticut, Delaware, Nevada and Rhode Island were there none.

The Grange was by no means the only farmers' organization, although its widespread diffusion and its national organization gave it great prominence. In various states, particularly in the Middle West, farmers' clubs and political organizations had been active before the Grange became prominent. As they had found themselves the prey to high warehouse charges for storing their crops and to the high rates which railroads charged them for carrying their produce, they began to demand government protection against these abuses. As the Grange was a social rather than a political organization, and devoted itself to discussion and propaganda, vigorous political organizations were called for to secure legislation. Some of these organizations were called Independents, others Farmers', Reform or Anti-Monopoly parties. The first of these were developed in Illinois, and as early as 1867, before the Grange had influence, or much organization, they had sufficient strength to get a Warehouse Act on the books. Heretofore railroads would only load grain from elevators which they owned or controlled. Under this law railroads had to pick up grain from any warehouse. By 1870 these farmers' clubs in Illinois were strong enough to put the power to regulate railroads into the new state constitution. Under this authority, the Illinois legislature fixed passenger and freight rates, and set up a railroad and warehouse commission to hear complaints and find facts. In 1871 a Granger law was passed in Minnesota which established a railroad commission to enforce rates set by the legislature.

The plight of both labor and agriculture, and the efforts in these ranks to organize for protection, had political implications which were recognized by those active in national as well as local politics. These implications seemed of particular importance to the Democrats for they might offer that party an instrument which it needed badly. The once-dominant Democratic party had emerged from the war years in confusion, and under a cloud. While the great majority in the North had been loyal to the Union cause, and had cooperated in the effort as War Democrats, a conspicuous minority of Copperheads had given aid and comfort to the Confederacy.

In 1865 the Southern Democrats had sought a comeback. Though various efforts were made to disqualify their leaders from activity, it was only too clear that the Democrats, North and South, added up to a great mass of voters. The Republican leadership feared this remobilization, and this apprehension lay at the basis of much Reconstruction politics. The Democrats must struggle to overcome the stigma of rebellion, the taunts of traitor, rebel, Copperhead. The Republicans had the advantage; they had freed the slaves, saved the Union, and beaten the rebels. They seemingly stood for all the virtues. How could such a phalanx of righteousness be shaken from control and the Democrats find any hope for success? It could not be done by reviving old issues such as state rights and strict construction. Some new reason for being must be found.

The "new" Democratic leadership, striving to revive the party, found in the plight of the poor, the distressed, and of some businessmen a possible answer. The people needed to be protected from Wall Street, from the money monopolists, from those who, by contracting the currency, sought to make money dear and thus easier for the speculators to control. They must be protected against gamblers and railroad pirates like Vanderbilt and Gould, Daniel Drew and the notorious Jim Fisk. The "Greenback" was the answer. This new issue had been raised in Ohio as soon as the deflation policy began to be implemented. There the Democrats seized upon the issue. They denounced the Republicans for contracting the currency and driving down prices at the behest of Eastern interests. They declared that as the nation's business was increasing, it needed more money rather than less. The greenbacks should be increased in amount to keep up wages and goods prices, and particularly to force the government to pay back the loans in the same medium which had been borrowed. It was rank injustice to make the taxpayers repay more than had been received. They proclaimed the Greenback as the great panacea for economic ills. Those facing debts, lowered income and unemployment found the idea appealing. The Democrats could see in this Ohio idea a program which offered the masses protection of their liberty, and a platform which would make people forget treason, rebellion and the Copperhead aspersion.

The Midwestern Democrats sought to make this the platform of the Democratic National Convention of 1868. They rallied behind an Ohio advocate of this program, "Gentleman" George H. Pendleton, and converged on New York City where the sessions were held. They succeeded in securing the adoption of their platform; the Greenback was to be their standard. But they failed to nominate their candidate. Eastern influences nominated a deflation-minded candidate in the person of the so-called "Copperhead" War Governor of New York, Horatio Seymour, who had sought to quell the New York draft riots by making a speech. Grant won handily, but students of the returns soon learned that his success had been achieved by the Negro votes in the South.

The Republican party was reorganized and victorious. National and state organizations had done their part. But it was Grant's popularity as the victor at Appomattox which probably was the decisive factor in his victory. This the General felt; he was the choice of the people. But it appears that there was little or no communication between the President-elect and the party managers after the election. He undertook to form his own Administration, and to determine his Cabinet and policies as though he were organizing an army. Interestingly enough his thinking, probably quite naturally, bore no relation to political organizing or power. This fact contributed not a little to the peculiar conditions which came to be denoted as "Grantism." Grant had few people around him with political experience. He had certain military friends and aides who were close to him and there was an unfortunately numerous supply of his own and Mrs. Grant's relatives. Then, too, General Grant had a naive respect and a totally unwarranted deference for wealthy businessmen, undoubtedly a reaction to his own life of financial failure.

The new President was going to play it by ear, but his ear had been attuned by civil failure and military success. It was utterly untrained to catch the soft music and the harsh instrumentation which together made up the confusing cacophony known as politics. Probably no advisers, no matter how astute, would have gotten through to him, wrapped as he was in the mantle of his taciturnity, and his determination to prevent communication. Whatever of a legislative program the new party high command might expect to achieve must be engineered by the Congressional leaders with little reference to the President. There were many indications that, for all its new strength, the Republican party was weak. It had no leader, its principal members were reactionary. Time was to expose the cancer in its body of "Grantism" which was going to contribute to its downfall. The Democrats had yet to find the formula for successful reorganization. But there was help coming from the South where another type of revolt was producing new power for the Democrats.

Unrest was not confined to the industrial cities and the Midwest. Many in the recently "reconstructed" South were miserably unhappy. Hardly had military reconstruction seemed to have established the Republican party firmly in power in the ex-Confederate states when signs appeared that this new political structure was built on rickety foundations. In 1868, the very year of the readmission of most of the seceded states, there were signs of instability. In Mississippi, a majority of the state voters rejected the newly drafted constitution, despite the fact that the Negroes outnumbered the whites. This document guaranteed Negro equality and the suffrage, but it was rejected largely because of the drastic penalties it imposed on the former Confederates, excluding them from politics and even from voting. In the Presidential election of that year, Georgia and Louisiana voted for Democratic electors, and Georgia chose a conservative legislature which expelled the Negro members when it met.

Congress took note of these alarming signs and acted. Georgia was put back under military rule. A Fifteenth Amendment was sent to the states making the Negro a voter. Mississippi, Virginia, Texas and Georgia, still out of the Union, were required to ratify this as well as the Fourteenth Amendment before readmission. After the Fifteenth Amendment was proclaimed as ratified in March 1870, Congress went to work on an Enforcement Act prescribing heavy penalties for any interference with the civil and voting rights of the Negro, greatly enlarging the jurisdiction of the Federal courts. Yielding to these pressures the four states still outside the Union complied. They ratified the amendment. Virginia and Mississippi adopted, by popular votes, constitutions providing for Negro suffrage, though the Confederate exclusion clauses, which were submitted separately, were defeated. Georgia, under the command of Federal law, submitted to a legislature sponsored by the Radical Governor. These last four states were admitted in 1870.

Despite the Constitutional Amendments and the Enforcement Act, the process of Republican disintegration proceeded. Various forces were at work. One was external to the Radical power. The disfranchised whites had created organizations to break down the voting strength of the Negroes by pressures not recognized by law. Late in 1865 a secret organization called the Ku Klux Klan had been mobilized under the leadership of ex-Confederates. By 1867, it was effectively influencing the Negroes not to vote. A similar group were known as the Knights of the White Camelia. The methods they used were designed to prey upon the Negroes' fears, superstitious or otherwise. In some instances, the klansmen wore ghostly costumes, and by visitations and warnings in the dead of night scared the Negroes away from the polls. In other instances, there were beatings as well as warnings. The result of this terrorism, psychological or physical, discouraged Negro political activity in many areas.

A second force was operating to weaken the Republicans within the ranks of the new Radical parties in various of the states, particularly in those where the white voters were in the majority. The "Radical" organizations were often not well-fused or skillfully managed, and their leaders were too self-seeking and venal. In such circumstances, therefore, jealousies and rivalries bred schism and disorganization. The reviving Democrats shrewdly kept in the background in some cases. When rivalry produced two candidates among the Republicans for the same office, instead of presenting one of themselves, they supported the milder of the two Republicans.

In 1870 the Democrats were able thus to regain much of their influence in Virginia and Tennessee, while in the same year the old Democratic party actually recaptured the legislatures in Alabama, North Carolina and Georgia. In the latter two states impeachment proceedings were undertaken. Governor Holden of North Carolina was removed from office though he was succeeded by a Radical lieutenant governor who was later elected to a full term. In Georgia, however, Bullock fled the state to avoid a trial, and in the special election ordered in October 1871 to choose his successor, a Democrat was voted in.

These developments, together with the increasing reputation for terrorism ascribed to the hooded order, the Ku Klux Klan, caused Congress to pass two more enforcement acts in 1871 to protect the Negro in his civil rights and in his voting privilege. The Ku Klux Acts gave Federal officials large powers of control over Congressional elections in the states, and authorized the President to declare martial law in any precincts in the South where he deemed Federal troops necessary to protect Negroes at the polls. Under this authority, President Grant declared nine counties in South Carolina as out of hand in October 1871, and sent in troops.

Despite these disquieting signs of party weakness, of revolt in the Republican ranks in the South, and of growing disaffection toward their rule among farmers and wage workers, the leadership paid little or no heed. They were listening to the new business interests. Grant's victory had been followed by a pronouncement by Congress that the bonded indebtedness of the nation would be paid in gold. In 1870 a funding act provided the machinery for this redemption. All that the labor and farm interests were able to achieve was to prevent any further retirement of greenbacks, or any exchange of them for gold at par.

The story was much the same in the matter of taxation, though some changes were accomplished. The accumulation of revenue made another limited tariff revision imperative. After a difficult battle, an unsatisfactory bill was passed in 1870, reducing the duties on some more items, most of which American industry did not manufacture, such as coffee, tea, wine, and spices, and others, particularly sugar and pig iron. On the eve of the election of 1872 the demands of the farmers were heeded, and a bill was passed providing for an across-the-board 10 per cent reduction. Here again the action was bitterly contested, and the end result careless.

Business objection to the plethora of taxes, including the income tax, got results more easily. Efforts at the reduction of excise taxes had begun in 1866, and the annual tax laws contained decreases until the law of 1870 brought these exactions down to a level which could be maintained for over a decade. Stamp taxes were largely eliminated, the income tax was abandoned. The excises remaining were largely the taxes on liquor and tobacco. The Republican leadership seemed eager to enact anything that the new business tycoons might wish.

But though the leadership made little response to the growth of discontent and defection in the ranks of the Republican party, the excesses, incapacities and rascalities of the political and business worlds were to assume a significant role in the election of 1872. As far back as 1869 a protest against excess and corruption had stimulated a "Liberal" movement among Republicans. This began in Missouri, under the leadership of Carl Schurz and B. Gratz Brown who shortly were elected United States Senator and Governor respectively. From Missouri this move spread to other states, north and south. These men spoke against the travesty of Reconstruction, the corruption rife in the Grant regime. They sought various types of reform, such as a merit system in the civil service, a lowering of the tariff, and the withdrawal of troops and Federal support from governments which were making a farce and a tragedy out of self-government in the South. They sought to arrest the tendency toward centralization in government by restoring state rights. Their chief objective was to replace Grant as the candidate for 1872.

The efforts of these Liberal Republicans to get control of the nominating machinery made little progress so they decided to set up a national organization of their own, and to nominate a candidate whom the Democrats might support, thus following the pattern which had been developing in certain Southern states. There was some possibility of this because a new movement, originating in Ohio and called "The New Departure," had appeared among the Democrats. The organizers of this faction called upon the party to forget the past, to accept the natural results of the war, and to demand a series of measures similar to those of the liberal Republicans. The ball was started rolling when the Missouri Liberal Republican state convention in 1872 called a national convention. This body duly assembled with the largest bloc supporting Charles Francis Adams, recently Lincoln's Minister to Great Britain. However, a group of professionals hardly meriting the designation "Liberal" gained control and nominated Horace Greeley, the famous editor of the New York *Tribune*.

This move had stirred considerable apprehension among the Radical leaders in Congress, and they had been moved to make some concessions. The "ironclad" oath designed to keep most Confederates out of politics and office-holding was repealed, and a general amnesty law was passed on the eve of the convention which would permit most of the Southerners previously excluded to return to political activity and service. But Grant himself was renominated. Vice-President Colfax, who had been associated with some unsavory finance, was dropped from the ticket, and Senator Henry Wilson of Massachusetts, an original Republican of antislavery days, was substituted. Despite Horace Greeley's notorious Republican fundamentalism, and high tariff enthusiasm, the Democrats accepted him in their national convention and the contest was fought between Grant and Greeley.

This did not mean that there were only two parties in the field. Protest did not come from these Liberal Republicans alone. Labor was seeking political organization as a remedy. The National Labor Union, despite the death of Sylvis in 1869, had held seven annual congresses, and was going into politics. In this year of 1872 it was instrumental in organizing a Labor Reform party. This group held a national convention and adopted a platform of broad scope. Its leaders were thinking in terms of the rights of man and the curbing of privilege. Their chief instrument was to be the greenback. They demanded that this currency should be kept in circulation, and furthermore that the bonds should be paid in terms of the original contract, not always in gold. Likewise there should be no tax-exempt bonds.

Next to money they were thinking in terms of the eight-hour day, the exclusion of Chinese labor, and the abolition of competition from prison labor. They wanted the public lands distributed only to those who had no land. They advocated a revenue tariff and demanded that money needed to fight wars should be assessed against the rich. They wanted civil service reform and the introduction of the merit system in place of spoils. The President should serve for only one term.

The time had come, they believed, for a general amnesty for ex-Confederates and the withdrawal of troops from the South; civil law should be supreme. Better patent laws should protect men of genius. A striking evidence of new thinking was presented by a demand that government should regulate railroad and telegraph rates. The convention, however, voted down government ownership, and the referendum method of enacting laws by submitting them to the voters. Judge David Davis of the United States Supreme Court and Governor Joel Parker of New Jersey were nominated for President and Vice-President, both of whom refused to run. But these platform-makers were looking further into the future than they dreamed. The time would come when their demands would be the valued currency of politics.

Other evidence of the complexity of the times was produced by the appearance in 1872 of other minor political organizations with their "isms" and their candidates. Some "hard shell" Democrats would have none of Greeley and nominated a ticket. The Prohibitionists made their first appearance. And it was in this year that women made one of their early efforts to secure the vote when Susan B. Anthony appeared at the Liberal Republican gathering to plead their cause. Despite these factions it was inevitable that the contest should be between the President and Greeley. The *Tribune* editor undertook to introduce an unusual note into national contests; he took the stump and attracted not a little support by his persuasive speaking.

All this opposition notwithstanding, Grant had an easier victory than in 1868, winning 700,000 more votes than Greeley. The votes of the third-party candidates were negligible. Nevertheless Grant's opponent carried three of the reconstructed states, Georgia, Tennessee and Texas, as well as the border states of Kentucky, Maryland and Missouri. In Louisiana the Radical Governor, Warmoth, had broken with the Federal appointees and supported Greeley. This meant that he certified that Greeley had carried the state. The rival faction arranged a certification that Grant's electors had won. Both the Greeley and Grant tickets met, and sent "certified" electoral votes to Washington. Congress, without any real hesitation, counted the Grant votes. This disputed result was an evil portent of 1876. Statistics showed that the Democrats were on the way back in the South, despite the fact that the Republicans had regained the Alabama legislature, and the Radicals had re-elected their gubernatorial candidate in North Carolina.

Thus the political fruits of the Union victory in the war were spoiling. The powers of the reorganized Republican party, seemingly given such emphatic endorsement in the elections of 1868 and 1872, were weakening. Large groups among labor, among Midwestern farmers, among Liberal Republicans and among Southern Republicans were in a mood to revolt. They were already giving aid and comfort to the Democrats. Might not these elements, discontented with the union of the Grant Republicans and the new money power, return the Democrats to authority and thereby, as they promised, restore the government to the people?

15

A Division of Power

THE REDISTRIBUTION of the power to govern the reconstructed Republic had passed through several phases. First, a new political power, the postwar Republican party, had been organized. Second, a nonpolitical power had emerged which frequently overshadowed those chosen by the voters to rule. This was the power of new business operators who controlled the use of the nation's resources. The third phase of this redistribution was a revolt against what was held to be a corrupt alliance between these two powers, a revolt designed to restore the purity of democracy. By 1873 the third phase seemed destined to failure and frustration. Grant, who was becoming a symbol of naive corruption as a tool of malign forces, had been emphatically endorsed in the election of 1872. At this point, however, disaster intervened.

Not the least of the factors complicating the period of postwar readjustment and reordering was the ending of another business cycle, marked spectacularly by a financial panic. Such financial convulsions in nineteenth-century United States were to recur all too regularly at twenty-year intervals. Already, three had occurred—in 1819, 1837 and 1857. Now the shattering Civil War appeared to have accelerated the cycle, and the next panic struck in 1873.

The principal factor precipitating the debacle of 1857, namely premature and unproductive railroad construction, was still operating, aggravated by the uncertainties of currency inflation. The value of the greenbacks was subject to constant fluctuation since the government was prevented by politics from enacting a permanent policy. Conservative financiers, businessmen, and citizens in general, still urged a return to a gold standard. But the agricultural interests, generally in the West, who now wanted to boost the price of grain, and others who felt that the growing business of the nation required more currency for its multiple transactions, opposed contraction. Such contraction would place too much power in the hands of Wall Street which could control and manipulate a fixed gold coinage.

The instability was further aggravated by the continuing lack of any central bank. The National Banking Act, while it had created a certain amount of guaranteed paper money in national bank notes protected by bonds deposited with the comptroller, had provided no machinery for central reserves which might be used to aid banks in trouble. All too large a part of·the nation's cash was on deposit in New York banks. If anything caused them to close their doors, a substantial part of the nation's business capital would be frozen and out of use.

A series of wars and accidents contributed to financial insecurity. Three conflicts, the Civil War, the Austro-Prussian War and the Franco-Prussian War had been expensive, speculative and destructive of reserves. Recessions and stringencies followed in England, France, and Germany, accompanied by failures, stagnation and liquidation. Many European holdings of American securities were dumped on American exchanges and drove down the price, likewise depreciating those held as collateral on loans, particularly by banks. In 1871 there had been a devastating fire in Chicago, and more recently one in Boston. Much capital had been destroyed in these holocausts and the insurance companies put under particular stress.

But the factor immediately precipitating disaster was railroad financing. The nation was subsidizing the construction of two transcontinental railroads. The Union Pacific had recently been

constructed, but by methods of doubtful propriety. Such operations had shaken public faith in the security of railroad invest-
ments. The renowned financier of the Civil War, Jay Cooke, was
having difficulty in finding the money necessary to build a Northern Pacific Railroad through a wilderness. He had planned to
sell bonds to secure the money but unfortunately he had not been
successful.

Investors were growing wary of such securities; there was a
feeling that railroads were overbuilt. Furthermore where was
there business in the Northwestern wilderness, how could such
a railroad earn any money with few passengers and little freight?
Also, the antagonism of the farmer, the rate wars and the sus-
picions stimulated by the Grangers that railroads were crooked,
all added to investors' reluctance. The result was that Jay Cooke
and others found themselves called upon to meet construction
costs without having been able to sell the necessary bonds to
raise cash. During the summer of 1873 various bankers had been
using up the deposits in their banks, leaving themselves only unsalable bonds as protection.

The inevitable happened. In the late summer of 1873, the crops
came on the market at harvest time, and money was needed to
buy them. So, large sums of money on deposit in New York,
where there was such a heavy concentration of cash, began to be
withdrawn. The New York banks could not pay these drafts;
they had frozen the money and were short. On September 8,
the New York Warehouse and Security Company which was
financing the Missouri, Kansas and Texas Railroad, closed its
doors. Five days later, Kenyon Cox & Co., "Uncle" Daniel Drew's
firm, involved in the Canada Southern Railroad, met a like fate.
But the climax came on September 18 when Jay Cooke & Co.
failed to open. This was a shocking calamity, emotional as well
as financial. Jay Cooke had built up a great reputation for in-
tegrity, financial skill and sound if ingenious enterprise. His
name was a household word, a symbol of reliability. People
trusted Cooke. His failure was a shattering blow to public con-

fidence. The next day, Friday, September 19, panic seized the
nation's business. It was indeed Black Friday, and on Saturday
the New York Stock Exchange closed its doors.

The panic was shortlived. President Grant and the Secretary
of the Treasury went to New York on Sunday and authorized the
purchase of government bonds with $20,000,000 held by the sub-
treasury. This transaction eased the cash shortage slightly. The
managers of the New York Clearing House Association set up
a committee of five who accepted approved securities from members, and issued certificates of deposit against them up to 75
per cent of their value which could be used to settle balances
without the necessity of daily transfers of cash. The immediate
panic was over by September 29, and by October 18 the deposits
and reserves of the New York banks were rising.

The depression, however, lasted for an unusually long period.
Business failures continued at a high rate. At the climax of the
Panic, during 1873, there were 5,000 failures with liabilities of
$228,000,000; this continued annually, increasing until in 1878
there were 10,000 failures though the total liability was but
slightly increased to $234,000,000.

The depression lifted slowly because the nation was still uncertain about its currency. Specie payment was not revived until
1879, and there were doubts as to its feasibility up to the first
day of resumption. The railroads were in debt and plagued by
strikes. Rate wars cut down earning capacity. The exposures of
railroad skulduggery caused states to attempt to regulate and
police railroad operations. Railroading continued to seem a highly
dangerous and even criminal form of operation, scaring off investors.

This depression hung over the nation like a pall during the
remaining years of "Reconstruction," 1873-1877. It stimulated
continued discontent among the farmers and wage workers, and
encouraged demands for further inflation, either through more
greenbacks or "free silver." The decline in employment and the
decrease in buying power made business sluggish, curtailed op-

timism and spread nervous apprehension. This atmosphere could
not fail to affect politics and the struggle for power. These disasters curtailed the political influence of businessmen. The discontented and the suffering demanded remedies, and reformers
gained greater strength.

The political situation developing between the Panic of 1873
and the election of 1876 was a complex one, reflecting the cultural
confusion of the times. Political behavior, then as always, was
merely a reflection of the society in which it took place. Since the
war period, American society had taken its tone from the swift
accumulation of wealth, from the burgeoning cities, from the
horde of European immigrants flocking to American shores. It
was a society of vivid contrasts, of great riches yet increasing
poverty. Huge fortunes were in the hands of men of great enterprise and power, but of imperfect taste. Their money was spent
ostentatiously, creating a "Gilded Age." Some of their ornate
homes could be stuffed with genuine "Old Masters" imported
from Europe, yet be simultaneously decorated with gingerbread
ornaments, showy turrets and iron animals on the lawns.

Inflation continued, and farmer and wage worker alike suffered from the resulting diminution of purchasing power in the
midst of plenty. City slums increased. But the poverty in America,
though disturbing to those who didn't think it possible, was mild
compared to European want. In large numbers the poor of that
continent sought to cross the Atlantic to a society where they
were led to believe the streets were paved with gold. Religion
seemed not so much concerned with preaching a gospel of Christian responsibility, as with fighting a battle against a science
which disturbed the literal-minded who missed the religious
strength and power which lay behind the mere uncomprehended
words of the Scriptures. The wealth, so quickly amassed and
concentrated largely in the hands of mighty though unlettered
men, was to unlock many doors. These masters of capital had
great respect for the education which they lacked, and no small
mite of their fortunes was invested in educational institutions

which they believed would justify the faith of the donors by strengthening the nation's capacity to provide opportunity for its youth to strive and succeed.

Men and women of intellectual perception and literary skill caught the spirit of this great surge of power, and put it into print between covers. It was an age of books and magazines and of an increasing newsstand-patronizing public. They could laugh with Mark Twain, for America, now that the war was over, was ready to laugh. Some could begin to comprehend the problems which the authors who were discovering a New Realism were delineating. They could grasp in some small measure the spirit of that great democracy of which Walt Whitman sang. But, in general, perhaps they were content with the prevailing materialism bred of wealth-amassing power. They could subscribe to Darwin's evolutionary doctrine, brought to America by Herbert Spencer, through such interpreters as William Graham Sumner who believed in the survival of the fittest. The masters of capital who succeeded did so because their power made them deserve success, and those who failed and sank into degradation because of failure were helpless victims of a biological predestination which determined the status of individuals according to an inexorable law which freed the successful from any great responsibility or qualms of conscience. There was little moral restraint to prevent politicos on small salaries in an age of inflation and panic from surviving by whatever devious means they found at their disposal.

The Panic of 1873 added to the political confusion, as it was well known that heretofore parties in power during panics had been defeated in the next election. Republicans therefore could not face 1876 with any overweening confidence. A second factor making the political situation unusual was the increasing evidence that a new politics was emerging in the South. There was evidence of a new white leadership in that section which was coming to be known as "Bourbon." In a sense, it reflected a renascence of the Old Regime. Ex-Confederates were undoubtedly prominent in it, particularly as the act of 1872 had removed the political disabilities of most of them. But the group was more diverse, representing a new society.

This society was no longer dominated by the wealthy cotton planters, almost feudal in their spirit. Smaller farms now became much more numerous. The old plantations were in certain instances divided into smaller units to be worked by the ex-slaves on shares, or as tenants. Frequently large plantations survived, worked by slaves as hired laborers, but the smaller farm was the new model. This change meant that farmers of relatively few acres were responsible for governing the rural areas. They did not have the power and the imagination of the large planters; they were men of small affairs and narrow horizons. The decline in the size of the farms meant a reduction in the bulk of the individual farmer's crops and money. A new method of marketing had to be devised, for no longer did a steamboat come up to a planter's wharf and load one man's crop of hundreds of cotton bales. Someone had to arrange to round up the few bales which each of the small croppers could raise, and then ship them to the cotton factors in the seaports. These men were often crossroads merchants who kept general country stores. They supplied the farmers with the merchandise they needed, and took their crops in payment. If the crop failed, or if the price was low, the farmer too often found himself in debt to the merchant at the end of the year. For this reason the storekeeper could have much influence in the rural community, and could upon occasion shape the political action of those in debt to him.

Reconstruction had stimulated enterprising Southerners to mobilize a new supply of capital. Either they transferred money from agriculture or, more particularly, took earnings from professional services, such as medicine and law, or cash borrowed on newly established credit to develop new economic interests. There were grants, sometimes extravagant, of tax money and state credit to new railroad construction, but there was investment of private capital in newly realized resources, in forests and in coal and iron mines. The possibility of textile and steel industries stimulated development. Mill towns began to flourish at the falls of the rivers and near the ore deposits, and in turn a new group of capitalists appeared. These men were thinking in terms of commercial advantage and proposed schemes for grants, subsidies and internal improvements. A number of these businessmen had been Whigs before the war, and could think more congenially in terms used by Northern Republicans than could many ante-bellum Democrats.

This expanding business activity was conditioning a more active politics with new leadership. The Negro was being eliminated, and with him went the Republican scalawag unless he changed his party. The carpetbaggers in large part were already gone. The Negro's political lot was most unhappy. He had not been accepted generally, even by the carpetbaggers, as anything but a dependent voter who would deliver on call. For this service few ex-slaves were permitted even minor offices, after the early extravaganza of military rule. The Radical governments had done little to establish the freedmen either economically or socially. They failed to expropriate land and establish the Negroes as independent landholders, and their status as sharecroppers, tenants, or hired farm laborers raised them slightly, if at all, either economically or socially, above slavery. When the freedmen lost their political opportunities, they found themselves with little chance to better themselves. Though free they must remain inferior and for the most part with slight hope of realizing any ambitions they might have. The Redeemed South was a White South.

The new leadership of the South was to be more enterprising, less cultured, but cautious and tight-fisted. It had reacted against the extravagance of the Radical governments by clamping down on local taxation. It attempted in various instances to reduce state debts by repudiation. On the other hand, these men did not share the ante-bellum Democrats' opposition to Federal appropriations. They were eager for waterways improvements and harbor works, while widely distributed groups were working for a subsidy for a southern transcontinental railroad, the Texas and Pacific. They would press steadily for the segregation of the Negro and his elimination from politics, and they were not particularly interested in providing improved educational facilities. There was a peculiar unity in their politics. They were of one party, solidly Democratic. though their Democratic party was to some extent more like the ante-bellum Whigs. But in Congress and in national conventions they finally were to bear the Democratic label, though this was not so inevitably fixed in the seventies as some historians have maintained. The Democrats had fused with the Liberal Republicans in 1872 and supported their candidate but, as will soon be seen, flaws were to develop in their monolithic unity in 1876. This then was the Southern Democratic party in a section not yet become "solid."

In the North, the Democratic party had developed characteristics quite in contrast to those of the Southern wing. North of the Mason-Dixon line the inflationary interests of wage workers and farmers had once caused the party to support the greenback, and to talk in terms of economy and of opposition to measures designed to increase the powers of wealth. The Panic of 1873 destroyed some of the effectiveness of these units of the Democratic organization.

Unemployment shattered much of labor's strength. A series of strikes started with a walkout of Pennsylvania coal miners in that year. The climax came in the severe railroad strikes of 1877. The trainmen, together with coal miners along the route of the Baltimore and Ohio, organized work stoppages in Pennsylvania, Ohio, Indiana and Illinois. Disorder mounted and the militia was called out. The local guard could not handle the increasing violence and at length Federal troops had to be summoned. The courts likewise intervened, and strikers were on occasion held in contempt of court.

Labor was indeed in difficulties. No effective organization had developed either by craft or in the form of a more general union like the Knights of Labor. The national political effort had to be abandoned as a separate venture. Those who were politically minded united with others who were discontented and formed a national Greenback party as the election of 1876 approached. The power of labor was not yet effectively mobilized, and the end of this era found organized labor in a position of weakness and disadvantage. Not until labor could achieve more efficient collective bargaining would its position be otherwise.

But the vigor of the disaffected farmers was stimulated and contributed to the power of the Democrats. The courts had begun whittling away at the newly devised state power to regulate railroads, notably in Illinois, and thereby hurried a reorganization among the Grangers. The founding group which had kept the management largely in Washington was retiring from the scene, and new and more vigorous men came into the leadership. They undertook a high-power organizing campaign.

Literally thousands of Granges began to spring up. The state federations took on new importance. Also, the farmers began a fresh effort to mobilize their political strength. Political meetings, outside the framework of the Grange, began to multiply. The Fourth of July, 1873, by common consent seemed to be set aside as a mobilization day. It became known as the Farmers' Fourth of July. At various patriotic meetings there was an impassioned reading of the Farmers' Declaration of Independence. This document, in language resembling the pronouncement of 1776, inveighed particularly against the railroads and the tyranny of monopoly. It demanded Congressional remedies and "purity, honesty and frugality" in government. Finally, its authors declared themselves independent of former party loyalties and announced they would vote only for avowed friends of the farmer. Their tactics can be illustrated by their action in Illinois where they organized a party called the "Reformers," and in 1873 carried 53 of the 66 counties.

Legislative effects of this political activity of the farmers increased in number. After a defeat in the courts of Illinois, the legislature then tried a second act seeking to regulate railroad

rates designed to meet the courts' objections. In 1874 Iowa and
Wisconsin passed acts by which the legislatures set the maximum
rates. Thus Illinois, Minnesota, Iowa and Wisconsin, together
with Kansas, became known as the Granger states. The railroads
fought back. They not only attacked the legislation in the courts,
but they made campaign contributions to the major parties. They
maintained expensive lobbies in the state capitals. They gave the
legislators railroad passes, and charges of bribery and intimida-
tion were rife. Their high-geared lawyers were oftentimes more
than a match for the farmers' attorneys in hearings before the
state railroad commissioners. But the right of states to regulate
public carriers was stoutly maintained up through the courts, and
in 1877 the Supreme Court upheld the power in the Granger cases,
notably Munn *v.* Illinois.

There were other political efforts, closely associated with
farmers' organizations in the popular mind, in which nonagricultural leadership was significant. The Greenback party which was
to run Presidential candidates in 1876 and thereafter, though it
had some farmer elements in it, was led by men of other interests,
like some of the Granges themselves. Certain businessmen and
others believed that there was not enough currency available for
the nation's growing business, and they thought greenbacks the
answer. The great ironmaster, Peter Cooper of New York City,
ran for President in 1876 on a Greenback ticket, and there were a
number of Congressmen, notably "Pig Iron" Kelley of Philadelphia, who supported paper money. Nonagricultural leadership of
some of the Granges, particularly in the Middle West, included
a number of former Copperheads and peace Democrats who
advocated Granger legislation in the postwar years and undertook to fight Eastern economic and political domination as they
had during the war.

Political efforts were by no means all that the farmers and
Grangers sought to exert. These organizations were essentially
nonpolitical, even social, and certainly economic. They had some
ambitions to use business methods to better themselves. In various

communities, Grange groups undertook to build their own co-operative elevators, and to handle their grain. They also under-took cooperative creameries and retail stores, in the latter case following the English Rochdale plan. In Iowa they even under-took to buy patents and set up a factory to manufacture farm im-plements, including a harvester. During 1873, and through 1875, there were a number of failures. By and large, the farmers proved themselves inexpert as businessmen. The Grange, which had been so prosperous and expansive in 1873, by 1875 was fading almost as quickly as it had grown.

But the Panic, and the continuing exposure of scandals which reached into Grant's official family, offset these losses in labor and farmer political effectiveness. The Democrats had an ad-vantage which they pursued assiduously. In the Congressional elections of 1874 they won the House of Representatives. This victory placed Northern Democrats, like Randall of Pennsylvania and Holman of Indiana, in strategic positions from which to work for a Presidential victory in 1876. They therefore made much of reform and economy. They watched appropriations tire-lessly, and were death on subsidies and extravagant appropria-tions. As the Bourbons were depending on this for Southern rehabilitation, the possibilities of disharmony were obvious.

Another cloud on the horizon which Democrats seized as an omen of hope was a silver one rising in the West. Those who sought advantage from cheap money as an aid to the farmer gained new strength shortly after the Panic of 1873. In the early sixties there had been new discoveries of precious metals in the Rockies, silver as well as gold. In 1873 it happened that a par-ticularly rich silver lode had been uncovered in the Comstock region of Nevada, and an increasing hoard of silver had been mined. So copious was it, and so inopportunely timed at a period when England, Germany and the Latin Monetary Union were failing to buy their usual amounts, that the price sagged viciously. The silver interest was in distress.

It was at this time that the idea of helping the miners and

the farmers by one operation began to appeal to politicos from mining and depressed agricultural states, particularly among the Democrats who were still seeking a compelling issue. The plan was to have the Treasury buy and coin large quantities of silver at the ratio current since 1835. Silver dollars should be sixteen times heavier than gold dollars, or three quarters of an ounce. As the market price of that amount was about 90 cents, the "free and unlimited" coinage of silver, if adopted as a Treasury policy, would mean that the silver miners would now be able to get a dollar from the Treasury for 90 cents worth of silver, and be making a profit again. Also, the money supply would be augmented by a mass of cheap dollars which would raise the price of the farmer's wheat and get him out of the hole.

Some Democrats sought to make political capital of the idea that Free Silver would offset the aid given to money dealers, Wall Street wolves, by the Republicans through the Resumption Act of 1875 which had been passed to bring back gold and enforce a degree of contraction. When the Democrats won the Congressional elections of 1874, a Western Congressman, Richard P. Bland of Missouri, became chairman of the Mines and Mining Committee. He proceeded to prepare a bill for Free Silver coinage which passed the House but, fortunately for those tired of inflation, failed in the Senate.

These contrasting developments in the two sections showed that the Democrats were not a united homogeneous party. The Southern wing was conservative, and not averse to government appropriations for improvements or for subsidies. There was a prominent element in the Northern wing which was radical, eager for reform, economical of expenditure and opposed to tight money. This group had many friends among farmers. And it attracted many from the ranks of labor who, in their opposition to their employers, worked against conservative measures and on behalf of cheap money which they believed could raise the wages of labor.

The Republican party too was divided. The wing which had

been in the ascendant during most of the Reconstruction period
was dominated by an oligarchic combination of United States
Senators, Representatives and state bosses. They were exploitive
in their psychology, eager for subsidies, and sympathetic with
the desires of the business tycoons. Some of them had been Civil
War radicals, opponents of Lincoln. Now, in general, they were
friends of Grant whose sympathy for wealth made them friends.
They were not too active in eliminating fraud, and they did much
to make ascendant capitalism stronger than ever. These men
included in their ranks Roscoe Conkling, Zachariah Chandler,
Oliver P. Morton, Simon Cameron, Schuyler Colfax, Ben Butler
and James G. Blaine. Upon occasion Charles Sumner was with
them, but his hatred of Grant, and a certain sense of moral
principle, made his association with them uncertain. These men
found Grant a convenient symbol of the triumph of the conquer-
ing North.

Opposed to these oligarchs was the Liberal wing of the Republican party. They were the men who had sought to defeat Grant
for renomination in 1872 and, failing that, had bolted and organized the short-lived Liberal Republican party. Among these men
were Charles Francis Adams, Carl Schurz, Lyman Trumbull and
some disappointed conservatives who were to be joined by others
who sought to combat the evils which were to be disclosed in
Grant's unfortunate second Administration.

Such Liberals were to continue to strive for civil service reform,
the elimination of graft and for financial policies, particularly a
lower tariff, which would benefit the average man rather than
the new money power. They wished to remove the troops from
the South, and to work for friendly reunion. Such division in
the ranks of the Republican party, together with the popular
distrust which followed in the wake of the Panic, had brought
victory to the Democrats in the Congressional elections of 1874.

This defeat aroused the Grant Republicans to attempt to settle
two legislative problems during the last weeks of their power in
the short session of 1874-1875. They brought the protective tariff

back almost to the high Civil War level, thus abandoning the attempts to lower the duties achieved in 1870 and 1872. They finally passed financial legislation checking the Civil War inflation by an act resuming specie payment. After January 1, 1879, greenbacks would be redeemable in gold, but those who felt that a larger supply of money was needed to take care of the nation's expanding business, and the embattled farmers, were given a concession in the requirement that the greenbacks so redeemed be constantly reissued. Thus more than $300,000,000 in paper was to be kept as a constant addition to the gold coinage. Tariff reformers and farm and labor interests had further witness that the ruling Republicans were agents of big business.

Southern political developments were further weakening Republican control in the reconstructed states. Texas and Alabama were carried by the Democrats in 1873 and 1874. Such "reconquests" had been achieved in most of the states in which the whites were in the majority. Only Arkansas, in this class, had not been regained by the Democrats. Success was yet to be won in all the states in which the Negroes were in the majority, save Alabama. Florida, Louisiana, Mississippi and South Carolina were still in the hands of the Republicans.

Arkansas was next to enter the Democratic ranks. This end was gained, however, only after a slight skirmish of civil war. Two rival Radicals took the gubernatorial election of 1872 to court. A Radical judge sought to oust the occupant of the Capitol by a shady decision. The candidate so favored ejected the incumbent by force, and fortified himself in the palladium to resist siege by the ousted statesman and his cohorts. President Grant settled the matter by sending troops to clear out the newcomer, and restore the original Governor. But this was the Radicals' last triumph. In the election of 1874 the Democrats got back the state.

In Mississippi, the last state to be reclaimed prior to 1876, the redeemers systematically organized the white voters into rifle clubs which acquired arms and drilled very ostentatiously. Their presence at the polls in the election of 1875 was decisive. As Grant was now tired of sending troops, the Radical Governor, even though he was Ben Butler's son-in-law, decided to resign rather than face impeachment. The state was, at last, in Democratic hands.

The misfortunes of the Republican party were further multiplied by new exposures in Grant's second term. This Administration was plagued by a series of unsavory revelations which exposed examples of distressing moral laxity and criminal carelessness in all branches of government. The Congress had shown a moral obtuseness that was disconcerting. In December 1872, the Crédit Mobilier scheme had been exposed by an investigating committee which revealed that Congressmen were willing recipients of the bounty of this doubtful venture. Also, the solons had increased their salaries and voted themselves generous back pay which meant each one would go home with a $5,000 gift, the Salary Grab.

There were further revelations of malfeasance in the Treasury, War and Navy departments, and in the Revenue Service. The Secretary of the Treasury had failed to interrupt the Sanborn contract racket. Under the law, if delinquent accounts owing the Treasury were collected by private individuals, the collector would receive half of the proceeds. The Secretary allowed Sanborn to collect current accounts which were perfectly good, and thus reap a handsome reward. The Navy Department seemed to be maintaining a fleet of outmoded warships for the benefit of contractors who were constantly paid for expensive repairs. Dealers of all sorts were reaping profits from supplying it, and the President's own brother was enriched as a "convenient" broker.

The Secretary of War was mixed up in an unsavory mess. A trader who was making enormous profits in the Indian service was permitted to keep his post by paying a large share of the profits to others, including a member of Secretary Belknap's family. For this Belknap was impeached. He immediately resigned, and Grant accepted his resignation with praise of his service. This enabled the Secretary to beat the impeachment for he was acquitted by the Senate, largely on the ground that as he was no longer in office, they had no jurisdiction.

Most appalling was fraud in the Internal Revenue Service. This was attacked by Benjamin Bristow, Secretary of the Treasury, who learned that a widespread system had been organized by distillers and revenue officials whereby false measurements were used in levying the tax on whiskey. This Whiskey Ring was deeply entrenched and, at first, Bristow was frustrated by spies in his own department who gave the Ring knowledge of his plans. However, he finally secured indictments and brought important political appointees to trial. In the course of his investigations, Bristow found that President Grant's private secretary, Babcock, was involved, and thereafter the White House did much to hinder the conviction of the Ring. General Babcock got off, but a number were convicted. Grant became convinced that Bristow was conducting this campaign against corruption to promote his bid for the Presidency. The President eventually forced his resignation. Bristow's valiant role won him a martyr's crown, and as 1876 approached it made him the candidate of the reform wing of the Republicans.

The lax moral sense of the times was to provide fuel to the political fires of 1876. The fact that the Republicans had been in control for a decade, and had grown arrogant and callous, was bound to raise intense opposition. The exposure of graft and corruption, and Grant's obvious inability to enforce honest administration, had encouraged some of those who had become active in the Liberal Republican move in 1872 to join with certain of the Regulars to attempt to "save" the party in 1876. They would nominate a reformer less subservient to business, more responsive to the needs of the average man, more honest, and truly interested in civil service reform. There was particular support among this group for the Secretary of the Treasury, Benjamin H. Bristow.

The Old Guard mustered several candidates. Senators Conkling and Morton, however, were overshadowed by James G. Blaine, the brilliant orator. Though besmirched by some railroad deals, he endeavored to restore the waning strength of the Republicans by arousing deep-seated prejudices. He charged that the Rebels were back in power in the South, and that they were depriving the Negro not only of the vote and of his civil rights but even of his freedom. Had the Union dead offered up their lives in vain, were their slayers to be permitted to return to power unpunished? Thus the "bloody shirt" was brought out and waved for political purposes.

At the Republican convention of 1876 Blaine and Bristow fought each other to a deadlock which was broken by the nomination of Ohio's reform Governor, Rutherford B. Hayes, on a platform denouncing corruption and promising clean government and a true reunion of North and South. The Democrats nominated the reform Governor of New York, Samuel J. Tilden, who had cleaned up Tammany in New York City, and Thomas A. Hendricks, an Indiana advocate of the Greenback. Their platform went to town on the scandals of the Grant regime. The Republicans were soon hard pressed. Tilden's nomination made it unlikely that they could carry his state, and their fortunes were very uncertain in the South, now so nearly redeemed. The result was bound to be close but no one foresaw how close. On election evening the returns generally favored the Democrats and most people with access to incoming news found that, as the night waned, Tilden had carried New York, New Jersey, Connecticut and Indiana, and certainly had 184 votes. As only 185 were needed, Tilden's victory might be conceded. But significantly *The New York Times* did not concede it, and an editor went from their offices to wake up the Republican Chairman, Zachariah Chandler, who had gone to bed discouraged. Three of the reconstructed states, Florida, Louisiana and South Carolina were still governed by that party. If their Republican vote counters would declare the right electors chosen, Hayes would have 185 and be President by one vote. The sleepy Chandler was persuaded to telegraph these canvassers to hold their states. In the morning he announced "Hayes has 185 votes and is elected."

The situations in these crucial areas made the problem of "holding" them not too difficult. In all three, Radical regimes were kept in power by the Army. And despite recent Democratic gains, the canvassers in each of these states, armed with full and final authority to count, accept or reject votes, and to declare the result, were still Republicans. They were generally men of desperate fortunes, facing political oblivion.

In the course of the next few weeks, in November 1876, various Democratic and Republican delegations went into these states and there was a vigorous effort to pressure the canvassing boards. It was alleged that some of them were for sale. Finally, by what seems to have been barefaced accommodation in which the will of the voters received scant heed, Republican electors were declared chosen at the same time that the election of Democratic state tickets was certified. The Radicals decided to pin their hopes of survival on Federal patronage, upon the salaries and perquisites of Federal jobs. By this drastic prestidigitation and manipulation of votes, the Republican canvassers believed they had insured Hayes' election. However, accident seemed to have destroyed their work. The Democrats claimed they had picked up the vote they needed to elect Tilden. In Oregon the Republicans had carelessly nominated a postmaster to be one of their electors, contrary to the express prohibition against Federal officeholders serving in this capacity laid down in the United States Constitution. Therefore this postmaster had been elected by the voters, but the canvassing authority, Democratic in this instance, disqualified him because of his Federal office and declared a Democrat elected.

Thus the regular state certifying officials from South Carolina, Florida and Louisiana sent Republican certificates to be counted by Congress, while a like authority sent a certificate including the needed Democratic vote from Oregon.* Certificates were received from these four states from contesting authorities, recording contrary results. Who would decide which were the legal certificates? There was no guide in the Constitution or the laws.

To complicate the situation, Congress was divided, the House Democratic and the Senate Republican. Was it going to be possible to make any decision, and if not what would be the consequences on March 4, 1877? Would there be anarchy? Moreover, if either man by some means was counted in, would the opposing party accept the result? Grant had command of the Army and the Republicans controlled the Senate. If these two forces combined to seat Hayes, might not the "Rebels" take arms and march on Washington? Democratic governors in numerous states were commanders of a large militia, well armed. Would an army be marshalled to seat Tilden?

Never had such a situation threatened the stability of the Republic. The nation was still vividly conscious of the war. Many veterans were available, equipped with war experience and not unused to weapons and battle. How could a peaceful constitutional way be worked out? Could any? Statesmanship was required in an era of rabid partisanship and crass corruption.

The Republican organization demanded that the matter be left in the hands of the presiding officer of the Senate, who under the Constitution was to receive and, before a joint session of Congress, present the electoral votes for tallying. He should decide which returns were legitimate. But he, like the Senate, was Republican, Senator Thomas W. Ferry of Michigan. The Democrats demanded that either a majority of the joint session, which was Democratic, should decide, or that "no election" be declared and the choice thrown into this same House as required by the Constitution. Naturally neither of these proposals was mutually acceptable. Some other way must be found.

* The two regularly qualified Republican electors designated a third to take the place of the one disqualified; these three cast the vote of Oregon for Hayes and sent in a certificate to contest that of the regular Democratic canvassing agency reporting the vote as two for Hayes and one for Tilden.

An answer was suggested by the divided state of the two major parties, particularly the Democrats. In the Southern states the leaders in revitalizing several of them, though ostensibly Democrats, had been Whigs before the war. As such they had been interested in internal-improvement appropriations. Now the South was in great need of such appropriations, but the Northern Democrats were economy minded and unwilling to vote such sums. Here was a possible line of cleavage between Southern and Northern Democrats, particularly as Tilden was of the economy group. The Republican James A. Garfield of Ohio, formerly a Whig, together with Murat Halstead, prominent Ohio newspaper editor, Henry V. Boynton, William H. Smith, and others connected with the Western Associated Press began working on an idea. Could not the old Whig element among the Southern Democrats be brought to support Hayes, also an old Whig, rather than Tilden, on the understanding that troops sustaining "Republican" Governors in the South be removed and appropriations and patronage be allotted to the South in generous measure?

Another element was to be found in the situation. Railroad entrepreneurs were interested in a third Pacific road, one to California via the southern route. During the twenty years from 1852 to 1872 a series of incorporation acts and financial operations had produced a bill somewhat like the Union Pacific and Northern Pacific legislation for a road finally named the Texas and Pacific to run from Marshall, Texas, to San Diego, California via El Paso. The land grant provided proved too small to ensure the construction of the road. Its two principal promoters, Thomas A. Scott of the Pennsylvania Railroad, and General Grenville M. Dodge, recently of the Union Pacific, saw a large Federal subsidy as their only hope. Would the South get behind such a move? If Southern Senators and Representatives would support it, could not an understanding be reached that these Southern Representatives join in keeping the Republicans in power by helping to seat Hayes, and by organizing the next House? If this body,

Democratic on paper, would vote for a Republican Speaker, he could appoint committees sympathetic to appropriations, and the Texas and Pacific would get its subsidy.

In an atmosphere like this, a certain proportion of the Southern Senators and Representatives, many of them complacent to the extravagances of Grantism, came to the conclusion that Hayes and the Republicans would probably do more for their section as beneficiaries of Southern support than would Tilden and his reforming, economy-minded associates. In a Tilden Administration they would be a minority group entitled to no particular concessions, a sort of step-child who was supposed to stand for economy and reform. In a Hayes Administration they would hold a whip hand, for they would be the allies that had made its existence possible. There were many talks and some vague understandings but, as is often the case in politics, no definite agreement was set down in a form which could later be cited or proved.

The procedure finally devised to solve the problem of who was to determine the validity of the returns from the Electoral College was to appoint an Electoral Commission which would consist of three Democrats and two Republicans from the House, three Republicans and two Democrats from the Senate, and two Republicans and two Democrats from the Supreme Court. The four Supreme Court Justices would choose a fifth from the Court to complete the membership of fifteen. On the court was one justice, David Davis, who was an independent. He had been active in the Liberal Republican movement and had support from farm and labor groups; it was expected that he would be chosen by his colleagues. All questions of disputed returns were to be submitted to this commission.

The Republicans in Congress were divided about this proposal, but the Democrats were almost unanimous in its support. Some thought that Davis, the independent Justice, would see it their way; others, particularly in the South, thought of the Commission as a means of seating Hayes and securing what the South wanted.

The hopes of the latter may well have prevailed because after the bill had passed the Senate, but before it was acted upon by the House, Judge Davis had been elected a United States Senator by Democratic votes in the Illinois legislature, and had declared himself ineligible for membership on the Commission. This meant that the Justices must choose a Republican as the fifteenth member; there was no other Democrat on the Court. Despite this fact the Democratic House passed the bill. A majority of the House Republicans voted against it, including some of Hayes' closest friends although a majority of the Senate Republicans had supported it before Davis left the picture.

On February 1 the count began. When Florida was reached, two returns were announced and duly submitted to the Commission. Counsel then argued for a week. The question at issue was whether the Commission would go behind the returns and accept evidence of fraud. Finally the Commission decided 8-7, 8 Republicans to 7 Democrats, that they would not. The question was merely which certificate was the one submitted by the duly constituted authorities. They decided 8-7 that the Republican votes were the valid ones. This decision was an indication of what the vote would be in the case of Louisiana. But how about Oregon? The return giving the Democrats the needed vote was sent by the duly constituted authority. If this had not been questioned in the other two states, how could it be questioned in this? Here the commission voted 8-7 that it could not be bound by the logic of the former reasoning. There was no investigation or taking of testimony necessary to discover that the Oregon voters had wanted to choose three Republican electors. The Commission voted 8-7 that a technicality could not be permitted to thwart their will.

When the decisions of the Electoral Commission became manifest the crucial question then was: would the Democrats organize and maintain a filibuster which would prevent finishing the count before the session expired on March 4, and leave the nation without an executive? The Southern Democrats, and Tilden himself, rejected this idea and the Democratic speaker, Samuel J. Randall of Pennsylvania, led the House, after a certain amount of filibustering, to accept the result. Finally, on March 1, the presiding officer of the Senate announced the election of Hayes. Without further ado he was peaceably installed.

Hayes immediately appointed a Southern Democrat as Postmaster General. Democratic state administrations were recognized as duly elected in Florida, Louisiana and South Carolina, although such recognition was a tacit admission that Democratic electors had likewise been chosen, and that Hayes was in the White House because of a political arrangement condoning fraud rather than by right of election. Generous allotments of patronage were made to the Southern Redeemers and the Federal troops were removed. Later on, whatever implied understanding there may have been to the contrary, none of the Democrats voted for Garfield for Speaker, and their party organized the House.

Who was really elected will never really be known. The fraud led many to believe that Tilden was counted out. On the other hand it can be argued that if the Negroes had been free to vote they might well have remained loyal to the party of their savior, Lincoln. Tilden himself, had he pursued a different course, might have been able to alter the result. But he was neither strong nor decisive in this crisis. He was never too well, and he was essentially an office man and lawyer. He issued no call to arms, no stirring manifestos. Rather, he sat at home writing briefs defining his rights and his position. His own preference would have been to have no legislation, to have the House withdraw from the joint session when alleged fraudulent returns were accepted. If no further joint sessions had then been held there could have been no election by the electors. In that event the Democratic House would have chosen the President, and the Republican Senate the Vice-President. However, Tilden assented to the Electoral Commission and urged his supporters to accept the result. He probably could have bought Louisiana's returning board, but this he would not hear of. Instead of calling his supporters to arms, he quietly accepted the verdict.

What had really happened had been a division of power, a compromise arrangement. Rutherford B. Hayes, Republican, was to be President. The Senate was so narrowly divided as to be practically nonpartisan. The House was to be Democratic with the Southern Democrats enjoying a good share of committee places allotted to them by Speaker Samuel J. Randall, re-elected by their votes. The Grant wing of the Republican party was not represented in the new Administration where William M. Evarts, John Sherman, Carl Schurz, and David M. Key, the Southern Democratic Postmaster General, were to waste little sympathy or patronage on them. The Radicals and the Negroes had been eliminated from party prominence. The South was in the hands of the Redeemers, and Hayes recognized the fact. The conclusion can hardly be avoided that the Southern Democrats preferred Hayes to Tilden, and for this preference they received a reward.

The Democrats had regained the South which for many years thereafter was to be solid for them. In the nation at large, Republican politicians were still nominally in control but they were going into an eclipse. Power was passing into the hands of men of enterprise outside of politics. Public attention was absorbed in the nation's growth and, for a season, failed to show much serious concern over new limitations on their powers of self-government.

For more than twenty years the American nation had been in the throes of changing its political leadership. In the mid-forties, the Democratic party, dominated by its Southern leaders, had been in control. This party wanted government to be strong and rambunctious in foreign affairs, truculent toward European powers. But at home it prescribed a policy of inaction, of hands off. Little was to be undertaken and a minimum spent. Such a government, however, was not in step with the times. The great continent and the restless mobile population produced a combination of forces which dictated action, and any government which refused to respond was doomed. The Democratic party under

Southern domination felt itself firmly enough established to defy the spirit of the times. The result was disastrous.

The individuals and groups who were frustrated by this negative policy only needed time to generate force sufficient to produce a new political alignment, strong enough to overthrow the party so long in power. The struggle for control was long and bitter, and in the end the means employed were so inflammatory as to cause a social war costing over a million lives and six billions of money. Even this great expenditure of life and treasure did not settle anything permanently. The hold of the Republican party was soon shaken and at the end of this period of conflict, power was shared in an uncertain compromise which left the issue of who was to control still undetermined. Never since has a new power been achieved with greater strength than that which had been in the ascendant from the 1830's to the 1850's. Later approximations of such power, 1897-1913 and 1933-1953, were no more lasting, and no such power exists today. But wherever the government of the United States functions or politics dominates there survive many evidences of the great mid-nineteenth-century contest for the stakes of power. The political strength of the South in Congress and in party convention, the social status of the Negro, the rivalry of sections, the conflicting claims of free enterprise and government subsidy or control, are never long absent from the consciousness of those devoted to operating that government which a century ago so many fought so valiantly to maintain.

Bibliographical Note

THE LITERATURE on this period of American History is extraordinarily various and new books are constantly appearing. There is something for everybody's taste; any selection such as this must be highly arbitrary. But it is certain that anyone who explores this selection will find many more suggestions for general reading in the period or in areas that specially interest him.

The stuff of which this history is made ranges from on-the-spot letters, diaries, and reports in the handwriting of observers to books published in today's centennial period, of which there have already appeared so vast a number. Many of the original manuscript sources are housed in the Library of Congress and in state historical societies, public libraries, museums, and university collections. The papers of Senators, Cabinet officers, diplomats, and men active in state politics, together with those of certain of the Presidents of the United States and a few Congressmen reveal much of what actually happened in politics. The papers of Abraham Lincoln and James K. Polk at the Library of Congress; James Buchanan at the Historical Society of Pennsylvania; William H. Seward and Thurlow Weed at the University of Rochester; Salmon P. Chase at the Library of Congress and the Historical Society of Pennsylvania; Edwin M. Stanton and Gideon Welles at the Library of Congress; Charles Sumner at

Harvard University; Stephen A. Douglas at the University of Chicago; Robert E. Lee at the Confederate Museum and Duke University; and George B. McClellan at the Library of Congress are only a few examples of such sources.

A great deal has survived in the correspondence of businessmen and in the records of firms and partnerships. The culture of the times is illustrated by the letters, diaries, and commonplace books of countless men and women who were literary and artistic, and those of many more of no fame. Such manuscripts as are in the nature of public records are to be found in the National Archives and the various state archives; see *Guide to the Archives of the United States,* 1961, Philip L. Hamer, ed. The war of 1861–1865 itself created a vast manuscript record, the bulk of which is found in the National Archives, but the thirty-four states had militia and literally hundreds of thousands of soldiers wrote countless letters now not only scattered among public depositories but often still cherished by descendants and collectors. Manuscripts are the most intimate and valuable sources, but they are not controlled and they must be searched for. The Library of Congress is endeavoring to build up a guide, "The National Union Catalogue of Manuscript Collections," but it is not yet complete.

The contemporary press likewise provides great quantities of historical data. From metropolitan dailies and country weeklies there exist innumerable files, scattered almost as widely as manuscripts. Journals such as the New York *Herald, Times,* and *Tribune;* the Springfield *Republican;* the Charleston *Mercury;* the New Orleans *Picayune;* the *Missouri Democrat;* and the *Chicago Tribune* are among those newspapers of which reasonably complete files have been preserved. The location of many of these files is listed in Winifred Gregory, *American Newspapers, 1821–1936,* 1937. Many now have been microfilmed and the films made available for purchase. There is an incomplete listing in G. A. Schwegmann, *Newspapers on Microfilm, a Union Check List,* 3d edition 1957, supplement 1959.

The operations of our democratic federal system have been recorded in vast numbers of federal and state documents. For the record of this epoch the great compilations are *The Congressional Globe* to 1873, at which point *The Congressional Record* began. Much of great historical importance is found in the eight series of Congressional Documents: *Senate Journals, Senate Executive Documents, Senate Miscellaneous Documents*, and *Senate Reports*, and the similar series published for the House. These are best collated in B. P. Poore, ed., *Descriptive Catalogue of the Government Publications of the United States, 1774–1881*, 1885. Another great source is *War of the Rebellion: a Compilation of the Official Records of the Union and Confederate Armies*, 130 volumes, 1880–1901 and its companion series for the navies. The Confederacy published no Congressional record but the journals of its Congress were printed by the U.S. Congress, "Journal of the Congress of the Confederate States of America, 1861–1865," *Sen. Document 234, 58 Cong. 2 Sess.*, 6 vols., 1904–1905; a compilation from Richmond newspapers of the proceedings of the sessions of the regular Congress is contained in *The Southern Historical Society Papers*, XLIV–LII, 1923–1959. Further details are in *Compilation of the Messages and Papers of the Confederacy*, 1905, and *Compilation of the Messages and Papers of the Presidents [of the United States]*, 1907, J. D. Richardson, ed.

A great microfilm compilation of state documents has been made by the Library of Congress and the University of North Carolina. These films are listed in *A Guide to the Microfilm Collection of Early State Records*, begun in 1950; the films may be purchased from the Photoduplication Division of the Library of Congress. Territorial documentation is found most conveniently in C. E. Carter, ed., *The Territorial Papers of the United States*, begun in 1934.

There are two multivolume treatments designed to cover the major portion of the time span of this book. James Ford Rhodes set a pattern of great influence in the first seven volumes of his *A History of the United States from the Compromise of 1850,*

1893–1906, but most of this was written in the 1880's and 90's. Allan Nevins is writing a more comprehensive work covering the same period, a work of great scope and scholarship to appear in ten volumes. Since 1947 *The Ordeal of the Union* (2 vols.), *The Emergence of Lincoln* (2 vols.), and *The War for the Union* (2 vols.), have brought the story down to 1863.

Other books about the period to 1865 are John Bach McMaster, *A History of the People of the United States,* 1883–1913, drawn largely from newspaper sources; *A History of the People of the United States During Lincoln's Administration,* 1927; and Edward Channing, *History of the United States,* Vol. VI, *The War for Southern Independence,* 1925. These are followed by Ellis Paxson Oberholtzer, *A History of the United States Since the Civil War;* the first three volumes, 1917–1926, continue the style of McMaster. A convenient single-volume work is James G. Randall, *The Civil War and Reconstruction,* 1937. The social history of the period is covered in Arthur C. Cole, *Irrepressible Conflict,* 1934, and Allan Nevins, *Emergence of Modern America,* 1927, volumes in *The History of American Life* series. An overall survey of how generations of historians have interpreted the war is Thomas J. Pressly, *Americans Interpret Their Civil War,* 1954.

The Mexican War era is covered most comprehensively by Justin H. Smith, *War with Mexico,* 1919. More popular accounts are Alfred Hoyt Bill, *Rehearsal for Conflict,* 1947; Robert S. Henry, *Story of the Mexican War,* 1950; and Nathaniel W. Stephenson, *Texas and the Mexican War,* 1921. A significant phase of the conflict is described in Norman A. Graebner, *Empire on the Pacific,* 1955.

The political ferment of the 1850's in its various phases can be better understood by exploring two volumes of the distinguished *History of the South*—Charles S. Sydnor, *The Development of Southern Sectionalism, 1819–1848,* 1948, and Avery Craven, *Growth of Southern Nationalism, 1848–1861,* 1953—as well as Gilbert H. Barnes, *Anti-Slavery Impulse,* 1933 (dealing with Middle Western enthusiasm); Ray A. Billington, *Protestant*

Crusade, 1800–1860, 1938; Jesse T. Carpenter, *The South as a Self-Conscious Minority,* 1930; David L. Cohn, *Life and Times of King Cotton,* 1956; and Dwight L. Dumond, *Anti-Slavery Origins of the Civil War,* 1939.

The sectionalism which contributed so much to the causes of strife is described in James T. Adams, *New England in the Republic,* 1926; D. G. Brinton Thompson, *Gateway to a Nation: The Middle Atlantic States,* 1956; Clement A. Eaton, *A History of the Old South,* 1949; John Hope Franklin, *The Militant South, 1800–1861,* 1956; William B. Hesseltine, *History of the South,* 1936; Francis B. Simkins, *The South, Old and New,* 1947; H. C. Hubbart, *Old Middle West,* 1936; Ray A. Billington, *Westward Expansion,* 2d edition, 1960; Thomas D. Clark, *Frontier America,* 1959; Frederick J. Turner, *Frontier in American History,* 1950, and *Significance of Sections in American History,* 1950; Walter P. Webb, *The Great Plains,* 1931.

The nature of the divergent cultures can be seen in Van Wyck Brooks, *Flowering of New England,* 1936; William J. Cash, *Mind of the South,* 1941; Merle Curti, *Growth of American Thought,* 1943; Ralph Gabriel, *Course of American Democratic Thought: an Intellectual History since 1815,* 2d edition, 1956; Bliss Perry, *American Spirit in Literature,* 1918; Oscar Handlin, *The Uprooted,* 1951; Marcus Hansen, *The Atlantic Migration,* 1940; Frank L. Owsley, *Plain Folks of the Old South,* 1949.

Significant economic interests in the ante-bellum era are described in Ulrich B. Phillips, *Life and Labor in the Old South,* 1929; John Hope Franklin, *From Slavery to Freedom: A History of the American Negro,* 1950; Kenneth M. Stampp, *The Peculiar Institution: Slavery in the Ante-Bellum South,* 1956; Paul W. Gates, *Fifty Million Acres, Conflicts over Kansas Land Policies, 1854–1890,* 1954; Philip Foner, *Business and Slavery,* 1941; Robert E. Riegel, *Story of Western Railroads,* 1926; Samuel E. Morison, *Maritime History of Massachusetts, 1783–1860,* 1921; George Van Vleck, *Panic of 1857,* 1943.

The approach of the crisis can be traced in James T. Adams, *American Tragedy,* 1934; Avery Craven, *Coming of the Civil*

War, 2d edition, 1957; Ollinger Crenshaw, *Slave States in the Presidential Election of 1860*, 1945; Dwight L. Dumond, *Secession Movement, 1860–61*, 1931; J. C. Furnas, *The Road to Harper's Ferry*, 1959; Samuel A. Johnson, *The Battle Cry of Freedom*, 1954; James C. Malin, *John Brown and the Legend of Fifty-Six*, 1942, and *The Nebraska Question, 1852–1854*, 1953; Roy F. Nichols, *Disruption of American Democracy*, 1948; David M. Potter, *Lincoln and his Party in the Secession Crisis*, 1942; P. Orman Ray, *Repeal of the Missouri Compromise*, 1909; Kenneth M. Stampp, *And the War Came: The North and the Secession Crises*, 1950.

Various phases of war conditions in the North are considered in Ephraim D. Adams, *Great Britain and the American Civil War*, 1925; J. Cutler Andrews, *The North Reports the Civil War*, 1955; James P. Baxter, *Introduction of Ironclad Warship*, 1933; Henry S. Commager, *The Blue and the Gray: The Story of the Civil War as Told by Participants*, 1950; Emerson D. Fite, *Social and Industrial Conditions in the North during the Civil War*, 1911; Wood Gray, *Hidden Civil War: the Story of the Copperheads*, 1942; Burton J. Hendrick, *Lincoln's War Cabinet*, 1946; William B. Hesseltine, *Lincoln and the War Governors*, 1948; Edward C. Kirkland, *Peace Makers of 1864*, 1927; Frank L. Klement, *The Copperheads in the Middle West*, 1960; Margaret Leech, *Reveille in Washington*, 1941; James G. Randall, *Constitutional Problems under Lincoln*, 2d edition, 1951; Fred A. Shannon, *Organization and Administration of the Union Army*, 1928; Richard S. West, Jr., *Mr. Lincoln's Navy*, 1957; Bell I. Wiley, *The Life of Billy Yank*, 1952; T. Harry Williams, *Lincoln and the Radicals*, 1941.

The way of the Confederacy is traced in E. Merton Coulter, *A History of the South: The Confederate States of America*, 1950; Clifford Dowdey, *Experiment in Rebellion*, 1946; Clement A. Eaton, *A History of the Southern Confederacy*, 1954; Burton J. Hendrick, *Statesmen of the Lost Cause*, 1939; Frank L. Owsley, *King Cotton Diplomacy*, 1931; Rembert W. Patrick, *Jefferson Davis and His Cabinet*, 1944; J. C. Schwab, *Confederate States of America,* 1901 (financial history); N. W. Stephenson, *Day of the Confederacy,* 1919; Richard C. Todd, *Confederate Finance,* 1957; Bell I. Wiley, *Life of Johnny Reb,* 1943.

The military phases of the war period are best followed from the Union side in Bruce Catton, *Mr. Lincoln's Army,* 1951, *Glory Road,* 1952, *A Stillness at Appomattox,* 1953, and *This Hallowed Ground,* 1956; in Kenneth P. Williams' five-volume *Lincoln Finds a General,* 1949–1959; and in T. Harry Williams, *Lincoln and His Generals,* 1952. Fletcher Pratt, *Ordeal by Fire: An Informal History of the Civil War,* 1948, is a well-written, interesting short history of the conflict. The Confederate story is in Alfred Hoyt Bill, *The Beleaguered City: Richmond 1861–1865,* 1954; Clifford Dowdey, *The Land They Fought For,* 1955; and Frank E. Vandiver, *Rebel Brass: The Confederate Command System,* 1956.

Biography, history's most fascinating revelation, has much to offer on this period. The three ante-bellum statesmen are portrayed by Charles M. Wiltse in his three-volume *John C. Calhoun,* 1944–1951; Glyndon G. Van Deusen, *Henry Clay,* 1937; and Claude M. Fuess, *Daniel Webster,* 1930. The Presidents are made flesh by Eugene I. McCormac, *James K. Polk,* 1922, and by Charles Grier Sellers' longer treatment of the same executive, of which the first volume appeared in 1957; by Holman Hamilton, *Zachary Taylor: Soldier in the White House;* by Robert J. Rayback, *Millard Fillmore,* 1959; by Roy F. Nichols, *Franklin Pierce,* 2d edition, 1958; and by Philip S. Klein, *James Buchanan,* shortly to be published.

The Lincoln bookshelf is very long; we can only be selective and alphabetical, listing Richard N. Current, *The Lincoln Nobody Knows,* 1958; David Donald, *Lincoln Reconsidered,* 1956; J. G. Randall, *Lincoln the President* (four volumes, the last completed by Richard N. Current), 1945–1955; Carl Sandburg, *Abraham Lincoln* (six volumes), 1926–1939; N. W. Stephenson, *Lincoln,* 1922; Benjamin P. Thomas, *Abraham Lincoln,* 1952.

Statesmen, publicists, and politicians are portrayed in Gerald

M. Capers, *Stephen A. Douglas,* 1959; George Fort Milton, *Eve of Conflict: Stephen A. Douglas,* 1934; Glyndon G. Van Deusen, *Horace Greeley,* 1953; Henry S. Commager, *Theodore Parker,* 1936; Stewart Mitchell, *Horatio Seymour,* 1938; David Donald, *Charles Sumner and the Coming of the Civil War,* 1960; Glyndon G. Van Deusen, *Thurlow Weed,* 1947; Richard S. West, *Gideon Welles,* 1943.

The Confederate statesmen deserve more attention than has been accorded them. Some important works are William E. Dodd, *Jefferson Davis,* 1907; H. J. Eckenrode, *Jefferson Davis,* 1923; Hudson Strode, *Jefferson Davis,* two volumes published (1955, 1959), one to come; Laura A. White, *Robert Barnwell Rhett,* 1931; Robert D. Meade, *Judah P. Benjamin,* 1943; Rudolph Von Abele, *Alexander H. Stephens,* 1946.

The generals have their volumes: Lloyd Lewis, *Captain Sam Grant,* 1950; Bruce Catton, *Grant Moves South,* 1960; Fred H. Harrington, *Fighting Politician, N. P. Banks,* 1948; Allan Nevins, *Frémont,* 1928, 1955; Lloyd Lewis, *Sherman, Fighting Prophet,* 1932; Warren W. Hassler, Jr., *General George B. McClellan,* 1957; Freeman Cleaves, *Meade of Gettysburg,* 1960; Russell F. Weigley, *Quartermaster of the Union Army, Montgomery C. Meigs,* 1959; Charles W. Elliott, *Winfield Scott,* 1937; Richard O'Connor, *Sheridan the Inevitable,* 1953; W. A. Swanberg, *Sickles the Incredible,* 1956. On the Confederate front, Douglas S. Freeman, *Robert E. Lee,* 1934–1935, and *Lee's Lieutenants,* 1942–1944; T. Harry Williams, *P. G. T. Beauregard,* 1955; William W. Hassler, Jr., *A. P. Hill,* 1957; Lenoir Chambers, *Stonewall Jackson,* 1959; Frank E. Vandiver, *Mighty Stonewall,* 1957; Gilbert E. Govan and James W. Livingood, *A Different Valor, General Joseph E. Johnston,* 1956.

Reconstruction is treated at length in Rhodes and in Oberholtzer. William A. Dunning, in his *Reconstruction, Political and Economic,* 1907, wrote the first comprehensive scholarly survey based upon modern research. Nevins, *Emergence of Modern America,* 1927, deals with the social phases. Coulter's volume in *A History of the South, The South During Re-*

construction, 1865–1877, 1947, elaborates the accepted story. Hodding Carter, *The Angry Scar, The Story of Reconstruction,* 1959, is the latest general history. C. Vann Woodward in his *Reunion and Reaction,* 1951, and *Origins of the New South,* 1951, sheds new light upon the politics of the era, particularly the election of 1876. Certain journal articles make significant reinterpretations, among them Howard K. Beale, "On Rewriting Reconstruction History," *American Historical Review,* XLV (July 1940), 807–28; Francis B. Simkins, "New Viewpoints on Southern Reconstruction," *Journal of Southern History,* V (February 1939), 49–61; T. Harry Williams, "An Analysis of Some Reconstruction Attitudes," *ibid.,* XII (November 1946), 469–86; and Bernard A. Weisberger, "The Dark and Bloody Ground of Reconstruction Historiography," *ibid.,* XXV (November 1959), 427–47.

Important phases of the reconstruction process are described in George R. Bently, *A History of the Freedmen's Bureau,* 1955; Mary R. Dearing, *Veterans in Politics: The Story of the G.A.R.,* 1952; Henderson H. Donald, *The Negro Freedman,* 1952; Jonathan T. Dorris, *Pardon and Amnesty under Lincoln and Johnson,* 1953; Harold M. Hyman, *Era of the Oath: Northern Loyalty Tests During the Civil War and Reconstruction,* 1954; Joseph B. James, *The Framing of the Fourteenth Amendment,* 1956; and Eric L. McKitrick, *Andrew Johnson and Reconstruction,* 1960.

The history of the changes in Northern economic activities during Reconstruction may be traced in Charles F. Adams, Jr., *Chapters of Erie, 1886,* 1956; A. F. Harlow, *The Road of the Century: The Story of the New York Central,* 1947; E. Hungerford, *Men of Erie,* 1946; R. E. Riegel, *Story of the Western Railroads,* 1926; John F. Stover, *The Railroads of the South, 1865–1900,* 1955. Paul H. Giddens describes *The Birth of the Oil Industry,* 1938. G. D. Lyman deals with mining in the *Saga of the Comstock Lode,* 1934. Reconstruction finance is treated in D. G. Barrett, *Greenbacks and Resumption of Specie Payments,* 1931, and Robert T. Patterson, *Federal Debt Management Poli-*

cies, 1865–1879, 1954. The farmers' plight is dealt with in Solon J. Buck, *The Granger Movement,* 1913, and *The Agrarian Crusade,* 1920; John D. Hicks, *The Populist Revolt,* 1931; and Fred A. Shannon, *The Farmers' Last Frontier,* 1945. Other significant recent studies are Robert P. Sharkey, *Money, Class and Party: An Economic Study in Civil War and Reconstruction,* 1959; George R. Woolfolk, *The Cotton Regency: Northern Merchants and Reconstruction, 1865–1880,* 1958; and Stanley Coben, "Northeastern Business and Radical Reconstruction," *Mississippi Valley Historical Review,* XLVI (June 1959), 67–91.

Reconstruction produced many interesting figures, and their stories liven many of the pages of history. Some of the many biographies are David S. Muzzey, *James G. Blaine,* 1934; Allan Nevins, *Hamilton Fish,* 1936; W. A. Swanberg, *Jim Fisk: The Career of an Improbable Rascal,* 1959; William B. Hesseltine, *Ulysses S. Grant, Politician,* 1935; Harry Barnard, *Rutherford B. Hayes and His America,* 1954; Allan Nevins, *Abram S. Hewitt, with Some Account of Peter Cooper,* 1935; George Fort Milton, *Age of Hate* [Andrew Johnson], 1930; Francis Brown, *Raymond of the Times,* 1951; Richard N. Current, *Old Thad Stevens,* 1942; Alexander C. Flick and G. S. Lobrano, *Samuel Jones Tilden,* 1939; Wheaton J. Lane, *Commodore Vanderbilt,* 1942.

Besides books, a variety of historical periodicals contains many articles dealing with the trends and events of this period. These journals report many of the latest findings of historians, many of which are not yet in books; they also have book-review sections which give an excellent means of judging historical literature as it is published. Important periodicals of this type are *The American Historical Review, The Mississippi Valley Historical Review, The Journal of Southern History, The New England Quarterly, The Pacific Historical Review, The Pennsylvania Magazine of History and Biography,* and many others. The location of articles and book reviews can be best found by consulting the files of the *Reader's Guide to Periodical Literature* and the *Book Review Digest.*

Index